Educational Programming and Student Learning in College and University Residence Halls

John H. Schuh
Editor

A book published by
Association of College and University Housing Officers —
International

TABLE OF CONTENTS

About the Editor

Editor's Notes

ABOUT THE EDITOR

John H. Schuh is professor of educational leadership at Iowa State University in Ames, Iowa where he is also department chair. Previously, he has held administrative and faculty assignments at Wichita State University, Indiana University (Bloomington), and Arizona State University. He earned his Bachelor of Arts degree in history from the University of Wisconsin-Oshkosh, and his Master of Counseling and Ph.D. degrees from Arizona State.

Schuh is author, co-author, or editor of over 140 publications, including 13 books and monographs. His newest book (co-edited with Allan Hoffman and Robert Fenske), *Violence on Campus*, was released by Aspen Publishers in August, 1998. He has served as editor and chair of the ACPA Media Board, and has served as a member of the editorial board of the *Journal of College Student Development*. Currently, he is editor in chief of the *New Directions for Student Services Sourcebook Series* and is associate editor of the *Journal of College Student Development*. Schuh has made over 140 presentations and speeches to campus-based, regional, and national meetings. He has served as consultant to 24 colleges, universities, and other organizations.

Schuh has served on the governing boards of ACPA, NASPA, and ACUHO-I. Recently, he was selected to join the Evaluator Corps of the North Central Association of Colleges and Schools. Schuh has received a number of awards for his research and publishing including a Fulbright award to study higher education in Germany in 1994. He has also been involved in international education exchanges in Scotland, Bulgaria, and Ukraine.

EDITOR'S NOTES

John H. Schuh

Within the past several years, calls for an increased emphasis on student learning have appeared in the literature (*Journal of College Student Development Special Issue* [March/April, 1996]; Kuh, Douglas, Lund, & Ramin-Gyurnek, 1994; Schroeder & Mable, 1994; Wingspread Report, 1993). It is incumbent that residence hall administrators, programmers, and others concerned about the quality of student experiences in residence halls have tools available to guide their practice. In an age of increasing accountability (see Bogue and Saunders, 1992), it is clear that colleges and universities and their staffs are being held responsible for providing an environment that is programmatically rich and fosters student learning outcomes consistent with the mission of their institutions.

The challenge to residence hall practitioners is obvious—their programs, services, and resources will need to be contemporary or they will face a variety of challenges from within and outside their institutions—including students and their parents, faculty and senior administrators, trustees, and private operators of student housing. Providing tools to meet such challenges certainly speaks to a fundamental reason for the development of professional organizations to help members meet the challenges of their daily work.

History and Purposes of the Publication

In 1977, ACUHO-I (then ACUHO) published a monograph (*Programming and Activities in College and University Residence Halls*) edited by this writer that addressed issues related to programming in college and university residence halls. This publication was designed to provide information about how programs and activities could be developed for the various groups of students who lived in campus housing. In many respects, this publication was designed to address the changing roles of residence hall staff, moving from having to supervise and control student life to developing experiences that would help them grow and develop.

The 1977 monograph was updated and published in a longer form in 1989 (*Educational Programming in College and University Residence Halls*). This book took an in-depth look at residence hall programming. At this stage of development, evidence abounded that indicated that residence halls were places where students could learn and grow, and as a consequence, programming was beginning to be focused more narrowly on the educational aspects of the residential experience. The book attempted to describe residence hall programs that worked.

This book builds on the second monograph and deepens the focus a bit further, with an emphasis on the learning that occurs in the residential environment. As will be pointed out in chapter 1, many studies conclude that given appropriate structure and interventions, the residential environment can contribute substantially to student learning. Substantial information exists on how to do this, and so this book has been developed to report on how this can be accomplished.

This book has been designed to assemble some of the best contemporary thinking on issues about residence hall programming and learning experiences. The various chapters tend to support one another and the publication is best used in its entirety. Without question, many of the chapters can stand alone, but to gain a more complete perspective, the reader is encouraged to read the publication in its entirety.

Organization of the Book

Chapter 1 outlines current thinking about student learning and highlights research about the effect of residential experiences on student learning. It provides a framework for the rest of the publication.

In chapter 2, Deb Grandner and John Foubert focus on several aspects of assessment as it applies to residence halls. They report on strategies for incorporating assessment in residential programming planning and measuring the effects of the residential experience on student learning.

Kris Hoffenberger and her colleagues focus on specific programs and learning outcomes from programs designed to assist students in making the transition to residence hall living and their first year at their institution in chapter 3. The chapter includes a discussion of the special needs of transfer students and international students in making the transition to the culture of the US.

Carole Henry and Susan Bruce address the historical development of residential colleges at Oxford and Cambridge in chapter 4. From the development of residential colleges in Great Britain, they move to the genesis of such units in the United States. They also provide a description of selected contemporary residential colleges.

In chapter 5, Bill Zeller and Mary Hummel discuss academically-linked student housing. Special purpose housing can involve units designed for students with specific majors, students who desire to improve their foreign language skills, or other units linked to unique academic programs or purposes.

Community development is the topic explored by Frankie Minor in chapter 6. The literature is replete with examples of the effect of the community on the student. This chapter discusses how community development can be fostered, and the learning that accrues from the development of a strong community.

Kathy Humphrey discusses issues related to serving students who have been under-represented on many campuses in chapter 7. Much of this chapter is devoted to discussing how the environment needs to be structured to meet the needs of historically under-served populations of students. In addition, several programs are described which make a difference in the experiences of these students.

Programs designed to enhance student-faculty interaction are reported by Mary Ann Ryan in chapter 8. Included in these programs are examples such as faculty fellows programs, classes offered in residence halls, and others which are designed to foster student-faculty interaction.

Ken Stoner reviews learning related to students' leadership experiences in chapter 9. At the core of residential programs are those related to student government. Working with student leaders and developing leadership skills are important elements of this chapter. The outcomes of serving as a student leader are described.

Chapter 10 serves to integrate the previous chapters so as to present a coordinated approach to developing programs focused on student learning. Conclusions and recommendations are offered.

The contributors and I hope that this publication takes the conversation about programs in college and university residences to the heart of the undergraduate experience: student learning. As was indicated earlier in this introduction, a wide variety of sources are calling for an increased focus on student learning and collaboration between student and academic affairs. We hope that this publication helps housing officers move from conceptualizing programs to implementation that enhances student learning in campus residence halls.

The authors and I would like to thank Norb Dunkel and members of the Media Board, and others associated with ACUHO-I for encouraging us to prepare this book. I would also like to thank Tom Dukes at Iowa State University for his invaluable help in preparing this book.

John H. Schuh
Iowa State University

References

Blimling, G. S. (1996). The student learning imperative [Special issue]. *Journal of College Student Development, 37*(2).

Bogue, E. G., & Saudners, R. L. (1992). *The evidence for quality.* San Francisco: Jossey-Bass.

Kuh, G. D., Douglas, K. B., Lund, J. P., & Ramin-Gyurnek, J. (1994). *Student learning outside the classroom: Transcending artificial boundaries.* ASHE-ERIC Higher Education Report No. 8. Washington, DC: The George Washington University, School of Education and Human Development.

Schroeder, C. C., Mable, P., & Associates. (1994). *Realizing the education potential of residence halls.* San Francisco: Jossey-Bass.

Schuh, J. H. (Ed.)., (1977). *Programming and activities in college and university residence halls.* Columbus, OH: ACUHO.

Schuh, J. H. (Ed.). (1989). *Educational programming in college and university residence halls.* Columbus, OH: ACUHO-I

Wingspread Group on Higher Education. (1993). *An American imperative: Higher expectations for higher education.* Racine, WI: Johnson Foundation.

Chapter One

Student Learning in College Residence Halls: What the Research Shows

John H. Schuh
Professor and Chair, Educational Leadership and Policy Studies
Iowa State University

Student Learning

Since the landmark publications of Arthur Chickering (1974) and Alexander Astin (1977), one of the most thoroughly researched aspects of the lives of undergraduate students has been the influence of residential living on college students. Books and articles have been written on how to improve the quality of student life in residence halls (Schroeder, Mable, & Associates, 1994; Winston, Anchors, & Associates, 1993;), how to strengthen educational programming in college residence halls (Schuh, 1977; 1989), the social benefits of living on campus (Pace, 1998, p. 32), and the effect of residential living on college students (Blimling, 1989; 1993). Marchese (1994, p. xi) observes the following: "here (in residence halls), opportunities to influence student learning and growth are highest."

In recent years, a renewed emphasis on student learning has been triggered by the publication of the *Student Learning Imperative* by the American College Personnel Association. This document urges, in part, that student affairs practitioners must ". . . seize the present moment by affirming student learning and personal development as the primary goals of undergraduate education" (1996, p. 121). The *Student Learning Imperative* further asserts: "student affairs programs and services must be designed and managed with specific student learning and personal development outcomes in mind" (p. 119).

One of the methods used to improve undergraduate education is the learning community. Gabelnick, MacGregor, Matthews, and Smith (1990) have identified the development of learning communities as a means of improving undergraduate student learning. They point out, "Learning communities . . . purposefully restructure the curriculum to link together courses or course work so that students find greater coherence in what they are learning as well as increased intellectual interaction with faculty and fellow students" (p. 5). Residence halls provide wonderful opportunities for the development of learning communities, which, in turn, should influence the quality of undergraduate learning. Are these communities worth the effort it takes to develop them? Gabelnick et al. conclude, "One of the strongest selling points for learning communities is their impressive record in retaining students" (1990, p. 63).

The body of literature on the influence of the residential experience serves as a tremendous resource for residence hall administrators who are interested in enriching the quality of the residential experience for their students. One of the challenges, quite honestly, is to try to develop a taxonomy for analyzing the literature and developing initiatives with the potential to enhance the quality of student experiences.

This chapter has been developed to identify and discuss aspects of the literature that examines student learning occurring in college residence halls. It is divided into three parts. The first part discusses resources related to the academic development of residential students. Included under the umbrella of academic development are topics such as persistence, cognitive development, and the intellectual orientation of residential students. The second part deals with topics related to the social development of students. In this section, research on the influence of residential living on those aspects of student learning that traditionally have been thought of as out-of-classroom experiences are examined. In the final section, recommendations for practice are identified. Among these recommendations are the development of living-learning centers and special assignments of homogeneous groups of students.

This chapter's method of organization is artificial. Students' experiences cannot be as neatly compartmentalized as this chapter suggests. "Most students perceive in-class and out-of-class experiences to be seamless" (Kuh, Schuh, Whitt, & Associates, 1991, p. 184). Kuh (1996) concludes that a seamless learning environment is what results from a series of conditions that contribute to educationally purposeful environments. "The word seamless suggests that what was once believed to be separate, distinct parts (e. g., in-class and out-of-class, academic and non-academic, curricular and cocurricular, or on-campus and off-campus experiences) are now of one piece, bound together so as to appear whole or continuous" (1996, p. 136).

As a caveat, I want to point out that this body of literature is extensive. It is virtually impossible to summarize all the studies that have been published on this topic. I have attempted to identify studies that were well-conducted and have particularly influenced our understanding of students. There is no question that other studies are available. The reader is encouraged to use this chapter as a place to begin an inquiry into this topic rather than assuming that little else is available in the body of literature.

The chapter does not discuss aspects of student learning or growth that may result from experiences or activities that would result from living in a residence hall that could be duplicated elsewhere on campus. For example, a student who serves as a floor officer could also be an officer of a club. Or, the student who organizes an event for the residence unit could also do such for a Greek letter organization. In short, this chapter looks at aspects of the residential environment that are unique and cannot be duplicated elsewhere on or off campus.

The reader should note one other aspect of this chapter which is a departure from the norm. Normally, in paraphrasing or simply recognizing sources, the page numbers of those sources are omitted. In the case of this chapter, the page numbers have been included so that readers can find the sources more easily if they are inclined to review the sources in primary form.

Academic Development

Academic development, as defined for the purposes of this chapter, includes a variety of outcomes related to student growth. Among the topics discussed in this chapter are the influence of residential living on academic achievement and persistence, the intellectual orientation and cognitive development of students, and their academic self-concept.

Academic Achievement

The literature on the influence of residential living reveals a variety of conclusions. For example, Blimling (1989, pp. 306-307) in his meta-analysis of the literature reported three conclusions:

1. Living in a residence hall has little effect on the academic achievement of students compared with students who live at home;

2. Living in a residence hall has a more positive influence on academic achievement than living in an off-campus apartment;

3. Living in a residence hall has a slightly more positive influence on academic achievement than living in a Greek letter house.

Blimling returned to the topic of the influence of residence halls on students in 1993 and reached essentially the same conclusions: residents perform no better than students who live off campus with their parents, but they perform marginally better than residents of the Greek letter houses (p. 287).

Other studies conducted on the influence of residential living on academic achievement have reported different findings. For example, Clodfelter, Furr, and Wachowiak (cited by Winston, Anchors, & Associates, 1993, p. 47) concluded that residential living has a negative effective on grade point averages. Fields in her dissertation (1991) found no difference in the grade point averages of African-American students who lived on campus compared with those living off campus. Pascarella and Terenzini (1982, p. 113) reported that living in a residence hall was a positive influence on the grade point averages for men. Winston et al.(1993, p. 47) cited the studies of May and Moos and Lee who concluded that living in a residence hall had a positive effect on the grade point averages of students although these studies were published over 25 years ago.

The influence of living-learning centers seems to have a positive influence on the grade point averages of students as reported by Winston et al. (1993, p. 47). They cite the studies of Pemberton; Vanderwall; Barnes, Pascarella, and Terenzini; and Felver— all of which concluded that residents of living-learning centers performed better academically than residents not associated with some kind of special residential programming. This is revisited later in this chapter. Special, enriched programming seems to make a difference in the academic development of residents, and provides a more advantageous living experience for students than does residing in a residence hall without this special emphasis.

In the final analysis, Upcraft (1989, p. 145) observed that there is an inherent goodness in living in residence halls if staying in college, graduating, and achieving personal development are inherently good. This observation supports the concept that living in a residence hall provides a substantial advantage for students, which other authors support as well (for example, see Astin, 1993, pp. 433-434).

Academic Persistence

Just getting good grades is not enough in an era where persistence ratings of college students are being called into question. "Half of those entering college full time do not have a degree within five years" (Wingspread Report, 1993, p. 5). As is the case with academic achievement, academic persistence has been researched a number of times, but the results are more consistent. In general, living in a residence hall seems to enhance student persistence to graduation.

In their summary of the effect of college on students, Pascarella and Terenzini (1991, p. 611) concluded that residential living is positively, although modestly, linked to persistence in the attainment of a bachelor's degree. Astin agreed. In his book, *What Matters in College* (1993, pp. 194-195), he concluded that residents are more likely to persist than commuters and that residents were more likely to report that they would re-enroll in their college if they had to begin the college education over again.

Blimling's 1993 report agreed with the research cited above. He concluded that residents were more likely to persist than students who have not had the experience of living in a residence hall and instead lived off campus. Earlier reports also supported the conclusion that living in a residence hall positively influenced persistence. Studies summarized by Winston et al. (Astin, 1973, 1975, 1977 and 1982; Herndon, 1984; Pascarella & Chapman, 1983; Velez, 1985) all supported the concept that living on campus enhanced persistence (1993, p. 27). Another earlier study conducted by Astin (cited by Pascarella, Terenzini, & Blimling, 1994, p. 27) concluded in 1977 that living in a residence hall added a 12% net advantage to a student's persisting to graduation.

Berger (1997, p. 451) examined the effects of social integration, student residence and persistence. He concluded his findings supported the work of Schroeder (1994) and others who have suggested that a sense of community in the residence halls can have positive effects for student success in other areas of campus; including increased contact with faculty and higher rates of persistence.

In general, then, the body of evidence supports the concept that living in a residence hall is linked positively to persistence. "The evidence reviewed so far clearly suggests that living on or near campus (versus commuting to college) facilitates integration into the campus social network of peers, faculty and and extracurricular activities" (Pascarella & Terenzini, 1991, p. 401). They went on to add, "This integration in turn has positive implications for persistence and degree completion" (p. 401). Whether this is a direct or in-direct effect of the residential experience is not entirely clear and may be beside the point. The fact that residential living has this positive influence is good news for students who choose to living on campus. If one considers Tinto's (1987, p. 150) conclusions about the factors that enhance student persistence, being integrated in the life of the institution in both an academic and social sense, and Pascarella and Terenzini's (1991, p. 48) conclusion that living on or near the campus is consistently among the most important determinants of a student's level of integration or involvement in the social system of an institution, then it is clear that residential living certainly improves a student's chances of persisting to graduation.

Intellectual Orientation

A number of studies have been conducted that have examined the influence of residence halls on the intellectual development of students. Winston et al. (1993, p. 49) summarized several of these studies (Bennett & Hunter, 1985; Lacy, 1978; Tomlinson-Keasay, Williams, & Eisert, 1978; Welty, 1976) by concluding that residential students show greater gains than off-campus students in the dimension of intellectual development. Pascarella, Terenzini, and Blimling (1994, p. 28) came to the same conclusion in their review of studies examining the influence of residence hall living on the intellectual orientation of students. They observed that students who live in traditional residence halls tend to make significantly greater gains in a number of areas, than their counterparts who reside off campus and commute, including intellectual development.

Recommendations are provided by Winston et al. (1993) in terms of how to enrich the residential environment. They suggest that residence halls be purposely structured so that communication to residents and potential residents is clear that living in residence halls is intended to be an extension and enhancement of classroom learning (p. 52). They also suggested that means be provided to recognize "individuals and groups who show commitment to and achievement in out-of-class learning" (p. 54). Added to these suggestions is the observation by Kuh, Schuh, and Whitt (1991, p. 351) that colleges desiring to promote student involvement provide small residences and classes so that faculty, staff and students are familiar with one another.

Cognitive Development

Another area which falls under the general umbrella of academic achievement is cognitive development. Pascarella, Bohr, Nora, Zusman, Inman, and Desler (1993, p. 218) found that resident students make larger freshman year gains on a measure of critical thinking than similar students who lived off campus and commuted.

Pascarella, Terenzini, and Blimling (1994, p. 26) also identified a number of studies (Chickering, 1974; Everett, 1979; Foster, Sedlacek, & Hardwick, 1977; Nelson, 1982) where residence hall students were found to have significantly more social interaction with peers and faculty. Interaction with faculty and peers can be a factor in accelerating cognitive development, so the residential environment might be interpreted as having an indirect effect on cognitive development, in that the environment provides the potential for residential students to have greater contact with faculty and peers than commuters. Greater contact with faculty and peers can result in growth in cognitive development. Kuh, Douglas, Lund, and Ramin-Gyurnek (1994) additionally reported that students who report greater gains in cognitive complexity are those who have developed close relationships with faculty, perceive faculty as being concerned about teaching and student development, and report that their peers have an important influence on their development (p. 27).

Conversely, Kuh et al. (1994, p. 26) concluded that, in general, the impact of residential living on cognitive complexity is mixed. They also reported that residing in a living learning center has a positive impact on the cognitive development of students. Once again, we return to the concept of specifically structured residential environments. As was the case with academic achievement, it seems likely that a structured environment has a positive influence on cognitive development.

Inman and Pascarella (1998, p. 564) found ". . . no significant differences in the development of critical thinking skills during the freshman year between resident and commuter students" when studying the effects of residence on critical thinking skills at predominantly commuter institutions. This study involved 671 students at six institutions. They observe that commuter students who attend predominantly commuter institutions that accommodate the lifestyles of commuter students may not be at a deficit compared with residential students.

In the final analysis, Pascarella et al. (1993, p. 219) concluded that ". . . the cognitive skills measured by the critical thinking test are more general in nature and less clearly tied to specific courses or curricula. This suggests the possibility that residential living may be most influential in fostering cognitive growth in areas that are not closely linked to specific course or curricular experiences." Thus, the residential experience, by encouraging the interaction of students with faculty and peers, seems to accelerate the cognitive development of students.

Summary

Residential living seems to have a positive effect on four areas of student-learning related to academic growth:

1. Students who live in specially structured experiences, such as living learning centers, seem to earn better grades than those who do not. The data are not clear as to whether students who live in conventional residence halls are more likely to earn better grades than those who commute. Residence hall administrators who have a goal of helping students improve their grade indexes would be well advised to develop special programs such as living-learning centers.

2. Living in residence halls seems to improve student persistence to graduation, compared with students who commute. This appears to be true whether or not students reside in special programs, such as living learning centers.

3. Living in residence halls also is associated with increased intellectual development. This may be a result of the indirect effect of residential living, meaning that living on campus enhances student contact with faculty and peers, which causes the increase in intellectual development.

4. Finally, living in residence halls seems to be associated with increased cognitive development. Again, this may result from the increased interaction with faculty and peers that residential living fosters.

Social Development

Under the rubric of social development are a variety of experiences that historically were characterized as extracurricular or out of class experiences. Research on students has demonstrated that it is very difficult to separate students' classroom and out-of-class experiences (Kuh et al., 1991, p. 334), but for the purposes of this discussion, an artificial boundary has been drawn.

Winston et al. (1993, pp. 40-41) identified a series of objectives for residence life programs committed to student development goals. Among these objectives are the following:

1. Promoting student development in becoming responsible, contributing members of a society of multiple communities;

2. Advocating commitment to the ideals of altruism and social justice;

3. Endorsing the cultivation of a healthy lifestyle, both physically and psychologically;

4. Encouraging students to examine their religious/faith/spiritual life;

5. Challenging students to confront moral and ethical issues.

Personal Development

Studies of a wide variety of aspects of personal growth that have been reported in the literature are included in this category. For example, Blimling (cited by Winston et al., 1993, p. 49) found in his meta-analysis that there were consistent but low magnitude differences that favored residents over commuters on issues related to personal growth and development. Pascarella and Terenzini (cited by Winston et al., 1993, p. 49) reported similar findings. Chickering (1974, p. 84) also found that the personal development of students who lived in residence halls exceeded that of commuter students.

Wilson and Anderson (cited by Winston et al., 1993, p. 49) reported that residents are more trusting, are better adjusted, show more initiative, and were less dependent on their parents than commuters. Chickering, McDowell, and Campagna, and Chickering and Kuper (cited by Winston et al., 1993, p. 49) reported that residents had larger declines in measures of authoritarianism than commuters.

Kuh et al. (1994, p. 33) concluded that living in a residence hall, especially coeducational residence halls, is associated with student gains in humanitarianism. They also concluded that the nature and strength of certain residential experiences have been associated with gains in intrapersonal and interpersonal competence (p. 38).

Psychosocial Development

Psychosocial development refers to the issues, tasks, and events that occur throughout the life span and to a given person's pattern of resolution of the issues, tasks, and adaptation to the events (Rodgers, 1990, p. 45, 55). A variety of studies have been reported that have examined the effect of the residential experience on student development. Welty (cited by White & Porterfield, 1993, p. 84) learned that residence hall students scored higher on tests of personal growth and developed more rapidly than commuters. This growth was attributed in part to the establishment of friendships and participation in extracurricular activities by residential students. Pascarella (1985b, p. 298) found that residential living had a direct effect on students' interaction with peers and faculty and their integration with people from these two groups. Finally, White and Porterfield concluded (1999, p. 85) that living in college residence halls had a positive impact on students' personal and social development.

Social Climate

Blimling (1993, p. 288) identified a series of conclusions about resident students compared with off-campus students. Among his conclusions were the following:

1. Residents participate in a greater number of extracurricular activities than commuters.

2. Residents show greater gains in various measures of personal growth and development.

3. Residents are more likely to change their attitudes and become more liberal.

4. Residents have a more positive view of the campus social climate than commuters.

Similarly, Winston et al. summarized several studies on student involvement in student organizations and concluded that residents are more likely to be involved than nonresidents (citing Astin, 1973; Chickering, 1974; Pascarella, 1984). Ballou, Reavill, and Schultz (1995, p. 19) reported that students who had never lived in residence halls had less contact with faculty members; less involvement with science and technology activities; participated at a lower rate in art, music and theater; had lower quality personal experiences; used the student union less; and participated less in athletic and recreational activities and clubs and organizations than students who had lived or were living in residence halls.

Academic and Social Self Concept

Pascarella, Terenzini, and Blimling (1994, p. 28) identified a number of studies where residents showed greater gains than commuters in academic and social self concept. Included in their summary were studies by Baird, Chickering, and Pascarella. They also cited a study conducted by Kuder which found that residence hall students have greater gains than commuters in autonomy and inner-directedness.

Affective Development

In his study of the affective development of over 5,000 students who attended 75 institutions, Pascarella (1985a, p. 659) found that social interaction with peers had significant direct effects on affective student development measures. He continued by observing that the strongest positive impacts on student affective development occurred at institutions that maximized social interaction among students. Pascarella, Bohr, Nora, Zusman, Inman, and Desler, M. (1993, p. 48) also observed that residing on campus or in certain planned residence arrangements, directly influenced different types of social interactions with peers and faculty, but that it was the social interaction that had direct effects on student development.

Institutional Satisfaction

Winston et al. (1993, p. 48) summarized a number of studies that compared resident and commuter students on their level of satisfaction with their institutions. They concluded that residents tend to be more satisfied with their institution and their educational experiences. Included in this set of studies were reports by Welty, Lundgren and Schwab; Goetz; and Nosow. Pascarella also summarized several reports on students' satisfaction with their institution and concluded that residents tend to be more satisfied with college than commuters (1985b, p. 292).

Applying Psychosocial Theory

Baxter Magolda (1993, p. 114) identified several reasons for the lack of theory-based residence life programs. Among them are the intensity of the work, a shortage of actual examples to guide the translation of theory to practice, a lack of understanding of the changes required by traditional student affairs organizations to implement such programs, and a lack of support from the university community for this function. Nevertheless, several examples of theory-based programs are available in the literature.

Locke and Zimmerman (cited by Magolda, 1993, p. 116) described a peer mentoring training program based on the concept that such programming would foster moral development. Student participation in this program resulted in higher moral development scores after the experience.

Student Learning

The Sierra project developed by Whitely and Associates was designed to foster moral development in its participants. The project was a study of freshmen who participated in academic courses and a laboratory that consisted of either serving as a paraprofessional counselor or in service roles in the surrounding community (Loxley & Whitely, 1986, p. 6). "There was a moderate improvement in the scores of Sierra freshmen on all three measures of character: ego development, moral maturity, and principled thinking" (Whitely & Associates, 1982, p. 283).

Ignelzi reported on an intervention designed to foster ethical development in a residence community (1990, pp. 192-198). A series of components were identified for participation in this community (called a Just Community), including guidelines for participation in it. Among these were that participation in the community was voluntary, the focal point of the community was the town meeting, meaningful decisions were shared with students, advisors acted as ethical advocates within the community, and community members shared responsibility for holding each other accountable to established community norms and policies (pp. 194-195). Ignelzi concluded that this ". . . approach holds promise as a useful companion to more traditional methods of ethical education in the formal curriculum" (p. 197).

One other report is worthy of note: The Olentangy Project. Reported by Rodgers (1990, pp. 155-180), the Olentangy Project was undertaken to assess students, their environment, and the degree of congruence in their interactions; to redesign the environment; and to evaluate the effects or outcomes of the redesigned programs over three years. The Myers-Briggs Type Indicator (MBTI) was used to assign students to residential suites, among other interventions. Rodgers concluded that in the MBTI suites "improved support and a sense of supportive community" occurred (p. 179). Rodgers also identified other positive outcomes, including a lower incidence of damage, fewer transfer requests for women, and fewer judicial sanctions for men.

Porterfield and White (1993, pp. 88-89) identified how theory can be useful to the residence hall practitioner. They identified the following applications of theory:

1. Understanding patterns of student behavior;
2. Training and supervision of staff;
3. Formulation of policies and procedures;
4. Development of programming, both in the assessment of need and the delivery of programming appropriate to the developmental level of students.

To this set are several other applications of theory recommended by Baxter Magolda (1993). These include:

1. Organizational structure;
2. Student group advising;
3. Counseling;
4. Behavioral norms and their management.

The reader is referred to Porterfield and White (1993), and Baxter Magolda (1993) for a detailed discussion of the application of student development theory to the residential setting.

Other Dimensions of Student Development

Astin (1977, p. 71) determined that affective changes facilitated by the college experience, including increased liberalism, interpersonal self-esteem, and artistic interests, are enhanced by the residential experience, as well as by attending a private college. Pascarella, Terenzini, and Blimling (1994, p. 29) citing a variety of studies concluded that in the areas of aesthetics, cultural and intellectual values, social and political liberalism, and secularism, evidence suggested that students living on campus experienced greater value changes than did their counterparts who lived off campus.

Conditions That Promote Student Development

Winston et al. (1993, p. 41-46) identified six conditions that are necessary for implementing residence life programs with student development goals in mind. The conditions they identified included the following:

1. The outcomes and goals of the housing programs are clearly conceptualized and articulated.
2. Values are owned publicly and acted upon.
3. Staff expectations of students are high.
4. Professional staff members interact regularly with residents.
5. Residence life programs promote active citizenship.
6. Facilities are well managed and well maintained.

These conditions are essential to providing a rich residential environment that will encourage student development.

Summary

Residential living appears to have a positive affect on the social development of college students in a number of areas. Among these areas are the following:

1. Personal development;
2. Humanitarianism;
3. Psychosocial development;
4. Academic and social self concept;
5. Affective development.

Residential living also seems to be associated with a more positive perception of the campus social climate, greater student involvement in the life of the campus, and increased student satisfaction with the institution.

Recommendations for Practice

Armed with this array of research on student learning in the residential setting, what is the residence hall practitioner to do to enhance the quality of students' experiences? Two direct interventions seem to make a significant difference in student learning, so they appear to be strategies that are extremely attractive for the practitioner to consider. These strategies include developing living-learning centers and using specific assignment strategies which appear to make a difference.

Living-Learning Centers

Living-Learning Centers (LLCs for the purpose of this discussion) are defined as specific interventions designed to tie living in a residence unit (floor, hall, wing) to a specific program sponsored by the institution. LLCs may include features such as a requirement that students submit a special application to live in the unit, a direct tie with an academic program, classes (credit or noncredit) offered for residents, and structured faculty inputs in the unit, such as meeting on a routine basis with students over a meal or in a lounge (Lorenz, Schuh, & Hanson, 1989, p. 74). Rowe (citing Commission III of the American College Personnel Association) defined an LLC as "a residence unit which seeks to integrate the student's academic experience with his or her living environment. The goals of affective, cognitive, and physical growth and development of the resident are pursued through intentional provision of formal and/or informal . . . learning experiences" (1981, p. 54). Love and Love (1995, p. 89, citing Ryan) identified six emphases of a living-learning center. Included in this set were ethics, citizenship, community, instruction, cocurricular programming and peer learning. The specific format of the LLC will depend to a great extent on the local needs of the campus. Regardless of format, the effects of LLCs on student growth have been shown to be very positive.

In their study of LLC students, Pascarella and Terenzini (1980) concluded that exposure to the LLC was ". . . significantly and positively associated with freshman year persistence..gains in intellectual and personal development and progress, and perceptions of the extent of intellectual progress and sense of community in freshman year non-academic life" (p. 351). They also point out that the benefits of the LLC ". . . accrued to students at the relatively highest levels of education aspiration" (p. 35). As levels of educational aspirations decreased, the benefits associated with exposure to the LLC concomitantly decreased.

In another study comparing LLC students with students living in more traditional residential arrangements, Pascarella and Terenzini (1981) found that LLC students have a higher degree of frequency of contact with faculty (p. 151). They also found that LLC students ". . . had significantly higher academic achievement. . ., were significantly more likely to persist into their sophomore year and had significantly more positive attitudes toward the academic program" (p. 152) than did students living in traditional residential arrangements. While they concluded that the difference between living environments may only indirectly influence student outcomes, the fact is that the LLC students had a more positive experience.

Pascarella, Terenzini, and Blimling (1993) identified several studies that examined the effects of LLCs on students. They concluded that LLCs ". . . exert most of their influence on student personal and intellectual development indirectly" (1994, p. 34). They concluded that "the impact of structural residence arrangements such as LLCs are indirect, being mediated by peer and faculty interactions they foster and that, in turn, exert strong, direct influences on various dimensions of student growth and development during college" (p. 35).

In their compendium of studies on college students, Pascarella and Terenzini (1991, p. 613) concluded that the residence climates that have the strongest impact on cognitive development and persistence are typically the result of purposeful programming efforts which integrate the intellectual and social life of students during college.

Pascarella, Terenzini, and Blimling (1994, p. 40) reached a variety of conclusions about the influence of LLCs on students compared with conventional residence halls. Their conclusions include the following about the LLC students:

1. They report a high quality social climate, engage in more informal contact with faculty, and report a more intellectual atmosphere in their residence arrangement.

2. They perform better academically.

3. They are more likely to persist in college.

4. They have a significant, positive indirect effect on student academic and personal growth and development, mediated by the living environments that they shape.

Blimling (1993, p. 288) observed that students who live in LLCs perform better academically, report a better quality of social climate, and indicate a more intellectual atmosphere than students living in conventional housing. He also concluded that students in LLCs are more likely to persist in college than students living in conventional residence halls.

Assignments

Blimling (1993, p. 290) concluded that "The homogeneous assignment of students to residence halls increases the trait on which students are assigned." He asserts that special assignment programs accentuate the common trait or traits of the students assigned to the unit. Students attracted to certain subject areas become even more interested in these areas. A variety of studies have been conducted on the effects of special assignment programs on students. Several of them are identified below.

Pascarella, Terenzini, and Blimling (1994, p. 37), summarizing the work of Chapple and Schroeder and Griffin, concluded that engineering and science majors are more likely to remain in college when they are assigned to live with students with the same majors rather than being assigned at random. Conversely, Blimling (1993) concluded that students homogeneously assigned by academic major do not perform better academically or report a better social climate than students in similar majors assigned randomly.

Pike, Schroeder, and Berry (1997, p. 616) studied the influence of Freshman Interest Groups (FIGs) on a variety of dimensions of the experiences of students who lived in them. They found that FIGs had substantial, positive effects on faculty-student interaction, social integration, and institutional commitment. Participation in a FIG program did not have a statistically significant influence on academic integration and persistence on students, however. Residential communities did not have a direct effect on student persistence, but they indirectly enhanced persistence through faculty-student interaction (p. 618). Another report on the FIG program concluded that FIG participants "demonstrate significantly higher levels of academic integration, social integration and institutional commitment than their non-Fig counterparts . . . FIG students also exhibited higher levels of integration of course information, and reported more involvement in out-of-class experiences" (Minor, 1997, p. 22).

Wasson (1994) compared first generation students who lived in a special program designed to enhance persistence with a similar group of students who lived in conventional housing. He found no significant differences between the two groups.

Hammond (1994) compared a group of students who participated in a special freshman year residential experience with a group of students who lived in a traditional residence hall. Even though the treatment group had weaker entry characteristics and were predicted to perform less well, the two groups performed equally well. The lack of difference between the two groups was attributed to the special program available for the treatment group members.

Cawthon (1995) compared women living in an all-freshman residence hall with first-year female students living in a female residence hall where all undergraduate classes were represented. The findings were mixed. The women living in the all freshman hall had higher scores related to the academic autonomy scale of the Student Development Task and Lifestyle Inventory (SDTLI), while the women in the mixed building had higher scores on the variable Establishing and Clarifying Purpose.

Konz (1989) studied students who sought to live on a "quiet" floor and were assigned to that unit with students who wished to live on a quiet floor but were assigned to a conventional floor, and students who did not want to live on a quiet floor and were assigned to a unit matching their preference. Grade point averages and probation, suspension and withdrawal rates were compared. No statistically significant differences were found.

Assignment by Gender

Housing assignments related to gender have been reported frequently in the literature. Murphy, using the SDTLI Mature Interpersonal Relationships scale, studied first year males and females. Students who lived in single-sex buildings had significantly higher scores, reflecting improvement, than students who lived in co-ed halls. Males who resided in a single-sex hall scored significantly higher than males living in the co-ed hall.

Blimling (1993, p. 288), in his analysis of studies on co-educational residence halls, concluded that students living in a co-ed residence hall have more social involvement with members of the opposite sex than students who live in a single-sex unit. He also concluded that co-ed living is not associated with gains in academic performance, greater personal growth and development, or participation in a larger number of extracurricular activities than living in a single-sex facility. Thus, the benefits of co-ed living appear to be modest at best.

Summary

Several conclusions emerge from this discussion of recommendations for practice.

1. Living-learning centers, or variations on the concept of providing an enriched environment which brings students and faculty together, either directly, or indirectly, result in good things happening for students. Although the precise reasons for this are still not completely clear, it appears the atmosphere created by such arrangements can result in educationally-purposeful outcomes. Terenzini and Pascarella (1997, p. 178) support this conclusion with the following observation, "Considerable evidence suggests discernible differences in the social and intellectual climates of different resi-

dence halls on the same campus; halls with the strongest impacts on cognitive development and persistence are typically the result of *purposeful, programmatic* efforts to integrate students' intellectual and social lives during college—living-learning centers are not only a neat idea, they actually work!"

2. The peer group, as was asserted by Astin (1993, p. 398), continues to be the "single most potent source of influence on growth and development during the undergraduate years." Moreover, "students' values, beliefs, and aspirations tend to change in the direction of the dominant values, beliefs and aspirations of the peer group" (p. 398). To these assertions Blimling adds, "The most powerful influence in residence halls is the peer environment" (1993, p. 290). Consequently, housing officers may be able to influence the student culture through the careful use of assignments (e.g, assigning students with similar interests and values to the same unit).

3. As Blimling (1993) has concluded, the homogeneous assignment of students increases the trait on which students are assigned. "Special assignment programs are successful in influencing students in the ways which would be expected" (p. 290). The converse of this strategy is also true. That is, the more students are assigned on the basis of a homogeneous trait, the less they are exposed to diverse points of view, values, and reasons for pursuing a college degree. So, a housing officer has to balance the extent to which a special assignment program complements or runs counter to the institution's mission and philosophy.

A Final Word

Love and Love (1995, p. 92) observe that ". . . conscious and deliberate actions must be taken to integrate intellectual, social, and affective elements of learning in the residence halls." Chickering and Reisser (1993, p. 400) add, "Residence hall arrangements can affect development of competence, purpose, integrity, and mature interpersonal relationships depending on the diversity of backgrounds and attitudes among the residents, the opportunities for significant interchange, the existence of shared intellectual interests, and the degree to which the unit becomes a meaningful culture for its members." This advice helps frame the agenda for those who administer student housing and work with students in residence halls.

Housing officers have the potential to benefit greatly from the large number of studies that have been conducted to measure the effect of the residential environment on students. Clearly, the development of living-learning centers and special assignment programs can have a positive influence on student learning. These programs are not without cost, however, in that they often require additional staffing, the development of relationships with faculty and academic administrators, and, perhaps, operating funds. But, the potential benefits seem to outweigh any of the administrative challenges associated with them, if the growth and development of students are of interest. Armed with the knowledge that these programs can make a difference, housing officers can influence student growth and learning for their residents.

References

American College Personnel Association. (1994). *The Student Learning Imperative.* Washington, DC: Author.

Astin, A. W. (1977). *Four critical years.* San Francisco: Jossey-Bass.

Astin, A. W. (1993). *What matters in college.* San Francisco: Jossey-Bass.

Ballou, R. A., Reavill, L. K., & Schultz, B. L. (1995). Assessing the immediate and residual effects of the residence hall experience: Validating Pace's 1990 analysis of on-campus and on-campus students. *The Journal of College and University Student Housing, 25*(1), 16-21.

Berger, J. B. (1997). Students' sense of community in residence halls, social integration and first-year persistence. *Journal of College Student Personnel, 38,* 441-452.

Blimling, G. S. (1989). A meta-analysis of the influence of college residence halls on academic performance. *Journal of College Student Development, 30,* 298-308.

Blimling, G. S. (1993). The influence of college residence halls on students. In J. Smart (ed.) *Higher education: Handbook of theory and research* (pp. 248-307). New York: Agathon.

Cawthon, T. W. (1995). The effects of residence hall living arrangements on the developmental level of freshman females (Doctoral Dissertation, Mississippi State University, 1995). *Dissertation Abstracts International, 56,* p. 2126.

Chickering, A. W. (1974). *Commuting versus resident students.* San Francisco: Jossey-Bass.

Chickering, A. W., & Reisser, L. (1993). *Education and identity* (2nd ed.). San Francisco: Jossey-Bass.

Durand, J. A. (1995). The relationship between academic achievement of university students and selected attitudinal, behavioral, and environmental characteristics. (Doctoral Dissertation, Illinois State University, 1995). *Dissertation Abstracts International, 55,* p. 3104.

Fields, V. (1991). An investigation into factors affecting academic success associated with on-campus and off-campus living experiences for African-American undergraduate students at Iowa State University (Doctoral Dissertation, Iowa State University, 1991). *Dissertation Abstracts International, 52,* p. 3834.

Gabelnick, F., MacGregor, J., Matthews, R. S., & Smith, B. L. (1990). *Learning communities: Creating connections among students, faculty, and disciplines.* New Directions for Teaching and Learning No. 41. San Francisco: Jossey-Bass.

Hammond, R. B. (1994). Effects of a first-year experience program on student academics, involvement and satisfaction (Doctoral Dissertation, Boston College, 1994). *Dissertation Abstracts International, 55,* p. 1483.

Ignelzi, M. G. (1990). Ethical education in a college environment: The just community approach. *NASPA Journal, 27,* 192-198.

Inman, P., & Pascarella, E. (1998). The impact of college residence on the development of critical thinking skills in college freshmen. *Journal of College Student Development, 39,* 557-568.

Johnson, W. G., & Cavins, K. M. (1996). Strategies for enhancing student learning in residence halls. In S. C. Ender, F. B. Newton, & R. B. Caple (Eds.), *Contributing to learning: The role of student affairs* (pp. 69-82). New Directions for Student Services Sourcebook No. 75. San Francisco: Jossey-Bass.

Konz, M. K. L. (1989). Comparisons between scholarly and collegiate living environments and academic success (Doctoral Dissertation, University of Wisconsin-Madison, 1989). *Dissertation Abstracts International, 51,* p. 39.

Kuh, G. D. (1996). Guiding principles for creating seamless learning environments for undergraduates. *Journal of College Student Development, 37,* 135-148.

Kuh, G. D., Douglas, K. B., Lund, J. P., & Ramin-Gyurnek, J. (1994). *Student learning outside the classroom: Transcending artificial boundaries.* ASHE-ERIC Higher Education Report No. 8. Washington, DC: The George Washington University, School of Education and Human Development.

Kuh, G. D., Schuh, J. H., Whitt, E. J., & Associates. (1991). *Involving colleges.* San Francisco: Jossey-Bass.

Lorenz, N., Schuh, J. H., & Hanson, A. (1989). Student-faculty interaction in the residence setting. In J. H. Schuh (Ed.), *Educational programming in college and university residence halls* (pp. 74-96). Columbus, OH: ACUHO-I.

Love, P. G., & Love, A. G. (1995). *Enhancing student learning.* ASHE-ERIC Higher Education Report No. 4. Washington, DC: The George Washington University, Graduate School of Education and Human Development.

Loxley, J. C., & Whitely, J. M. (1986). *Character development in college students. Volume II: The curriculum and longitudinal results.* Alexandria, VA: AACD.

Magolda, M. B. B. (1993). Intellectual, ethical and moral development. In R. B. Winston, Jr., S. Anchors, & Associates, *Student housing and residential life* (pp. 95-133). San Francisco: Jossey-Bass.

Marchese, T. J. (1994). Foreword. In C. C. Schroeder, P. Mable, & Associates, *Realizing the educational potential of residence halls* (pp. xi-xiii). San Francisco: Jossey-Bass.

McMahon, J. P. (1998). A comparison of the development of mature interpersonal relationship among freshmen who live in coeducational residence halls at the University of South Carolina (Doctoral Dissertation, University of South Carolina, 1993). *Dissertation Abstracts International, 54,* p. 3344.

Minor, F. D. (1997). In Practice: Bringing it home: Integrating classroom and residential experiences. *About Campus, 2*(1), 21-22.

Pace, C. R. (1998). Bottom line: Getting more for less. *About Campus, 3*(1), 31-32.

Pascarella, E. T. (1980). Student-faculty informal contact and college outcomes. *Review of Educational Research, 50,* 545-595.

Pascarella, E. T. (1985a). Students' affective development within the college environment. *Journal of Higher Education, 56,* 640-663.

Pascarella, E. T. (1985b). The influence of on-campus living versus commuting to college on intellectual and interpersonal self-concept. *Journal of College Student Personnel, 26,* 292-299.

Pascarella, E. T. (1989). The development of critical thinking: Does college make a difference. *Journal of College Student Development, 30,* 19-26.

Pascarella, E., Bohr, L., Nora, A., Zusman, B., Inman, P., & Desler, M. (1993). Cognitive impacts of living on campus versus commuting to college. *Journal of College Student Development, 34,* 216-220.

Pascarella, E. T., & Terenzini, P. T. (1980). Student-faculty and student peer relationships as mediators of the structural effects of undergraduate residence arrangement. *Journal of Educational Research, 73,* 344-353.

Pascarella, E. T., & Terenzini, P. T. (1981). Residence arrangement, student/faculty relationships, and freshman-year educational outcomes. *Journal of College Student Personnel, 22,* 147-156.

Pascarella, E. T., & Terenzini, P. T. (1982). Contextual analysis as a method for assessing residence group effects. *Journal of College Student Personnel, 23,* 108-114.

Pascarella, E. T., & Terenzini, P. T. (1991). How college affects students. San Francisco: Jossey-Bass.

Pascarella, E.T., Terenzini, P. T., & Blimling, G. S. (1994). The impact of residential life on students. In C. C. Schroeder, P. Mable, & Associates, *Realizing the educational potential of residence halls* (pp. 22-32). San Francisco: Jossey-Bass.

Payne, R. W. (1998). Predicting voluntary student departure from Northern Arizona University (Doctoral Dissertation, Northern Arizona University, 1995). *Dissertation Abstracts International, 56,* 1680.

Pike, G. R., Schroeder, C. C., & Berry, T. R. (1997). Enhancing the educational impact of residence halls: The relationship between residential learning communities and first-year college experiences and persistence. *Journal of College Student Development, 38,* 609-621.

Porterfield, W. D. & White, D. B. (1993). Psychosocial development in college. In R. B. Winston, Jr., S. Anchors, & Associates, *Student housing and residential life* (pp. 65-94). San Francisco: Jossey-Bass.

Rogers, R. F. (1990). An integration of campus ecology and student development: The Olentangy project. In D. G. Creamer & Associates, *College student development: Theory and practice for the 1990s* (pp. 155-180). Alexandria, VA: American College Personnel Association.

Rowe, L. P. (1981). Environmental structuring: Residence halls as living learning centers. In G. S. Blimling and J. H. Schuh (Eds.), *Increasing the educational role of residence halls* (pp. 51-64). New Directions for Student Services Sourcebook No. 13. San Francisco: Jossey-Bass.

Schuh, J. H. (Ed.). (1977). *Programming and activities in college and university residence halls.* Columbus, OH: ACUHO-I.

Schuh, J. H. (Ed.). (1989). *Educational programming in college and university residence halls.* Columbus, OH: ACUHO-I.

Schroeder, C. C., Mable, P., & Associates. (1994). *Realizing the educational potential of residence halls.* San Francisco: Jossey-Bass.

Terenzini, P. T., & Pascarella, E. T. (1997). Living with myths: Undergraduate education in America. In E. J. Whitt (Ed.), *College student affairs administration* (pp. 173-179). ASHE Reader series. Needham Heights, MA: Simon & Schuster.

Thompson, J., Saniratedu, V., & Rafter, J. (1993). The effects of on-campus residence on first-time college students. *NASPA Journal, 31,* 41-47.

Tinto, V. (1987). *Leaving college: Rethinking the causes and cures of student attrition.* Chicago: University of Chicago Press.

Upcraft, M. L. (1989). Residence halls and student activities. In M. L. Upcraft, J. N. Gardner, & Associates, *The freshman year experience* (pp. 142-155). San Francisco: Jossey-Bass.

Wasson, W. D. (1994). A study of first-generation freshmen in a residence hall retention program (Doctoral Dissertation, University of Georgia, 1993). *Dissertation Abstracts International, 55,* p. 49.

Whitely, J. M., & Associates. (1982). *Character development in college students. Volume 1: The freshman year.* Falls Church, VA: ACPA.

Wingspread Group on Higher Education. (1993). *An American imperative: Higher expectations for higher education.* Racine, WI: Johnson Foundation.

Winston, R. B., Jr., Anchors, S., & Associates. (1993). Student development in the residential environment. In R. B. Winston, Jr., S. Anchors & Associates, *Student housing and residential life* (pp. 25-64). San Francisco: Jossey-Bass.

Chapter Two

Assessment Issues and Practice
in Residential Education

Deborah Grandner
Assistant Director of Resident Life
University of Maryland-College Park

John Foubert
Assistant Dean of Students
University of Virginia

Assessment Issues

As professionals in college and university housing departments, we desire to know if our educational programs make a difference in the quality of our students' residential experience. In addition, the competing demands on our institutional resources often require that we know and can provide evidence that our residence hall program contributes to the mission and priorities of our institution. A well-designed assessment strategy is essential for any organization that seeks to build a residence hall program based upon an accurate understanding of the needs and expectations of its constituencies, and for any department that cares to compete effectively for university resources and recognition.

This chapter addresses a number of issues associated with developing and implementing assessment practices in residential education. Residential education is a term we will use to refer to the combination of programs and services that make up a residence life department's efforts to enhance and enable student learning. This includes, but is not limited to, educational activities, academic environment initiatives, faculty involvement programs, physical environment improvements, living-learning programs, and specialty housing. We focus on practices which assess groups of students as opposed to individual assessments.

The issues are organized under five topics to consider as a department of residence life plans an assessment process. We describe the value of assessment, organizational planning strategies, types of assessment, logistical and ethical issues, and results reporting. We emphasize practical considerations of the planning process and offer numerous examples and suggestions.

The Value of Assessment in Residence Life

Assessment efforts make demands on an organization's time, energy, funds, and technical expertise; in addition, there can be unforeseen risks associated with the outcomes. Given the liabilities, one might ask what makes the effort worthwhile. Assessment practices are valuable because they enable a department to improve organizational decision making, enhance department credibility, identify and correct service or program deficiencies, and potentially acquire institutional resources.

Organizational decision making is improved by having specific and current information regarding issues, programs, or services. Assessment practices increase the likelihood that the organization's decisions will be based on accurate information and less on untested assumptions. A department of residence life can design studies to measure satisfaction with programs and services, assess needs for program improvement and service delivery, gather data relative to university retention, identify qualitative and quantitative differences of living-learning programs, and measure progress toward learning outcomes defined for residence education. The information gained from such assessments can be used to determine program goals, decide the most appropriate distribution of resources, or make modifications to improve practices. If studies are conducted routinely, they can identify trends that may influence decisions about long-term priorities.

Assessment efforts can demonstrate program success to students, faculty, parents, and senior administrators. These constituencies often request information about programs and are generally more convinced by data than opinions. Organizations that are able to produce such information are likely to enhance their credibility. Even when studies produce less desirable information about a program, it is better to be the first to know this information. Identifying problems before they become significant can assist in making decisions to improve a program or service. This reduces the risk that others will make those decisions for the department providing the service.

Assessment practices can position a department of residence life to influence institutional priorities for resource allocation. This particularly may become true if information can be provided that relates to the specific goals of the institution. Data on retention rates, outcomes, or student satisfaction provides persuasive information in a formal proposal for resources. Recently, assessment at the University of Maryland helped the Department of Resident Life gain campus support for the expansion of its living-learning programs, acquire funding for renovations, earn recognition in campus retention efforts, and stimulate new partnerships between Residence Life and Academic Affairs.

Other intangible benefits result from conducting assessments. When students participate in evaluative studies of department services, a vehicle is created for their voice in the community. Collaborative discussions of results between administrators and students often strengthen relations between them. Residence hall staff can develop new skills through data collection, survey development, or evaluation reporting.

While the benefits of assessment cannot be underestimated, there are some risks to consider and not all attempts at residence hall assessment are worth the effort. Questions such as what information needs to be known and what will be done with it, should be asked. If these questions are not asked, the information obtained may not be useful. A review of the program goals will more clearly define what is learned from departmental research efforts. It is imperative that achievable and measurable outcomes are established. Of greater concern is the potential for obtaining results that cannot be addressed. For instance, when a department participates in a study that compares its program to that of another campus, the comparison dimensions should be reviewed carefully to ensure they are realistic and important. The participating department and the institution should anticipate and know how to respond to results that may be programmatically or politically undesirable. Put simply, care should be taken in preparing the assessment.

To what degree will assessment efforts contribute to the mission and goals of the institution? If this connection is not understood data may be produced that are interesting but irrelevant. For example, if the campus initiates plans to develop "learning communities," a study that shows how special interest housing programs contribute to this goal may gain institutional support and recognition for the department. However, if the campus is struggling with security issues that are dominating the agenda of student groups, campus administrators, and parent associations, a study on special interest housing may not receive any institutional support despite its merits. A better course might be to delay the plan for a year and dedicate this year's assessment to security related issues. A department of residence life is most effective when it predicts issues or agenda the campus will address over the next few years, and positions assessments to obtain the right information at the right time.

Planning an Assessment Strategy

A strategy to guide departmental assessment efforts will greatly increase its value and success. This is true whether evaluators are considering a simple one-shot program evaluation or a strategic plan for a comprehensive assessment of departmental initiatives. It is important in either case to develop a plan well in advance, organize a team of individuals who can help design and implement the assessment, and gain the approval or endorsement of significant players at the institution.

Before launching into the development of a research strategy, it is necessary to consider the level of investment all participants are able to make. What other agenda currently face the evaluating department? What are the levels of expertise and experience of staff? What is the current stage of evaluation or assessment employed by the organization? The answers to these and other questions will determine whether to construct a foundational commitment to program evaluation or prepare to construct a more intricate, multi-leveled, five-year plan. Poorly conducted research will end well-intentioned efforts.

A long-term plan for assessment can help guide efforts and decision making regarding specific studies. This plan should be developed by a team of individuals who, collectively, have access to institutional information regarding priorities for information and research, expertise in research methodology, practical experience in implementation, and leadership skills. Such a team might include the Director or Assistant Director of Residence Life, a faculty member or campus research specialist, a representative from the Vice President's office, and a Community Director or Resident Director responsible for supervising Resident Assistants.

The team should dedicate the first year to define the goals of the plan and to consider the content and methodology of major studies to be undertaken. They should collect and review any available material for inclusion: institutional mission statement and strategic plan; department of residence life goals and priorities; evidence of external pressures on the institution, such as recent legislation, campus issues reported or relevant in professional literature; and research trends in other residence life departments across the country (Hanson, 1997). It is important to understand institutional priorities and organization as research priorities are developed. These materials can provide the basis for discussion and goal setting at this stage in this process. The team should clearly define and agree upon a set of research priorities that will help guide decision making.

A range of research topics should be considered and evaluated against research priorities. The team may desire to evaluate student satisfaction with programs and services, study perceptions of alcohol awareness initiatives, collect data on student interest in faculty involvement programs, evaluate a new math tutoring program, study retention rates in special living learning programs, or assess learning outcomes for the residence education program. This is an imposing list of possibilities! The list can be narrowed based on priorities and the need for a realistic timetable. It is important to consider how frequently each of these areas need to be assessed. Satisfaction data collected each year over five years can help define consistent patterns of information. Studies need to be conducted with the same population over time in order to measure change. The resources to conduct several of these studies over the five-year time period may be limited, so it is important to make the best possible choices. Depending on the size of the department or institution, it may be necessary to merge the efforts of all departments so as to gain the required resources, tools, and expertise.

The team should plan to meet routinely over the course of the year to successfully manage the process to completion. Consider the best methods, surveys, and instruments to accomplish study objectives. This will require some investigation or consultation with others who stay current with their knowledge in this area. Some professional associations provide a resource guide that detail available options. One particularly helpful guide is *Learning Through Assessment: A Resource Guide for Higher Education* (AAHE Assessment Forum, 1997). In addition, planning will require careful consideration of logistical issues such as timing, resources, and funding. Last, but not least, the research team should plan how to analyze, prepare, and communicate assessment results to the department, campus, or professional community. These areas of planning are discussed more specifically in the remainder of this chapter.

What Types of Assessments Are Available to Residence Hall Staff?

There are many assessment methods and instruments available to the residence hall practitioner. Be informed of your options and make good choices on which assessment tools are needed. For the purposes of this chapter we also describe three categories: needs assessment, environmental assessment, and outcomes assessment.

We will identify what each method is designed to assess and how it can be useful to residence hall practitioners.

Needs Assessment

Needs assessment has traditionally been viewed by residence life departments as a process where groups identify tangible and intangible needs they want met through programs and services. More recently, needs assessment has been described as a means to identify and focus on institutional problems which inhibit the accomplishment of goals (Kuh, 1982). By conducting a needs assessment, an organization can more clearly define problems and address them through program development, physical improvements, or policy changes.

It is important for an organization to routinely challenge its assumptions regarding student needs. This is particulary true with the passage of time or significant changes within the institution. When the racial, socioeconomic, or academic profile of the residence hall population shifts, so will needs and expectations. Changes within a residence hall program such as the introduction of living learning programs also require us to reassess the needs of the newly formed populations. Such programs usually alter the traditional assignment of students to housing spaces or attract students who may have unique characteristics.

As residence life departments strengthen their partnerships with academic affairs, they may find that assessment can be a useful tool in merging efforts and improving relations. Georgia Southern University assessed areas of partnership effort between faculty and student affairs professionals to identify where their initiatives were successful and which ones needed improvement (McClellan, 1999). Based on the results and further assessment, they developed a Partnership Process Model for their campus. Living-learning programs also engage campus faculty, whose needs and expectations regarding information, programs, and services should be understood to ensure program success in residence education. You may find it beneficial to conduct a needs assessment with students and faculty in the early stages of planning and routinely after a program is implemented.

Residence hall staff generally are active players in residence education efforts. Needs assessment efforts conducted with residence hall staff enable an organization to discover problems which may have inhibited their ability to serve. Results can be an important guide in designing changes to staff orientation, training, and supervision.

Needs assessment can be conducted through a variety of methods including surveys, phone interviews, focus group discussions, or even through electronic communication. One method may not be adequate to assess needs accurately and you may find that a combination of methods can be most effective. The tools to conduct an assessment range from self-constructed surveys to more formal assessment instruments. Informal assessment can be as simple as distributing a survey at a floor meeting. Focus groups provide a structured discussion format to gather more descriptive information such as when and how security information can be most useful to students. Standardized instruments are an option for more formal assessments. For example, the Student Development Task and Lifestyle Inventory (Winston & Miller, 1987) can help gauge the needs of residents from a student development perspective. This instrument provides staff with a developmental profile of the student body on which to base developmental programming efforts and gives students information about their own development for personal planning and goal setting.

Whenever a needs assessment is pursued, it is important to distinguish between "needs" and "wants." A group of students may indicate that they "need" a programmatic change that is not feasible to implement. A clear understanding of students' needs may reveal more feasible avenue. It is also critical to balance what students want, or think they want, with what can be provided realistically. For example, students may say that to enhance the educational environment in residence halls they need to have air conditioned rooms for study and cable television for educational viewing. At the same time, they may also want lower housing rates. While either of these additions could be valuable new features, the housing professional must balance these wants against what is truly needed and what can be afforded. Thus, it is important to consider each suggestion, but balance it with the bigger picture. A mission statement can be instrumental in guiding significant changes.

Environmental Assessment

The physical, social, and institutional influences on student life in residence halls can be considerable. Environmental assessment provides information regarding how these influences contribute to the quality of the students' experience. A fundamental assumption of environmental assessment is that behavior is a function of the interaction between a person and his or her environment. Additionally, environmental components are interdependent and synergistic—whereby change in one component of an environment brings about change in other components—and environments exist in a larger environment of reference in which each environmental component has intersecting areas with every other component (Coyne & Clack, 1981). As an illustration of these points, consider a situation in which the institution changes its admissions policies to improve the academic profile of students. Simultaneously, a behavior change may occur in another environment, such as an increase in the demand for on-campus housing, a decrease in the amount of hall vandalism, or an increase in the use of study space.

Environmental assessment involves choosing a particular environment and examining the physical, social, and institutional components (Coyne & Clack, 1981). Physical components of an environment include the natural (weather and climate) design features of an environment (buildings and open space). In residence halls, the physical components might include lobby and recreation areas, Resident Assistant rooms, dining facilities, security entrances, or exterior space such as picnic tables or basketball courts. The social dimension involves the demographic and personal characteristics of people, their behavior, and relationships. For example, where do students congregate? Who are the informal leaders and how do they communicate with other residents? Are students more likely to attend a program on their floor or in the dining hall? Finally, institutional components of the environment may include policies, student handbooks, tuition rates, and registration procedures. In residence halls, this might include room assignment procedures, drug and alcohol policies, standard sanctions for violations, or the number of Resident Assistants assigned per floor.

An instrument which can be particularly helpful in residence hall environmental assessment is the Student Residence Environment Scales (SRES) (Winston, Lathrop, Long, McFarland, & Bledsoe, 1998). Developed by Winston and associates at the University of Georgia, this instrument is designed to evaluate aspects of community development within a residence hall setting. The subscales on this instrument measure such areas as citizenship and academic achievement. If the intent is to better understand the components of the overall housing program as they relate to citizenship and academic achievement, these two subscales could be used as part of your assessment. It is important to note that the SRES focuses on community, not personal, development. To rate citizenship for example, ask residents whether they perceive the living unit as tight-knit and socially integrated with students who care about each others' welfare. The scale does not ask students to self-report behavior that might correspond to their individual development in the area of citizenship. This scale could be used as an indicator of the citizenship present on a floor community, but is not necessarily an indicator of individual citizenship development.

Outcomes Assessment

Outcomes assessment becomes increasingly important in residence education as institutions focus on educational goals and objectives. Outcomes assessment in residence life should involve the gathering data to assess the organization's goal achievement progress. Erwin (1993) suggests three ways in which outcomes assessment can be useful. First, outcomes assessment improves practices designed to achieve specific ends. Second, outcomes assessment serves as an accountability tool. Third, outcomes assessment provides a means for students to self-assess their progress in various developmental areas so as to determine their next steps.

Outcomes assessment should focus on three main areas: knowledge, skills, and growth (Erwin, 1993). In order to assess these areas, outcomes need to be clearly identified and defined in measurable terms. For example, if the assessment goal is to determine how well students are developed into being responsible citizens, citizenship should be described in terms of observable behaviors, characteristics, or attitudes that could be measured.

One of the more commonly used and well-established models of outcomes assessment is the Input-Environment-Outcome (I-E-O) model (Astin, 1993). This model suggests that those who are looking to assess outcomes in higher education should closely observe three variables. Input variables consist of students' pre-college characteristics—what was the student like before entering the institution? Environment variables refer to all of the programs, policies, people, and educational experiences the student has during college. Outcome variables consist of the student's characteristic post-college attendance. To adequately assess change using this model, outcome characteristics are compared to input characteristics. Astin's framework can be applied to residence hall assessment. Within that framework, questions such as these may be asked. What characteristics do our residents have before they come to us? What experiences do they have in residence halls that modify these characteristics? How are they different when they move out of residence halls?

Another instrument which can assist the residence hall practitioner in outcomes assessment is the College Student Experiences Questionnaire (Pace, 1993). The CSEQ is a well-validated instrument used to measure student progress and the quality of student experience, both in and out of the classroom. It gives the researcher an indicator of how students spend their time and the nature and quality of their daily activities. The CSEQ provides information concerning students' backgrounds, activities, opinions about college, ratings of their college environment, and how students evaluate themselves against important objectives. The instrument aims to identify the quality of effort students put into their college education.

Logistical and Ethical Issues

After your research team has determined what types of assessments are most appropriate for your plans, it should carefully plan how to implement the studies. This section reviews a few of the more critical issues to consider during the planning phase.

First, research often requires an investment of money and resources. At first, it may seem that the costs would outweigh the benefits. However, as discussed in the first section of this chapter, conducting an assessment project has the potential not only of substantiating team efforts, but also of becoming a part of an articulated rationale for further resources. When considering an assessment project, financial resources have to be determined and formally requested for inclusion in the budget.

A typical department research budget should include funding for labor, administrative, and programmatic requirements. Labor considerations might include consultant fees, graduate assistant compensation for managing data collection, or specialist fees for data entry and analysis. Administrative considerations would include the cost of surveys, copying fees for letters and information to participants, and incentives required to encourage subject participation. Program considerations might include funds for a brochure to report findings to the campus community or a creative marketing strategy to get a high return rate.

The hidden costs of staff time and energy required to successfully conduct a study need to be considered. The process of motivating, training, and supervising a staff through a research project requires an investment of time and often a reorganization of priorities. In addition, the time and effort required to distribute and collect data can be considerable, especially if Resident Assistants or front line staff are involved. It is especially important to be mindful of the time of year in which the assessment project is conducted. Conducting a comprehensive assessment project during a month when the RA selection process is being completed, when preparing for room selection, or when staff are attending conferences may not be the best time to undertake a project. While the timing of data collection is driven by the specifics of the study, the return rate may have a lot to do with the energy level of staff who are involved. Look at the yearly calendar to plan each step of the process so that the assessment takes place when staff are less burdened. Remember students' schedules too.

There is much to gain by thinking creatively about how to use resources available on campus to implement the research project. A staff member who is seeking a professional development opportunity might be eager to take on the project. Talented graduate students might be willing to do a thesis or dissertation on a topic about which the housing department is interested. There may be faculty members seeking participants for a publishable research study who would like to be a part of an assessment effort. Win-win possibilities exist from many sources if the project is planned appropriately.

Avoid conducting too many assessments, particularly with the same students. If multiple surveys are administered throughout the year, staff, residents, and others begin to question whether these projects are valuable. Coordinate studies with other departments on campus who may be administering independent studies, but are involving residence hall students as subjects.

It is very important to research policies on your campus and ensure that guidelines for ethical practice are adhered to. For example, participants in any research project should be guaranteed anonymity and confidentiality of results, and they should be given sufficient information before they consent to participate. In most cases, a proposal to your Institutional Review Board or Human Subjects Committee for research studies must be submitted. Also, who will have access to the data and who will maintain the data base? Many individuals on campus may seek access to assessment data, necessitating thought as to whom it should be shared and how this might be accomplished.

Interpreting and Reporting Results

Once the study has been completed, the next step is to carefully interpret assessment findings and decide how to report the results. A complete version of the study in a general report may be prepared, and smaller reports tailored for specific audiences such as parents, senior administrators, students, or staff can be extracted. It is important to remember that while some (very few) individuals are interested in reading the complete version of any research study, most appreciate short, accurate, and concise reports. Charts and graphs help the audience connect visually with the information; a one page summary enables them to review the results and decide if they want to read further. Scheduling a meeting to report assessment also draws attention to the findings and is a great way to involve others in discussing implications.

Advice on how to interpret and report your results may be desired. An experienced researcher can locate statistical errors or inaccurate interpretations of the data. Three critical errors that should be avoided are generalizing results inappropriately, identifying participants inadvertently, and assuming too much from the data. A mistake that is easily made is to generalize results to the larger residential population on the basis of qualitative methods. The use of qualitative methods such as interviews and focus groups can be highly effective in identifying the proper questions to ask in a quantitative, paper and pencil assessment, or to illuminate the findings of a survey research project. However, qualitative methods, by their very design, are not intended to be generalized (Patton, 1990). In short, qualitative methods should be used to discover and illuminate, not confirm and generalize quantitative methods.

Carefully review all summaries and charts in the report to be certain that research participants are not identified indirectly in research findings. Check sample size and return rates for specific populations where this oversight will most likely occur. For instance, if only one Native American student lives in a residence hall and you report all findings by race, that resident's responses could be traced directly.

It is easy to get caught up in the enthusiasm of positive results. But there are limits to what can be implied from the study. Specifically, a basic rule of statistics is to never assume that correlation equals causality. While variables may appear to be related, it cannot be assumed that one causes the other, unless your research was specifically designed to determine this. For example, it may be found that the number of residence hall programs offered in a hall positively correlates with residents' satisfaction with that hall. However, it cannot be assumed that more programs caused greater hall satisfaction. If two variables are correlated, this may point to some promising directions. It may make more sense to put energies into areas where desirable variables are correlated than where they are not correlated.

A Final Word

This chapter was written to stimulate your interest in assessment opportunities in residence education and offer helpful guidelines for practice. One concluding piece of advice that transcends any research planning process is offered. Borg and Gall (1989) advise that research should be used to influence policy making and practice, but only with the exercise of careful judgment. They remind us that most, if not all, research knowledge is value-laden. The practical implementation of research findings means putting into practice a particular set of values. By doing so, one set of values rather than another may be implemented, intentionally or inadvertently. The primary role of residence life professionals is to enhance the development of students in our halls and to build strong academic communities out of the collective groups of students who live in them. Assessment efforts should have a direct connection to this mission.

References

Astin, A. W. (1993). *What matters in college.* San Francisco: Jossey-Bass.

Borg, W. R., & Gall, M. D. (1989). *Educational research: An introduction.* New York: Longman.

Coyne, R. K., & Clack, R. J. (1981). *Environmental assessment and design: A new tool for the applied behavioral scientist.* New York: Praeger.

Erwin, T. D. (1993). Outcomes Assessment. In M. J. Barr and Associates, *The handbook of student affairs administration* (pp.230-241). San Francisco: Jossey-Bass.

Gardiner, L. F., Anderson, C., & Cambridge, B. L. (Eds.). (1997). *Learning through assessment: A resource guide for higher education.* AAHE Assessment Forum. Washington, DC: American Association of Higher Education.

Hanson, G. R. (1997). Workshop presentation. NASPA National Workshop: Assessment in Student Affairs, September 27, 1997, Portland, Maine.

Kuh, G. D. (1982). Purposes and principles of needs assessment in student affairs. *Journal of College Student Personnel, 23,* 202-209.

McClellan, M. (1999). Partnership Process Model. Paper presented at the meeting of Academic Affairs—Student Affairs: Creating Synergy for Learning, University of Miami, Miami, FL.

Pace, C. R. (1993). *College Student Experiences Questionnaire.* Bloomington, IN: Indiana University.

Patton, M. Q. (1990). *Qualitative evaluation and research methods.* Newbury Park, CA: SAGE Publications.

Winston, R., Jr., Lathrop, B. J., Long, J. C., McFarland, M. L., & Bledsoe, T. (1998). *The student residence environment scales.* Athens, GA: Student Development Associates.

Winston, R., Jr., & Miller, T. (1987). *Student developmental task and lifestyle inventory manual.* Athens, GA: Student Development Associates.

Chapter Three

Transition Experience

Kirsten Hoffenberger
Assistant Director for Residence Life

Robert Mosier
Director of University Housing

Bobbie Stokes
FIG Coordinator

University of Wisconsin-Stevens Point

For a number of reasons, many colleges and universities are currently focused on helping students make successful transitions into their institutions. As a result, student affairs staff members are placing greater emphasis on the use of theoretical models that can aid transition, and develop strategies to implement the models. Within this context, residential living environments can have a positive impact on transitioning students and help them deal with the major changes they are experiencing.

The transition process discussed in this chapter is examined from the perspective of four populations: traditional first-year students, international students, women students, and transfer students. Program strategies will be explored as practiced at various schools. The implications for finances, staffing patterns, technological issues, facilities, marketing, and relationships with faculty and administrators will also be discussed.

It is important to recognize the difference between *change* and *transition*. Change is situational, such as moving to a new location or learning new procedures. Transition is the psychological process that one undergoes due to a change (Bridges, 1991). Change and transition are common experiences for many generations of students. However, the current generation of students may be experiencing more rapid change in their world than many previous generations. Levine and Cureton (1998), when describing today's college students, view them as existing in a time of profound change and discontinuity. Researchers view change as so broad and deep in our society that ordinary cycles have stopped or been altered. Vaill (1996) describes our current era as a time of "permanent white water," when the one major constant is rapid change. This change is occurring in social institutions, the economy, political institutions, in technology, and in other areas. These same themes are repeated in a recent work by Strauss and Howe (1991), in which they see a generational change from our current "Generation X" to the "Millennial" Generation. Given the enormity of the current change being experienced, it is not unexpected that our current students would experience significant stress. Levine and Cureton (1998) report that current college students are characterized as tired, frightened, desirous of security, pragmatic, consumer-oriented, career-oriented, and disenchanted with politics and the nation's social institutions. Many current students view college as a means to an end, focusing on goals of getting a better job or making more money, rather than developing a meaningful philosophy of life. They report being confused with the degree of change occurring in their lives. Further, they feel pressure to achieve at a very high level, in terms of grades, to prepare for a vocation. These students focus on the need to have a better paying job as one definition of a successful career.

With this increased preoccupation with career success have come greater academic pressures. And as academic pressures mount, students are finding themselves underprepared for some aspects of college.

Culture Shock and College Students

In order to prepare students to make a successful transition into the residence halls and their respective college or university, educators can help students better understand their campus culture and develop strategies for dealing with the stress of integrating into a new culture. As students move into an academic culture, they may experience a clash between the values of their academic and home environments. These students experience a culture shock similar to that of students entering colleges and universities in a new country. Transfer students also experience a form of culture shock when entering a new post-secondary environment. The better campus educators are at facilitating students' encounter with culture shock and the transition process, the more successful these students will be.

Many people have experienced culture shock when traveling in a foreign country. Individuals in a foreign environment are no longer able to understand what appropriate responses to situations are, how to read the cultural cues that would better assist them, or how to respond appropriately to rituals and traditions. This misinterpretation causes feelings of stress and a loss of equilibrium as persons experience great confusion. Their expectations for achievement are still present, but these individuals feel that significant obstacles exist to achieving success in that culture.

This same process, and the accompanying feelings, can occur as the first-year student arrives on campus. The differences between high school and college are accentuated during the first few weeks as first-year students struggle with new terminology, roommates, unfamiliar campus environments, language, and expectations of professors. Kuh (1993) and Kuh and Whitt (1988) have described the difficulty of understanding a university culture, as many of its characteristics are not clearly spelled out. To people immersed in the culture its assumptions and underlying values are obvious, while newcomers may feel that the culture is mysterious or hidden from them. This is especially the case when no one in the student's family has previously been in college. Campus staff can help new students understand and join a college or university culture by making explicit its values, norms, and assumptions.

Many colleges and universities are strongly value driven. They value the search for truth; the growth of human resources; the development of intellectual, cultural, and human sensitivities; the advancement of expertise in specific fields; and the improvement of the human condition. Universities support an ethic of inclusion and membership, of valuing their historical roots and traditions, of supporting a shared conceptual framework of goals, and of sending messages to new students that this is an opportunity to learn and develop.

However, according to Levine and Cureton (1998), current students may possess a value system based upon a strong consumer mentality, which focuses on convenience, quality, service, and cost. Further, they view the college experience as primarily vocational training, enabling them to begin a career at the end of their education.

When these somewhat inevitable clashes of values and expectations occur, students may experience a strong sense of culture shock. Zeller and Mosier (1993) suggest that the role of residence hall staff is to help first-year students better understand this transition process by providing guidance and mentoring to focus on the positive aspects of integrating into the new culture. The transition model of Gullahorn and Gullahorn (1963) and its adaptation by Lewis and Jungman (1986) is pertinent to this understanding.

Transition Models and the First-Year Student

Gullahorn and Gullahorn "W Curve"

Gullahorn and Gullahorn (1963) propose a "W curve" model to describe the transition process of movement into and out of a foreign culture (*Figure 1*).

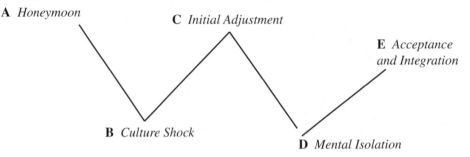

Figure 1. The Gullahorn and Gullahorn W-Curve is one of the earliest and best known models for describing culture shock (1963).

Stage A: Honeymoon Phase

A number of positive factors work together to produce a sense of excitement in first-year students. The university staff and faculty are very welcoming, with mentors available to offer help during arrival and orientation. The students also enjoy the sense of freedom of being on their own, making independent decisions away from parents and other past authority figures.

Stage B: Culture Shock

As students begin classes and as the academic rigors of university life begin to appear, less positive feelings begin to emerge. Students must deal with the differing expectations of faculty. Schroeder (1993) found that students liked the following kind of teaching styles: direct concrete experiences, moderate to high structure, practical and immediate learning, and active methods of learning. Faculty, on the other hand, valued global and theoretical concepts, dealing with abstract relationships of ideas, and passive methods of learning. These differing expectations contribute to students feeling as if they have entered a foreign culture with confusing customs, rituals, myths, traditions, ceremonies, and language.

This confusion over customs and traditions impacts first-year students as they try to deal with a myriad of challenging tasks. In addition, discovering their expectations differ from those of the faculty, the students find cultural differences between the university's values and those of their high schools, their values and those of roommates and floor mates, their comfortable ways of problem solving in high school through a known network compared with the mystery of the university's bureaucratic structure, and the values of family as opposed to those in the university environment.

Stage C: Initial Adjustment

When first-year students become more comfortable with the university through the use of environmental mapping and transitional skills, they feel more confident about adjusting to the new culture. However, the gap between home and community customs and values and the university's customs and values persists.

Stage D: Mental Isolation

As first-year students move deeper into the first semester, they experience a second cultural shock as differences between their new culture and their home environment remain unreconciled. They may retreat to their home environment in attempt to reestablish previous high school status, strong friendship ties, and social relationships that brought them a general level of comfort and confidence. Dissonance grows as the feelings of frustration, isolation, and loneliness they presently experience clash with their idealistic vision of the university environment. They feel they are losing stable values, rather than developing more flexibility in integrating new ones.

Stage E: Acceptance, Integration, and Connectedness

Finally, first-year students continue to connect with students, faculty, and staff in their new environment, and become more integrated into the university culture. According to Astin (1993), colleges and universities can have their greatest impact on students' learning and development by integrating a strong student orientation throughout their programs. This impact can be accomplished by espousing the values of a strong commitment to undergraduate learning, a positive residential learning environment, close student-student and student-faculty environment, an emphasis on diversity, and opportunities for direct student involvement in the learning process.

Lewis and Jungman's Modified "W Curve"

Lewis and Jungman (1986) have modified the "W curve" of Gullahorn and Gullahorn (1963). In their model of the first-year experience, new students approach the beginning of school with a normal amount of intensity, making decisions to leave home, and saying goodbye to the home community. This behavior is characterized as the preliminary phase. After entering the university, first-year students may feel greater intensity about their experience, but initially enter a passive spectator stage. The third phase, the participatory phase, involves a great deal more activity on the part of first-year students. The greatest degree of conflict of cultures between first-year students' home communities and the university occurs during this phase. If this conflict is not resolved, it can lead to the fourth phase of the transition—culture shock. As first-year students move through this fourth phase, they experience the final phases of adaptation and reentry. As students successfully negotiate the final phase they become integrated into the university and experience a strong feeling of connectedness.

Residence Halls and the Transition Process

Residence halls represent a human-scale organization with "small spaces and human places." The hall staff and student leaders must continue to transmit caring and concern to entering students, and help them transition into the university community. Residence Life staff can facilitate this process through efforts such as:

- Planning a sequence of programs, through student orientation and residence hall orientation, focusing on the transition of first-year students.
- Encouraging involvement in programs and activities through student governance meetings and programs sponsored by hall governments, Residence Hall Association, and others.
- Participating in purposeful intervention strategies in the halls, utilizing the knowledge of the phases of the "W" curve.
- Facilitating connections between first-year students and the university community through faculty mentor programs, invited lectures, informal meetings between faculty and students in the halls, meal invitations to faculty, and other mechanisms.
- Providing opportunities to build skills in situations such as conflict resolution, assertiveness, reading and studying, and stress management.
- Using the initial positive phase to prepare first-year students for the down turn during the onset of cultural shock (providing resources and contacts).
- Assisting the first-year students in understanding the university's cultures and confronting or adopting its values.
- Many colleges and universities are offering first-year programs to incoming freshmen to assist with their transitions.

The University of Wisconsin-Stevens Point (UWSP) has two first-year programs established for this purpose. The Freshmen Interest Group (FIG) is a program that allows incoming freshmen who live in the same hall to enroll in two to three classes together for both semesters of their freshman year. Each of the six FIGs on campus includes 16-25 participants. The program assists with social and academic growth. The "ARC to Success" program is a one-semester program that matches a freshman student with an upper-class peer staff member to discuss study skills and other transitional concerns. The student and the peer meet one-on-one biweekly. Both residential programs have been successful in meeting their goals.

Morgan State University has a project named CARE (Caring Adults for Residents' Existence). The focus of the program is to assist with the transitions of both students and parents during the students' first year. Mentors who are graduates, faculty, professional staff, and advocates are matched with residents according to criteria of mutual interest.

Adaptation of the "W Curve" to International Students

Just as students entering colleges and universities in their own countries experience culture shock and transition through the "W Curve," so too do international students as they arrive in another country. This culture shock is intensified because they simultaneously are confronted by new values, beliefs, attitudes, and styles of the country in general, and the culture of the college or university in particular. Rong and Turk (1994) have developed a comparison of culture shock issues between American and international students. They portray the similarities and differences experienced by the two groups of students as it relates to the transition through the "W Curve."

A Comparison of the "W Curve" between American and International Students

Stage A: Honeymoon Phase

Turning first to the honeymoon phase of the "W Curve," American students experience a sense of freedom and excitement as they deal with the prospects of being on their own. The recruitment and orientation process is generally favorable as the university staff work to provide positive information about the school. Making new friends and meeting faculty and staff can be very positive. International students have similar experiences in dealing with admissions and the orientation process, as host families and international student offices welcome them. However, they also must resolve passport/visa issues and recover from the fatigue of extensive travel. Additionally, they may be exposed to unfamiliar advanced technology systems with a very complex set of social customs and attitudes.

Stage B: Culture Shock

While both American and international students may experience bureaucratic obstacles, academic challenges, living environment conflicts, personal maintenance challenges, and loss of family contact, the international student may additionally face language difficulties, unfamiliar teaching and academic styles, roommate customs and traditions, personal care regimes, and a greater loss of family contact. In addition, whereas American students lose some personal esteem as they move from high school seniors to first-year college students, international students may feel they have moved from being people with significant status in their own country to individuals with very little status in the new country.

Stage C: Initial Adjustment

The initial adjustments to these challenges are fairly similar for both groups of students. They both attempt to establish structure and routine in their lives. They focus on academics and understanding the expectations of professors. Also, they are interested in meeting new people and making friends. Again, however, the international student face some additional challenges, as mentioned previously, in these endeavors.

Stage D: Mental Isolation

Both groups will experience homesickness and question decisions they have made about attending this particular school. However, international students' ability to have physical contact with their families is severely diminished. While the American student may simply reconnect with high school friends, the international student must seek out people from the same or a similar culture. International students may respond negatively when the beliefs or actions of their home country are challenged by professors. Finally, they may view Americans as more aggressive and feel uncomfortable with this style.

Stage E: Acceptance and Integration

While both groups work to develop positive relationships with various people on campus, the international students will more likely focus on the International Students Office and other international students. Most international students will grow to appreciate various aspects of the American culture, while realistically accepting its limitations and more negative features. Both groups find that their original home becomes more remote and they become less dependent on their family and earlier friends.

Resources and Research on Aiding International Students with Transitions

Reiff (1986) discusses the concept of culture shock and its impact on international students and provides programming ideas for hall staff. To provide more successful transitions for students from various countries, Reiff provides ideas for international centers, curricula, programs, and resources for staff training and development. He also discusses ideas for staff selection and development. Oamek (1992) also provides suggestions for residence hall staff in assisting international students.

Several researchers have examined the impact of roommates on college students from the same or different cultures. Saidla and Grant (1993) compared residents from traditional male and female halls with residents from an international hall housing international/American roommate pairs. They found that American/American pairs did not have a better rapport or understanding than international/American pairs. Saidla and Parodi (1991) had similar findings.

Training Staff to Work with International Students

With respect to training staff, Rong and Turk (1994) have a series of recommendations.
First, they suggest, make people feel welcome.
- Pick up people at airport, bus, or train.
- Make sure to have flexible arrangements for check in for early and late arrivals.
- Offer information in writing.
- Post a huge welcome sign that includes a welcome in many languages.
- Post a welcome note or sign on room door or in the room with names of staff members and how to reach staff.

Second, demonstrate interest in the person.
- Ask what they look forward to in this country and/or at your college/university.
- Ask about their interests, family, and culture.
- Ask if they would be interested in presenting a program on their country/culture (formal or informal).

Educational Programming

Third, offer support in every way that you can and encourage them to get support from others as well.

- Use paraphrasing and empathetic statements so they feel understood.
- Introduce them to others of the same or similar culture.
- Introduce them to other internationals—from their country and other countries—who have adapted or found their niche.
- Encourage them to practice their faith and get involved in a church, temple, or mosque. These communities are a great source of support and they usually encourage individuals to be the best they can be.
- Allow translators and support people for hearings, mediations, and consultations.

Fourth, challenge your residents to put their feelings into perspective.

- Make sure they know about culture shock and that it is normal to feel this way.

Finally, remember that people who have adapted to another culture can be wonderful role models, mentors, and sources of support for those experiencing culture shock.

- Encourage networking, socializing, and support groups.

Programming for International Students

Programming for international students is intended to address a number of their unique needs, according to Rong and Turk (1994). Below is a list of some recommended programs.

- Family, weekend travel programs;
- Language tutoring, tips of classroom interaction;
- Values and traditions of American culture;
- Discrimination and racism in the U.S.;
- On-going "American experience" program (include American students in the process);
- Community tour (how to shop in a grocery store, how to do laundry, etc.);
- Safety and security tips;
- Immigration issues;
- A comparative perspective on finance issues in the U.S. and developing countries;
- Classroom etiquette;
- Homesickness counseling sessions;
- Dating etiquette;
- Gender issues in the U.S.;
- AIDS and STDs;
- International student government and organizations;
- Religious organizations in the community;
- Employment in the U.S.

Women Students

According to Straub, "in the last 15 years, research on women's development has provided evidence that men and women may follow different developmental pathways and, within those pathways, address different developmental issues or concerns" (1987, p. 198). However, despite increasing evidence that men and women may have different developmental "pathways," not one particular woman's college transitions model has emerged to guide Student Affairs professionals in creating strategies or designing programming to assist women in their transitions to and within college.

Until recently, transition programs and practices were based on male models. This approach generalized the findings from studies conducted with white male students, largely from elite colleges, to the female student population. Theorists Josselson (1973, 1987); Gilligan (1993); Belenky, Clinchy, Goldberger, and Tarule (1986); and Magolda (1992), among others, have researched women's development directly—their psychosocial identity, their moral development, and their epistemology. Their work offers some insights for Student Affairs professionals concerned with designing programs to assist women students with their transitions as incoming freshmen of traditional age, as transfer students, and as graduating seniors.

The Transition Phase for Women Students

It seems reasonable to assume that women students, as well as men students, undergo and are affected by transitions to and within their collegiate experience. And while no theorist or theory, at present, focuses primarily on women's transitions related to college, the work of the women's development theorists mentioned in this section offer insights that could be usefully applied in Student Affairs' work. What these theorists have in common is that they judge women's development to be different in kind and degree to that of men's. What follows is a very brief summary of their theories and major findings.

Women's identity. As Evans, Forney, and Guido-DiBrito (1998) explain, women's identity has not been researched thoroughly. Women's identity researcher P. Josselson (1973, 1987) uses Marcia's (1966) four identity groups or states—*foreclosures, identity achievements, moratoriums, and identity diffusions*—to construct a model for women. He asserts that women are much more focused on "the kind of person to be" (1973, p. 47) rather than on personal and professional achievements predicted by the male model.

Women's cognitive-structural development. The work of Gilligan (1993), Belenky et al. (1986), and Magolda (1992) provides insights into women's development in the moral, cognitive, and epistemological domains. In *In a Different Voice,* Gilligan asserts that women generally do not follow a strict hierarchical path, from lower to higher moral thinking, as is usually attributed to men. Instead, women define their moral development along relational lines—as attachment to others. Gilligan classifies the moral voice in both women and men as either "a care voice" (traditionally female) or "a justice voice" (traditionally male). Baxter Magolda reflects the differences in two general reasoning and learning patterns (although these are not exclusive gender patterns). Males, generally speaking, prefer to process individually. They need the mastery and competence of being autonomous and are less socially connected. Females are socialized to be more relational, subjective, socially connected, and learn to process in a group setting.

Belenky et al. (1986) focus on the metaphor of a woman's voice in relation to her development. As they define the concept, a woman's voice is her vehicle for making sense of the world or constructing her epistemological self. The researchers offer five perspectives (as opposed to fixed stages or permanent states) that describe each episte-mological voice: *silence, received knowledge, subjective knowledge, procedural knowledge,* and *constructed knowledge.* For example, the silent voice has no power or ability to create meaning, while the voice that constructs knowledge integrates both subjective and objective knowledge and employs feeling *and* thought in the process. A constructing knower has the power to create, to be fully a part of the world of knowing.

Baxter Magolda (1992) provides a four-stage theory, the Epistemological Reflection Model, that explains, in part, how men and women make sense of their worlds. The first three stages have "patterns" that *may* be related to gender differences (with the first pattern usually associated with women's knowing): absolute knowing (*receiving knowledge* and *mastering knowledge*); transitional knowing (*interpersonal knowing* and *impersonal knowing*); independent knowing (*interindividual* and *individual*); and contextual knowing. Her study found that absolute knowing was more common among freshmen and transitional knowing among sophomores, juniors, and seniors.

Program Strategies and Models for Women Student Transitions

Josselman's Implications

The four states refined by Josselman (1973, 1987) are yet another classification scheme that Student Affairs practitioners may find useful in placing a particular women student's locus of identity.

Belenky et al. Implications

It is important to realize that some women feel powerless in relation to how and what they know. Active knowing or learning is not a redundancy. The more women students are involved in questioning, synthesizing, and applying knowledge, the more they are in control of their own epistemological voices.

Magolda Implications

Evans, Forney, and Guido-DiBrito (1998) summarize Magolda's (1992) suggestions for Student Affairs practitioners working with absolute and transitional knowers:

For absolute knowers: create opportunities for positive peer interaction and student responsibility, and balance opportunity for responsibility with support. For transitional knowers: encourage the development of support networks of friends, help students respond to peer influence and learn as much as possible about diversity. Promote leadership development, offer opportunities for practical experience, recognize student organizations as a source for forming friendships and dealing with diversity, and organize living arrangements around themes of responsibility and community. Use internships and employment to build human relationship skills and offer practical experience, provide direct experience and stress management assistance to help students make decisions, provide opportunities for self-discipline, and use international and cultural exchange to provide direct encounters with diversity.

Program Models

The apparent needs for a woman freshman vary, but primarily emphasize her need to feel included and to have an environment that is both relational and one where she feels comfortable to step "out of the box" and examine or explore all options available to her.

Programs to meet these needs include:
- Informal discussions with faculty and peers about the issues faced by women students;
- Support groups;
- Women's studies courses dealing with career issues;
- Career counseling;
- Programs on gender and sexual harassment;
- Personal health and wellness programs;
- Safety and security programs;
- Involvement and leadership opportunities.

A search of the published literature offers a dearth of information on transition programs for women that includes a partnership with or a contribution by residential housing professionals. Further, the 162 abstracts from the conference proceedings for both the inaugural and the second National Conference for Students in Transition, held in 1995 and 1996 respectively, mentioned not one transition program for women that was situated in residence halls or that involved residential housing staff.

Despite the scarcity of program information in publications, it may be that some transition programming for women that is connected to residence halls is nonetheless occurring. For example, the Freshman Interest Group Program (FIG) at University of Wisconsin-Stevens Point inaugurated a Women in Science FIG for 1998-99. This program gives female students who are interested in going into the field of science the opportunity to interact with female faculty from science departments and others with similar interests.

At Penn State (Chapman, 1990), the Center for Women Studies has designed several programs to address some of the needs of the woman student. These programs include using films to address interpersonal relationships and provide panel discussions on male feminism and on egalitarian relationships.

Transfer Student Transitions

Studies indicate that about one-third of full-time entering freshmen nationwide are not at the same institution one year later (Beal & Noel, 1980; Noel & Levitz, 1983). This movement may be due to students transferring from a community college to a four-year institution, from one four-year institution to another, or from a four-year institution to a community college. In 1967, 13% of all new freshmen students estimated that chances were very good that they would transfer to another college. The number was 14% in 1996. Women, at a slightly higher rate than men, upon entering college believed that they would transfer. In 1996, 14.3% of freshmen women forecast their eventual transfer, while 13.7% of freshmen men did so (Astin, Parrott, Korn, & Sax, 1997).

Although transfer students may not experience the same transition of leaving high school and acclimating to a college environment, their need to adjust to a new culture or environment is still present. Unlike new freshmen, transfer students oftentimes do not receive the transition assistance they need or they may be overlooked. However, student affairs professionals need to remind themselves that transfer students, like freshmen and international students, are in a state of transition. They too need assistance designed to help them adjust academically, personally, and socially; such assistance is an integral part of assuring the success and retention of these students. Transfer students are embarking on a new experience that may leave them feeling like an outsider, looking in on an already developed or formed culture.

Academically, the transfer student may have acquired useful experience and have already learned many of the academic and social skills necessary to be successful. Yet, the relationships that had been formed at a previous institution have now been abolished and the student is starting over. Learning the campus layout, establishing new relationships, and becoming involved in the community are a few of the challenges the transfer student has in common with an incoming freshmen or international students.

Comparison of Transfer Student Transitions to the "W-Curve"

The culture shock of a transient student, as outlined by Barna defines this period as "a combination of emotional reactions brought about by sudden immersion in a new culture" (1976, p. 20). Much like the stages of Gullahorn and Gullahorn's "W-Curve," Adler (1975) identifies five stages of transfer student adjustments.

Contact

Transfer students often find the new environment intriguing and exciting. The student may be curious and want to integrate into this new environment. Already having some of the basic knowledge of being a post-secondary student, transient students feel a certain amount of confidence that provides security.

Disintegration

Transient students begin to see the differences between the "old" and "new" environment. The culture, values, and means to an end, which was once familiar now become abstract and confusing. A period of withdrawal and loneliness or perhaps depression ensues.

Reintegration

During this state the students feel angry and frustrated as to why there may be a difference between the two cultures—old and new. Transfer students may experience tendencies to rebel and question their decisions as well as the practices of the current institution.

Autonomy

The students begin to regain their balance and recognize the difference between the "old" and "new" environment. Feeling more a part of the current culture, the students become less hostile and opinionated.

Independence

During this final stage, the students begin to value the new environment, thus supporting the decision to transfer schools. The students become more positively expressive and self-actualizing.

In order to assist transfer students' transition, student affairs professionals may need to address the following areas.

- Academic expectations;
- Level of study skills that are needed to be successful (theoretical vs. practical);
- Community re-establishment;
- Community involvement and re-orientation;
- Involvement in extracurricular activities;
- Relationships;
- Living environment (especially if transitioning from living at home to living on one's own);
- Values.

Frequently, we assume that because transfer students previously have attended a post-secondary institution, that the need to acclimate to the new institutional culture is gone. This assumption supports why transfer student orientations or residence hall orientations are more geared toward the traditional first-year student. Yet taking into account the similar transitional needs of the transfer student, universities as well as residential staff should consider the following three needs of the transfer student when building their programs:

- The need to belong.
- The need to become involved.
- The need to feel a part of the community (academic and residential).

Ideas to achieve these needs may include:

- Longer transfer student orientations;
- Mentorships (academic and peer);
- Residential acclamation into the residence halls;
- Establishing support groups;
- Gearing faculty advising toward making use of previous experiences and academic record;
- Providing leadership opportunities (belonging);
- Establishing a relationship with the community outside the university;

Although transfer students' experiences during their first six weeks are not as predictive of success as they are for freshmen, it is a time of great change. University personnel who attend to transfer students' *transition process* help them succeed personally and academically.

Programs for Transfer Students

TRIG (Transfer and Returning Student Interest Group) Program. In 1991, the University of Washington initiated a learning community program for new transfer students and students returning to college after an absence of two or more years. The program groups students who are in the same major (psychology in this instance). The TRIG students are coregistered in two courses and attend a weekly non-credit group meeting. The group meetings have been used as a time for students to interact socially as well as academically (Crampton & Holm, 1993).

Transfer Days. Illinois State University (ISU) offers the "Transfer Days" orientation program so that transfer students may have the opportunity to speak with representatives from the many different offices on campus. In addition, ISU has a student organization, the Transfer Student Association (TSA), which provides social, educational, and professional programs to transfer students.

Summary

Each of the four student populations discussed in this chapter demonstrate similar transition needs as they adjust to their new academic and personal environments. The "W-Curve" provides an awareness of the various stages through which transitioning students might. Such an awareness also enables student affairs personnel to design strategies and programs that can best serve student populations in transition.

Seeking additional funding for transition programs may not be necessary. Rather, university personnel should evaluate their current practices and programs to determine if they meet the various needs of incoming students. Such self-examination should reveal whether our transition strategies are meeting the needs of individual groups of students or are simply a one-size-fits-all programming effort. Many traditional orientation methods, whether campus-wide or residential, are well established and effective; nonetheless, special populations' benefit when strategies to meet their needs are incorporated into our ongoing programs.

As indicated in the beginning of this chapter, the students of this "millennial" generation will be different than any of their predecessors. University student affairs staff members who develop an understanding of these changes will be prepared to accommodate the needs of tomorrow's students. Such understanding and accommodation is not achieved without cost. The resources required may include an investment of time to develop new programs and, in some cases, funds to involve additional staffing. Most importantly, staff members should reassess their current thinking about the special needs of transitioning students.

References

Adler, P. (1975). Transitional experience: An alternative view of culture shock. *Journal of Humanistic Psychology,* (1975, Fall), 13-23.

Astin, A. (1993). *What matters in college?* San Francisco: Jossey-Bass.

Astin, A., Parrott, S., Korn, W., & Sax, L. (1997). *The American freshman: Thirty year trends.* Los Angeles: Higher Education Research Institution.

Barna, L. (1976). *How culture shock affects communication.* Paper presented at the Communication Association of the Pacific Annual Convention, Kobe, Japan.

Beal, P. E., & Noel, L. (1980). *What works in student retention.* Iowa City, IA: American College Testing Program and National Center for Higher Education Management Systems.

Belenky, M. F., Clinchy, B. M., Goldberger, N. R., & Tarule, J. M. (1986). *Women's ways of knowing: The development of self, voice, and mind.* New York: Basic Books.

Bridges, W. (1991). *Managing transitions: Making the most of change.* New York: Addison-Wesley.

Chapman, S. (1990). Women studies. In M. L. Upcraft, J. N. Gardner, & Associates (Eds.), *The freshman year experience* (pp. 287-302). San Francisco: Jossey-Bass.

Crampton, B. P., Holm, K. (1993). A learning-community program for transfer and returning students. *Journal of College Student Development, 34*(6), 439.

Evans, N. J., Forney, D. S., & Guido-DiBrito, F. (1998). *Student development in college: Theory, research, and practice.* San Francisco: Jossey-Bass.

Gilligan, C. (1993). *In a different voice: Psychological theory and women's development.* Cambridge, MA: Harvard University Press. (Original work published 1982)

Gullahorn, J. T., & Gullahorn, J. E. (1963). An extension of the u-curve hypotheses. *Journal of Social Issues, 19,* 33-47.

Josselson, R. (1973). Psychodynamic aspects of identity formation in college women. *Journal of Youth and Adolescence, 2,* 3-52.

Josselson, R. (1987). *Finding herself: Pathways to identity development in women.* San Francisco: Jossey-Bass.

Kuh, G. (1993). *Cultural perspectives in student affairs work.* Lanham, MD: University Press of America.

Kuh, G., & Whitt, E. (1988). *The invisible tapestry: Culture in American colleges and universities* (AAHE-ERIC/Higher Education Research Report No. 1). Washington, DC: American Association for Higher Education.

Levine, A., & Cureton, J. (1998). *When hope and fear collide: A portrait of today's college student.* San Francisco: Jossey-Bass.

Lewis, T. J., & Jungman, R. E. (Eds.). (1986). *On being foreign.* Yarmouth, ME: Intercultural Press.

Magolda, M. B. B. (1992). *Knowing and reasoning in college: Gender-related patterns in students' intellectual development.* San Francisco: Jossey-Bass.

Marcia, J. E. (1966). Development and validation of ego-identity status. *Journal of Personality and Social Psychology, 3,* 551-558.

Noel, L., & Levitz, R. (1983). *National dropout study.* Iowa City, IA: American College Testing Program, National Center for Advancement of Educational Practices.

Oamek, M. E. (1992). *Residence life strategies for proactively meeting the needs of international students.* Unpublished master's thesis, Colorado State University, Fort Collins, Co.

Reiff, R. (Ed.). (1986). *Living and learning for international interchange: A sourcebook for housing personnel.* Washington, DC: National Association for Foreign Student Affairs.

Rong, Y., & Turk, S. (1994). *A comparison of culture shock between American and international students.* Paper presented at the meeting of the American College Personnel Association, Indianapolis, IN.

Saidla, D., & Grant, S. (1993). Roommate understanding and rapport between international and American roommates. *Journal of College Student Development, 34,* 335-340.

Saidla, D., & Parodi, R. (1991). International and American roommate relationships. *College Student Affairs Journal, 10,* 54-69.

Schroeder, C. S. (1993, September-October). New students—new learning styles. *Change,* 21-26.

Straub, C. A. (1987). Women's development of autonomy and Chickering's theory. *Journal of College Student Personnel, 28,* 198-205.

Strauss, W., & Howe, N. (1991). *Generations.* New York: William Morrow.

Vaill, P. (1996). *Learning as a way of being: Strategies for survival in a world of permanent white water.* San Francisco: Jossey-Bass.

Zeller, W., & Mosier, R. (1993). Culture shock and the first-year experience. *The Journal of College and University Student Housing, 23,* 19-23.

Chapter Four

Residential Colleges

Carole S. Henry
Executive Director of Housing and Food Services
University of Connecticut

Susan Bruce
Former Interim Assistant Director of Residence Life
West Virginia University

Residential Colleges

There must be a richer experience for students at the university than to be left entirely to their own devices, and rewards for all in conversation across the gulf of age and habit. The cultivation of common ground is a significant educational enterprise. In the process we might see signs of the value of work; a higher level of civilized behavior; greater interest in intellectual work; a greater degree of engagement in the university's wealth of cultural variety; more effective guidance of youth; and deeper respect and sympathy on all sides (*Annual Report of Monroe Hill College*, University of Virginia, 1991, p.3).

This chapter presents an historical narrative on the development of the residential college model in England, its adaptation in the United States, and its relationship to the changing goal(s) of American higher education. It provides historic and contemporary examples, and discusses several considerations and challenges that may await higher education administrators who are contemplating designing their own residential college programs. Questions that will be addressed in this chapter are:

- What is a residential college?
- What was the origin of the residential college?
- What is the purpose of a residential college?
- What are the characteristics of a residential college?
- What are some modifications of and alternatives to the traditional residential college model?
- What important factors should be considered to determine if a residential college (or a modified version) is right for a particular institution?

Forward to the Past

Live and learn programming is not unusual on university campuses. Nearly every college and university residence hall offers some sort of organized learning opportunity and stresses the importance of community. The very term "residence hall" is a deliberate replacement for the more narrowly defined term "dorm." This change in terminology was an intentional effort on the part of student affairs professionals to broaden the concept of undergraduate education; it expresses the belief that higher education should acknowledge that learning reaches beyond the realm of the classroom.

If the philosophy is not new, why then does Appalachian State University's initiative merit special mention? It is worth noting because it portends a sea of change in the provision of undergraduate education across campuses of American universities. It is more than the traditional "dormitory." It is even more than a residence hall with special academic programming. It is a living and learning "center" and, most importantly, *it will be brand new*.

According to its promotional literature, Appalachian State University's Living-Learning Center will be built on a "mountain site" in Boone, North Carolina. It will house 330 students and provide planned areas for studying, computing, dining, meeting, and entertaining. The Center will provide five classrooms and offices for professors. It also include apartments for a resident director and at least one faculty member.

Clearly, the center's architectural style and layout is intended to attract and envelope students and faculty alike, inviting them to join in a fellowship of learning. The architect's very description evokes a misty sense of ancient academe and a faint longing to prove oneself worthy of belonging to a centuries-old fraternity of scholars. Consider the following: "Drawing on European hilltowns and English residential colleges as precedents, the design responds to its unique site with a series of terraced outdoor spaces including an entry plaza, gateway, piazza/campanille, quadrangle, and formal entry court" (Little & Associates, 1998). One can almost see Isaac Newton, Charles Darwin, and Adam Smith sitting on the sun-drenched steps.

Appalachian State University might do well to ask Newton, Darwin, Smith, and other intellectual luminaries conjured up on its proposed center's terrace to ponder the potential returns on an investment of $15 million (academic costs notwithstanding). Would these scholars envision increased and expanded interest in applying to the university? Would they see undergraduate academic achievement levels rise? Would they predict higher retention and graduation rates? Would they point out probable correlative benefits such as fewer incidents of student misbehavior; increased student, staff, and faculty commitment to service-learning opportunities, both on and off campus; an improved regional image; a better national reputation; proud and involved graduates; happy trustees and (since Appalachian State University is a publicly supported institution), a satisfied, even appreciative state legislature? Appalachian State University is betting that, if they could be asked, those great minds would predict all these positive results and more.

Appalachian State University definitely stands out, but it is not alone in its commitment. Several universities have a strong undergraduate focus. One in particular, Michigan State University, has instituted a type of residential college program epitomized by the well-known, tradition-laden systems found at Harvard and Yale (themselves modeled after Cambridge and Oxford). Another, West Virginia University, for example, has adapted the traditional concept, incorporated resident faculty, and initiated efforts to capture a common program to enhance the student experience. It has set itself on an educational path for the future, and is willing to invest the resources to ensure that it stays the desired course. Still another, Salisbury State University, offers specific programs that promote increased out-of-classroom contact between faculty and students. With strong economic disincentives in their immediate future (and maybe even in the face of them), it is likely that many universities soon will follow these examples to remain competitive with their peer institutions.

The Living/Learning Connection

The relationship between living and learning programs and the outcomes mentioned above are the result of considerable research conducted over the past twenty-five years regarding the effects of residential life on undergraduate students. (John Schuh presents a detailed discussion of this research in chapter one, "Student Learning in College Residence Halls: What the Research Shows"). This growing body of knowledge has sparked in-depth reviews of the state of higher education as it approaches the end of the century. Publications such as the National Institute of Education Report, *Involvement in Learning: Realizing the Potential of American Higher Education* (1984); *An*

American Imperative: Higher Expectations for Higher Education (1993), a report by the Wingspread Group on Higher Education; the *Student Learning Imperative* (1994), prepared by the American College Personnel Association; and the recent *Reinventing Undergraduate Education: A Blueprint for America's Research Universities*, presented by the Boyer Commission on Educating Undergraduates in the Research University call for a renewed commitment to undergraduate education and set out suggestions as to how that objective could be achieved.

A strong theme that runs through the research and the reviews regards the notion of creating an environment for undergraduates where teaching and learning transcend classroom walls and traverse disciplines, and where students and professors both teach and learn together. Many ways are avaialble to cultivate such an environment especially within a large university setting. One method is the creation of a residential college program.

The Definition of a Residential College

What is a residential college? First and foremost, it is a living/learning community. Its physical space, standards, and traditions serve to foster a sense of belonging and loyalty to the smaller college and, by extension, to the larger university as a whole. Its community includes students, staff, and faculty whose daily and primarily informal interactions personalize learning by softening traditional role boundaries and promote the shared discovery of knowledge on a human scale.

If asked to close our eyes and envision the traditional residential college, many of us might imagine ivy-covered Gothic buildings, arched stone passageways, and secluded gardens. We might see a student crossing an empty courtyard, his gown flapping as he hurries to his weekly tutorial, late as expected. We might see his tutor standing at the window of a comfortable study, book in hand, waiting. And then we might hear music and realize that our imagination has been usurped by a movie we cannot quite identify. Is it "Love Story?" Is it "Chariots of Fire?" Or could it be "Good-bye Mr. Chips?"

It is difficult to stay out of this trap; the stereotype can be overwhelming. Harvard, Yale, Cambridge, Oxford, and even English prep schools all seem to blend together when thinking about the characteristics of a traditional residential college. The image is so familiar that we seem to know it intuitively. However, by jumping over the process of understanding and going straight to recognition, we risk the benefit of analysis.

According to Alex Duke (1996) in his book, *Importing Oxbridge,* the inability to analyze in an organic way how and why Oxford and Cambridge residential colleges "work" makes it difficult to anticipate how they would translate to another setting, especially to one in another country. Duke surmises that this inability is why many of the earlier residential college programs in the United States had a rough time finding initial support or sustaining themselves over time.

Duke's Oxbridge Model

Most twentieth-century residential college programs in the United States have taken their inspiration from the colleges at the ancient universities of Oxford and Cambridge (or from their earlier adaptations at Harvard and Yale). Use here of the term "inspiration" is deliberate; the model chosen to emulate was more a wistful fabrication by the English themselves than one made of hard fact. It was wrought from a mixture of reality, selective historical memory on the part of mid-nineteenth century English social critics and educational reformers, and romantic notions popularized by books such as *Tom Brown's Schooldays* (which forever infused Oxford's image with prep school charm) and its sequel, *Tom Brown at Oxford*.

These revised histories of Oxford and Cambridge smoothed over the rough spots in centuries of change. They downplayed periods of disaffection and inattentiveness to scholarship, incidents of internal strife, and other bumps along the way from past to present that might belie a newly applied veneer of venerability. In fact, they seemed to ignore Oxford's entire eighteenth century which historian Lawrence Stone named "The Great Depression" because of its limited scholarships, declining enrollments, and an undergraduate population that was "a squalid mixture of laziness, waste and vice" (Midgley, 1996, pp. ix-x).

The repackaging of Oxford and Cambridge universities in the mid-nineteenth century was a defense of an aristocratic order that seemed to be slipping away. Oxford and Cambridge were touted as the bedrock of Anglo-Saxon culture upon which generations of leaders had found their footing. These medieval educational institutions were dressed up in neo-gothic attire, often "more ornate than the original Gothic edifice[s]" (Duke, 1996, p. 37), and presented to all the world as *the* calming influence against the churning forces of industrialization and encroaching pluralism. According to Duke, "gothic style became a metaphor for a culture under siege" (p. 51).

This is the residential college of Oxford and Cambridge that many United States higher education reformers, administrators, and scholars encountered in the last half of the nineteenth century; this is the model that they attempted to copy within their own universities. Inspired more by image than by substance, the model was a better vision than an actual plan. Add some American-style independence, individuality, and ingenuity, and it is easy to understand how, over the next century, several permutations cropped up around the country with varying degrees of success (Duke, 1996). It is why, to this day, many of us hear music and experience a wave of nostalgia when we think of the ideal residential college.

In light of Duke's hypothesis, it may be beneficial for university administrators who are considering implementing a residential college program to look back before they look forward, way back to when a *universitas* was a brotherhood of scholars. It is important to understand that the philosophical underpinnings of the present day living/learning movement in undergraduate higher education are wider than an ocean and several centuries deep.

Residential Colleges

The University/College Relationship—Oxbridge Style

A sure sign of the autonomous nature of the colleges at Oxford and Cambridge universities is the layout of their websites. Consider Oxford (Oxford University website, 12/15/98). There are no central residence life or housing department links to the individual college web pages as is a common practice in the United States. For example, click on Colleges and Halls at the University of Oxford home page. A short introduction leads directly to a list of individual college web pages. Click on a few. They are quite different in style, content, and technical sophistication. All Souls College simply lists its members' addresses, while Corpus Christi College invites one on a virtual tour of its buildings and grounds.

It is clear from the start that these colleges are not subordinate to a university-wide department or even to the university. They are individual and independent. They know of no other way of being because they have always been autonomous entities. They each have their own roots; they did not stem from the university. Rather, they and the university have grown up together and around each other, intertwined, yet comfortably distinct.

Most of the college websites have at least two items in common: a coat of arms and a description of the history of the particular college. Clearly, the unique character of each college is very important to its members. Founders and historical events are highlighted in a concerted effort to connect generations of students with each other along a strong cord of tradition. Merton College is a typical example. It introduces its home page with a description of its origin. It states, "[i]n 1262 Walter de Merton, Lord Chancellor of England, made over the income from certain of his estates in Surry to a community of scholars" (Merton College website 12/15/98). The very simplicity and matter of fact presentation of this historical event underscores a long-held presumption of college autonomy.

Merton College was chartered in 1264 and built in 1270. It is the oldest organized college in Oxford. Merton chose Oxford as his site, but he also had considered Cambridge as a location. Cambridge was already well established at the time, having been officially organized as a seat of higher education in the early 1200s by a group of dissatisfied Oxford scholars.

The source of these scholars' dissatisfaction is not clear. Either they were mistreated by the Oxford townsmen (Cambridge University website, 12/15/98) or they were unhappy with Oxford's academic organization (Westmeyer, 1997). Whatever the reason, thinking it prudent to move on, certain disgruntled scholars packed up their meager belongings and headed along the River Cam to settle in Cambridge. By 1231, these scholars had organized themselves well enough to have a monopoly on higher education in Cambridge as well as protection from unscrupulous landlords, each courtesy of King Henry III (Oxford University website, 12/15/98).

Senior scholars, known as regent masters, licensed each other to read and explain texts to the students who came to town to learn from them. Every student had to be listed on a regent master's *matricula* or roll to verify that he was an officially enrolled student who was working toward attainment of a certain level of scholarship. The regent masters also established standards of achievement by which to judge the competency of the lesser scholars' disputations (oral examinations where the student defended a thesis against senior opponents and then against the regent master) (Cambridge University website, 12/15/98).

Initially, scholars came to Oxford and Cambridge to pursue studies that would enable them to secure positions "in the Church or in the Civil Service (as diplomats, judges, or officers of the royal household)" (Cambridge University website, 12/15/98). Teaching and living took place in private homes, churches, and hostels until the senior scholars secured enough financial support to purchase common space for lectures and disputations.

Eventually, the senior scholars acquired more permanent housing for themselves as well. Groups of senior scholars, known as fellows, were given safe quarters and a living stipend in exchange for praying for a certain benefactor's soul. Many scholars were able to continue their studies indefinitely with this arrangement. Some benefactors were more forthcoming with funds than others. This led certain colleges to seek to subsidize their living expenses by providing housing to undergraduate students. Others took in special students who were relatives of or otherwise favored by a benefactor. As Anne Matthews states in her book, *Bright College Years*, "Street crime and sordid rooming houses [drove] early scholars to attempt communal living. . . . At Oxford and Cambridge, a quadrangle enclosing dining hall, chapel, study areas, and dormitories [proved] an efficient plan for keeping young men supervised and aggressive townies at bay" (Matthews, 1997, p. 117).

Buildings and land, degree standards, and money required continued accountability. Organization was inevitable. It was structured on the rights and responsibilities given to the regent masters by the Crown, local Church authorities, and various other benefactors. These responsibilities gradually evolved into a complex arrangement for the administration of university and college functions. Fellows elected officers to manage their various colleges. One officer, the Head Master, also served on the university governing council. The position of Chancellor of the university was filled by the college head masters who served in that role on a rotating basis.

According to Matthews, "[g]entlemen's sons discover[ed] higher education in the late Middle Ages, chiefly as an excuse for parties and peer bonding; a two track college experience result[ed] . . . [a] struggle for the scholarship student and subsidized indolence for the rich and social" (Matthews, 1997, pp.116-117). King Henry VIII facilitated these changes in the student body with his actions to reduce the external control of the Catholic Church; he opened up the curriculum and mandated degrees for certain court nominees, a practice that persisted into the eighteenth century.

Not-so-studious students flooded the towns of Oxford and Cambridge in the mid-sixteenth century with an itch to spend the newly acquired riches of their merchant fathers. Following in their wake were "their servants, and the tailors, fencing-masters, tennis-court-keepers, riding-masters, and the like, who came to profit from them" (Cambridge University website, 12/15/98). The towns were overrun with people, activity, and a significant number of students who were more interested in getting a degree than in excelling in a scholastic endeavor. Many of these students had enough free time to engage in drinking, gambling, and even an occasional deadly street riot. Colleges soon felt compelled to institute detailed rules of student behavior to control all aspects of student life, such as New College's (Oxford) prohibition "against throwing stones in chapel" (Haskins, 1957, p. 61).

By the seventeenth century, math and science were thriving, especially at Cambridge. In residence was Sir Isaac Newton "who with his followers pursued scientific investigations of all sorts" (Cambridge University website, 12/15/98). Collections and experiments called for a lot of physical space. Museums, the Botanic Gardens, an observatory, lecture halls, laboratories, and a central library all required more land and new buildings. Jointly acquired and utilized by many scholars from a variety of colleges, these resources generally were controlled by the university rather than by the colleges.

Life in the separate colleges in the eighteenth century found contented senior scholars, otherwise known as "dons," whiling away the afternoon and evening hours in the senior common room, a gathering place reserved for senior fellows all of whom were Masters of Arts. Often with them, however, were the young noblemen students whose station in life enabled them to claim many of the same privileges that the senior fellows had earned with their scholarship. These noblemen "dined at the high table with the dons. . . . They were excused any supervision by a tutor and the work or examination he might have set for them, nor did they need to take a degree or present themselves for the university exercise which qualified a man for his degree, formal and scandalously lax as those exercises were" (Midgely 1996, p. 1).

In his book, *University Life in Eighteenth Century Oxford*, Graham Midgely presents detailed first-person accounts of the daily life of students and fellows. In particular, he discusses the many views of the role of the senior common room and notes that some dispute the popular notion that it was reserved for high-minded debate and deliberation on innumerable scholarly questions. Rather, Midgley notes that life in the common room was often contemporaneously described as a "mixture of pedantic chat, learned quippery, and current affairs, blending finally in the supposed brilliance of alcoholic self-assurance" (Midgely, 1996, pp. 50-51).

In the 1860s, the university and most of the colleges determined that they needed to reclaim the teaching function from private tutors. Among other concerns, they wanted to address the fact that small colleges did not have adequate teaching personnel to aid their undergraduate members in successfully meeting the increasingly more weighty educational demands of the university.

In an effort to "inspire life into college teaching" as well as "make the colleges more competitive and university-minded," a new system of teaching was proposed (Rothblatt, 1968, p.205). First, a college lecture would not be limited to the membership of the particular college. This enabled students from smaller and poorer colleges to take advantage of the expertise and resources of the other colleges. Second, small college lecturers would be able to draw their attendees from a larger population of students. Third, small colleges would no longer have to spread their resources in a vain attempt to cover all subjects; they could specialize. Finally, a new cadre of university lecturers would be hired to ensure that any remaining educational gaps would be filled.

In order to effect these changes, college teaching had to become competitive with private tutoring. Toward this end, it was recommended that the traditional college lecturer requirements of celibacy and ordination should be removed and adequate remuneration for teaching services should be ensured. Although college and university officials wanted to retain a free market tension between lecturer and student to enhance quality, they also wanted to ensure that the colleges had some control over education. Fearing that quality might be sacrificed if lecturers were given a completely guaranteed income, a formula of part base salary and part fee per student was proposed (Rothblatt, 1968).

Reform took time. The lore of the private tutor was difficult to overcome even with conscious efforts toward reform. It lured students away from the college community, away from joint inquiry and shared learning. Rothblatt characterizes the private tutor as "a sophist-utilitarian hired to produce results" (1968, p. 209). In modern day terms, such a characterization made the private tutor the educational equivalent of a hired gun. No wonder teaching reform took time at Oxford and Cambridge. Such a formidable opponent must have been hard to stand down.

The relationship of the tutor to the undergraduate began to take on moralistic, even heroic overtones. It was fostered by public school influences carried to the colleges in the expectations of cohorts of schoolboy chums brought up on the philosophy of Matthew Arnold. Arnold believed that England was in a state of "spiritual anarchy" and his remedy was to create a political, intellectual, and social "new elite" (Duke, 1996, p. 30).

At the turn of the twentieth century, some educational reformers and prominent statesmen from England and the United States would respond to what they saw as a popular threat to these ideals by supporting programs such as the Rhodes Scholarship (1902).

College tutors began to make themselves available to undergraduates well beyond the bounds of their traditional role as disciplinarian and lecturer. They taught lessons of life and character and they attempted to do so by example. The model tutor was one who "acquired a piano, asked after rowing results and cricket scores, [and] made his rooms a meeting place for undergraduates" (Rothblatt, 1968, p. 223). This "new don," this "muscular Christian," replaced the older, more aloof don. His relationship with the student became the essence of a revitalized college.

World War I decimated the university communities across England and Europe. Teaching was reduced drastically and colleges lost income. Cambridge University suffered severely and had to accept its first systematic financial support from the government in 1919. The university began to rely on an annual grant from the government; with such support, however, came increased government oversight and control over both the determination and administration of university functions. For example, Cambridge University was obliged to "take over responsibility for lectures and practical teaching" (Cambridge University website, 12/15/98). It is important to note, however, that the colleges did not receive government funding. They remained independent and they continued to provide individualized teaching to their respective student members.

Cambridge University experienced a wave of "unprecedented expansion" after World War II. Its scientific contributions to the country during the war were well known and it drew many top students eager to learn from some of the best scientific minds in the world. Four new colleges were established to "provide fellowships for some of the growing number of teaching and research staff, as well as . . . research students" (Cambridge University website, 12/15/98). Female students also bolstered undergraduate enrollments. They had established their own colleges in the last quarter of the nineteenth century—Girton in 1869 and Newnham in 1872—however they did not gain full status until 1947.

Cambridge University took more responsibility for the quality of student life on campus. It established a social center for the entire community of students, staff, and faculty. It built a music school and a concert hall and refurbished a theatre for undergraduate student productions. "Such developments . . . showed an increasing awareness of the wider responsibilities of the University, both to its own members and to the community at large" (Cambridge University website, 12/15/98).

Oxford and Cambridge Today

The colleges of Oxford and Cambridge have not lost their individuality as they approach the twenty-first century even though they have continued to adapt to the changing needs and sensitivities of their respective universities and society as a whole. The Girton College website links visitors to a description of the current Cambridge collegiate system (which it suggests is similar to that of Oxford). The site is especially useful to persons unfamiliar with the characteristics of residential colleges, specifically persons whose experience is limited to United States higher education. Although brief, the site's information provides a sense of the fundamental differences between the Oxford and Cambridge universities and a typical university in the United States. It is recommended as an initial reference for those university administrators who are considering developing their own residential colleges or modifications thereof.

It is important to note that the colleges of Oxford and Cambridge have a heritage of individuality and autonomy that comes naturally. They were never faced with the awkward and risky task of trying to separate themselves from a larger entity (a university) or even of having to distinguish themselves from one another.

The Girton College website states that "[t]he University itself predates the Colleges, scholars gathered in Cambridge for some time before they started grouping together in mutual fellowship" (Girton College website, 10/15/98). The early university did not see itself as a guardian of student welfare or as an administrator of co-curricular activities. As noted earlier, individual scholars were often the victims of unscrupulous landlords and rowdy townsmen, even to the point of being driven out of town. The scholars learned that their needs and their very safety could be addressed more effectively by joining together. In time, these practical associations drew individuals of like mind and interest whose scholarship and fellowship garnered the sustained financial support necessary to establish them as residential colleges.

According to the Girton website, individuality has been a consistent theme among all of the residential colleges at Cambridge from its oldest, Peterhouse established in 1284, to its newest, Robinson established in 1979; it flows naturally from the fellowship that is at their core. A few colleges are known as some of the "wealthiest institutions in Britain" while others have the reputation of being as "poor [as] the day they were founded." Some colleges have as few as 30 undergraduate members, while others have more than 200. Many colleges emphasize a particular focus or tone even though they meet the needs of what may be a very diverse membership. The very fact of these and other differences underscores the individuality of the various colleges (Girton College website, 10/15/98).

The notion of fellowship also speaks to the autonomous nature of an Oxford or Cambridge college. Most members (undergraduates) must be reviewed and accepted by the college. Each college is self-governed. All members have a voice, but certain advantages of seniority serve to stabilize the impact of decisions over time. Consider a few of the words typically used to describe a college: "fellow," "senior member," "junior member," and "common room." All of these factors connote an association of individuals whose interrelationships are intentional and functionally purposeful relative to the perpetuation of the association.

The enduring strength of the colleges of Oxford and Cambridge comes from their individuality and their autonomy. Their respective members belong to something unique, something that sets them apart in a fellowship. That special something holds them together in real time and also connects them with past and future members through a common tradition.

A strong sense of integrity has enabled the colleges to hand over to the university and to each other some responsibilities that had been theirs alone originally. Although undergraduates become members of the university only by virtue of their matriculation with a particular college, graduate students are admitted to the university first and then placed with a college. Also, colleges refer proposed students to each other when they cannot meet the needs of their own qualified applicants. Students even have the convenience of taking meals in the dining halls of several colleges (Girton College website, 10/15/98).

Examinations and the conferring of degrees remain the purview of the university; teaching, which was once the primary responsibility of the colleges, is now handled by the various university departments whose resources have grown to be greater than any of the individual colleges. The colleges still arrange for the academic supervision of their undergraduate members, however, it is the responsibility of the university's departments to provide that supervision or tutoring. Supervisors, who are often postgraduates, meet on a regular basis, usually in a college facility, with a few undergraduate students at a time to "go over particular [academic] areas in detail" (Girton College website, 10/15/98).

Rote, Research, and the Renaissance of the Scholar—American Style

As late as 1884, mental discipline was the typical teaching methodology in the colleges of the United States (Veysey, 1965). It was based on an educational psychology known as faculty psychology. It relied on a controlled curriculum that was perpetuated by the denominational "old college" movement that peppered the United States with more than 800 small colleges from 1776 to 1861 (Westmeyer, 1997).

The primary function of mental discipline was to instill mental and moral power in students rather than to impart specific knowledge. The proponents of mental discipline believed that the human soul was comprised of certain "faculties" or potentialities that, in order to be realized, needed to be rigorously exercised through a series of increasingly strenuous "mental gymnastics." According to educational historian Laurence Veysey, in his 1965 seminal work, *The Emergence of the American University*, "[t]he psychologists of the soul did not always agree in their catalogues of these faculties, but prominent on such lists were will, emotion, and intellect" (1965, p. 22-23).

It was believed that a youth's faculties were prey to malformation and needed to be molded by expert manipulation. This need for intervention was a rationale for formal education; advocates held that only a properly designed program would bring the faculties into full form and balance (with respect to each other) within the student's soul. Veysey dubbed this balance the "divine recipe for a successful human being" (1965, p. 23).

The acquiring of specific knowledge or as it was called, "the furniture of the mind," was considered to be of minor importance in the mental discipline process. Knowledge was regarded as temporary and elusive and not fundamental to the core of the individual. In fact, too much knowledge was thought to get in the way of the intellect's development.

The objective of intellectual development was to sharpen the student's deductive capabilities. Through the diligent analysis of abstract problems, the student was supposed to acquire a certain tenacity or mental toughness that would enable him to meet and conquer similarly difficult challenges throughout his life. Many orthodox advocates of mental discipline even believed that "well-honed, razor-sharp mental faculties" were not as important as "the exertion of will which was required in the process of developing them" (Veysey, 1965, p. 24).

The majority of small colleges existed on the edge of financial collapse, especially toward the end of the nineteenth century. Sectarian and rural by design, they were initially quite small and beholden to their immediate communities and religious denominations; their support was local, limited, and generally inelastic. But needs grew and costs rose. To remain relevant and viable, many small colleges reached beyond their "natural" base for more support. They enrolled a more diversified student body from a larger region and reluctantly accepted a watered-down denominational image and increased secular control in exchange. This merger of "rural piety and urban wealth" created a tension that eventually weakened a once firm commitment to a prescribed and purposeful curriculum and ultimately loosened the grasp of the mental discipline doctrine (Leslie, 1992, p.144).

College students began to identify with a general collegiate culture that crossed campus boundaries. Rich and organized alumni from ever-widening (Protestant) backgrounds reinforced the new cultural ideals. Strict denominational "distinctiveness and piety" were swallowed up by an all-inclusive Protestantism that championed a generic muscular Christianity (Leslie, 1992, p. 241).

In the second half of the nineteenth century, debate began between the orthodox and the more open proponents of mental discipline over what constituted an appropriate and complete curriculum. This debate was characterized by Veysey as the opening of higher education's Pandora's box. "It was this growing willingness partially to re-examine the content of the curriculum which foreshadowed the ultimate downfall of the disciplinary outlook in education altogether" (Veysey, 1965, p. 25). Once the contribution of knowledge to higher education was accepted as a legitimate topic for discussion, it was only a matter of time before the debate turned to how much knowledge and what kinds of knowledge.

By the late nineteenth century, higher education in the United States began to focus on original research having been influenced by the "two great innovations of the German system, the laboratory and the seminar" (Kennedy, 1997, p. 26). Pursuing an advanced education, American scholars had gone to study in Germany. When they returned to teaching positions in the United States, they were dissatisfied with their limited opportunities. They grew impatient with the pedantic methods of the old colleges and advocated for increased choice and greater relevance in the higher education curriculum. They wanted independence and the freedom to seek new knowledge.

New institutions such as Clark University, Chicago University, and Stanford University offered graduate programs. Johns Hopkins was designed primarily for advanced study and research. Some older colleges quickly added graduate schools, such as Harvard's Graduate School of Arts and Sciences (1889). Others, like Princeton and Yale, were reluctant to give in to what they regarded as the amoral forces of science.

Large universities, both public and private, sprang up especially in the Midwest. They were fueled by the passage of the Morrill Act of 1862 (and its subsequent Act) as well as a growing community service commitment on the part of successful industrialists who eagerly spread their "gospel of wealth" in the form of an "unprecedented rush of philanthropic attention to higher education" (Kennedy, 1997, p. 27). Many of the universities had neither the inclination nor the resources to attend to the basic daily requirements of undergraduates, let alone the capacity to monitor their moral growth. Meeting personal needs such as housing, meals, guidance, and supervision were often left to the individual student.

Educating the "Whole Man"

Gaze up toward the top of Branford Dining Hall at Yale University and you will see several "inaccessible" windows "set in the roof" (Branford College website, 9/21/98). These windows are quiet reminders of the end of a period when American higher education found itself caught between two seemingly disparate goals—the development of knowledge and the development of character. It was a time when several prominent educational leaders, such as Harvard President Abbott Lawrence Lowell (1909-33) and Princeton President Woodrow Wilson (1902-10), had attempted literally to set in stone their conviction that the modern American university's expanding focus on research and its apparent acquiescence to vocationalism would not overshadow the education of what Wilson termed the "whole man."

The time was the late 1800s and the early 1900s. The issue was whether universities, in their quest to serve the advancement of knowledge through the German ideal of scientific inquiry as well as their increasing willingness to cater to the utilitarian needs of a new generation, had sacrificed an important ingredient in American higher education: the collegial environment. Higher education reformers felt that these two seemingly disparate goals—purity and practicality—were tugging at the extremities of Wilson's whole man and tearing him apart. Wilson, Lowell, and other similarly concerned educational leaders sought to put him back together again with a dose of liberal culture and a lot "strength, sweetness, and light" (Veysey, 1965, p. 215).

Wilson and his fellow "reformers" were in an odd position; their calls for change were often regarded as obstructionist rather than progressive. In fact, sometimes they were misinterpretted as merely being advocates of a return to the rote learning of mental discipline. However, their mission was more complex. They did not want to slow the discovery of new knowledge through scientific inquiry. Also, they were uneasy in advocating too strongly against utilitarianism for fear of appearing elitist, undemocratic, and reactionary. Rather, they sought to establish a controlled balance in the provision of higher education, the loss of which they believed was epitomized by the current free-wheeling elective "non-system" of courses and an overwhelming proliferation of extracurricular activities that Wilson described as "[t]he side shows . . . that have swallowed up the circus" (Leslie, 1992, p. 194).

W. Bruce Leslie suggests in his book, *Gentlemen and Scholars: College and Community in the "Age of the University," 1865-1917,* that "[a]n autonomous, and sometimes underground, student life developed [in the United States] in the 1870s and 1880s. . . . [It was] a romanticized version of life in which peer-group prestige outweighed academic prowess" (Leslie, 1992, p. 189). Wilson and fellow reformers thought that it was unwise to allow students such a free reign in finding their own paths in the world, academically and socially. They believed that students needed a more unified direction and they sought to provide it to them through the establishment of a core curriculum and a vital community of scholars. Veysey (1965) notes that in Wilson's inaugural address at Princeton in 1902, he emphasized his conviction that " 'the true American university' " should have a college of liberal arts " 'at its very heart.' " Wilson advocated that Princeton and other universities should effect within their institutions " 'a pervading sense of unity and an unbroken circle of learning' " (Veysey, 1965, p. 246). This concept was so central to Wilson's philosophy of higher education that he proposed to build Princeton's first graduate school in the center of the campus and make it residential in design, an atmosphere reflective of the colleges of Oxford and Cambridge.

Cultivating a "Garden of the Mind"

Woodrow Wilson College at Princeton University calls itself the "College of Destiny." This must refer to the circuitous route it traveled on the way to becoming Princeton's first residential college, at last fulfilling Woodrow Wilson's dream to integrate the social and academic lives of Princeton's students and create what he called a "garden of the mind." Woodrow Wilson College is, according to its website, "the oldest and the hippest" of Princeton's five residential colleges. It was officially established in 1966, but it really began in the late 1950s as the Woodrow Wilson Lodge, an alternative to the selective eating clubs that had developed, in part, as a response to housing shortages on campus in the 1860s.

Wilson tried to put an end to the exclusive eating clubs during his tenure as president of Princeton (1902-1910). He sought to create a unified intellectual community on the Princeton campus. He complained that students were more loyal to their various extracurricular activities and clubs than they were to the university's academic ideals. Wilson felt that there was not enough order and direction in students' lives. He believed that the university's responsibility was to instill in its students shared and lasting principles that would connect them to each other throughout life in spite of their individual differences and regardless of their chosen career paths. Wilson referred to it as the " 'ideal of truthful comradeship.' " A supporter of the goals of the Rhodes Scholarship, Wilson advocated that wherever students go when they leave Princeton, they always should have the " 'feeling that they are men of a common country and put into it for a common service' " (Veysey, 1965, p. 243).

In furtherance of his goals, Wilson reorganized the curriculum to enable students to prepare more effectively for advanced study. In addition, he established a preceptorial program adopted from the Oxford tutorial system in what Duke (1986) describes as an effort "to import to the great university the methods and personal contact of the small college and so gain the advantages of both" (p. 83). The preceptors were hired to conduct small group discussions on readings that corresponded with the material covered in the larger lecture courses. The preceptors were chosen not so much for their scholarship, but rather for their ability to inspire through example a life "beyond the intellectual sphere" (p. 84). Wilson modeled his preceptors on the tutors of Oxford and Cambridge in the last quarter of the nineteenth century.

Wilson's last plan was to develop a residential college program housed in four newly built quadrangles. The colleges were to have live-in masters as well as live-in preceptors. Each was supposed to have its own dining room and commons room where house members could gather informally and enjoy friendly conversation and lively debate. Finally, Wilson wanted the university to assign members to the various colleges to ensure diversity and equality of opportunity.

Wilson's clear intent was to diffuse the power of the elite and divisive eating clubs and turn allegiance back toward the institution. Since his plan took such blatant aim at the club system, it was not surprising that Wilson raised the ire of students and alumni alike. Refusing to modify his plan, Wilson chose to leave Princeton rather than to compromise with his adversaries. He resigned in 1910 to seek the governorship of New Jersey (Duke, 1996). It was not until 1966 when Woodrow Wilson College—the "College of Destiny"—received its charter as Princeton's first residential college, that Wilson's last plan finally began to take shape.

Princeton University Today

All first and second-year students at Princeton University live and dine in one of five residential colleges. Each college consists of a cluster of buildings that house between 450 and 500 students and a dining hall. The colleges also have libraries, seminar rooms, reading rooms, lounges, coffee houses, theaters, computer clusters, study spaces, and recreation/game rooms.

A senior faculty member serves as the master of each college. Each college also has a staff that generally includes a director of studies who is responsible for academic advising (decentralized), an administrator who supervises the programs of the college; an administrative secretary, and juniors and seniors who serve as resident advisers and minority affairs advisers. Graduate assistant masters and a resident faculty member live in the college's residences with the students. Faculty fellows, graduate student fellows, visiting faculty members, as well as building and dining personnel are all critical to the college's sense of community.

Forbes College exemplifies the residential college program at Princeton. It uses the former Princeton Inn (built in 1924 and acquired by the university in 1970) as the centerpiece of its cluster of buildings. Although renovated, the ambiance of an old inn adds warmth and history to the relatively new college. The master's residence is next door to the inn and an assistant master and some students live in another house. The facilities at Forbes College include a computer cluster, a library, a large screen television room, a coffee shop, a fitness center, a dark room, a ceramics studio, and a music practice room. The college also maintains a guest suite for visiting faculty members.

The Fellows Program of Forbes College consists of faculty, staff, and graduate students who come from a wide range of departments. They maintain close ties with the college, using its facilities for casual and occasional formal gatherings with each other and with the student members of the college. Each student has a faculty adviser who is a fellow of the college. Each advisor works closely with the director of studies who provides advice and administrative assistance regarding programs and course offerings (Princeton University website, 10/19/98).

Interested students may enroll in freshman seminars that are designed to explore a specific interdisciplinary topic in close collaboration with a faculty fellow. Also, review sessions for large courses are offered by graduate student fellows. Other programs include a peer tutoring program administered by the director of studies, various presentations on academic departments and career opportunities, special luncheons for fellows and undergraduates, and regular field trips.

A Full Range of Living and Learning Programs

A residential college is only one of several examples of a live and learn program. In fact, there are so many variations on the theme, especially across the United States, that over-categorization may do a disservice to many innovative programs that are still evolving. However, certain features of live and learn programs have begun to crystallize as identified by the ACUHO-I Residential Task Force in 1996 and listed below (The Residential Nexus, 1996-April).

Sometimes, features stand alone as a single program. Sometimes, they are only one of several components of a larger program. The more familiar features are detailed below (and discussed more fully from an academic involvement perspective by William J. Zeller and Kathy L. Hummel in chapter 5).

Current Examples of Residential Colleges and Modified Residential Colleges

As noted earlier, Oxford and Cambridge universities often are mentioned as the inspiration for the residential college movement across the United States. However, it is important to remember Alex Duke's warning. Though such a universal inspiration may serve as the spark, it is individual institutional inventiveness that brings shape to the program. The following systems of higher education may be quite different, yet they all have one thing in common: a desire to provide live and learn opportunities to their undergraduate population.

The Residential Colleges of Yale University

Yale University has a system of 12 residential colleges, each consisting of a community of about 400 men and women. Founded in 1701, Yale has a long history of providing a liberal education to its undergraduates. Although students choose an area of concentration, they are encouraged to experiment with courses outside their majors. In addition, Yale promotes diversity and breadth in all co-curricular student activities and programs (Yale University colleges website, 9/21/98).

The Residential College system officially began in the early 1920s after years of discussion as an effort to personalize the ever-growing institution. The discussion culminated in a decision to "alleviate a housing problem and . . . make an ever-growing college seem smaller and more intimate" (Branford College website, 9/21/98). The decision required Yale to undertake a massive renovation of its just decade-old Memorial Quadrangle to accommodate two newly designed residential colleges, including student and faculty living space, libraries, dining halls, commons rooms, and gated private courtyards.

The initial emphasis of Yale's residential college program was not on curriculum support or enhancement. Rather, as noted by Duke, "Yale's residential colleges . . . were conceived primarily as places where faculty and students could interact away from the classroom" (Duke, 1996, p. 154).

Yale always has stressed the importance of a liberal education for its undergraduates. It advocates that learning how to learn is especially vital in a diverse and rapidly changing world. It desires to "instill in its students an affection for learning that leads to the development of their intellectual, creative, and moral capacities throughout the whole of their lives" (Yale University academics website, 2/5/98).

Today, Yale's colleges continue to have no particular academic theme or focus. Rather the goal of the residential college program is to facilitate the exploration into unfamiliar areas of study and militate against a student's potential inclination toward social exclusivity. College membership is deliberately diverse. This enables new students to be introduced—without being overwhelmed—to the variety of cultures and ideas that are found within the larger university population. Toward these ends, freshmen and sophomores are required to live on campus and receive most of their administrative and academic support services through their colleges.

Each of the twelve residential colleges has it own dean and master who live in the college. The master oversees the social and cultural life of the student. The dean addresses student academic interests and assists in course scheduling. Faculty fellows also are affiliated with each of Yale's residential colleges. They serve as academic advisors for individual students. In addition, the fellows teach seminars, dine with students, play on intramural teams, and generally participate in the daily life of the college. Also critical to the academic success of the students are the writing and math/science tutors assigned to each college.

"The most important component of academics at Yale is the faculty's commitment to undergraduate teaching," states the Yale faculty website (10/28/98). Even the most prestigious Yale faculty members teach introductory courses and some members are involved in the Residential College Seminar Program that "sponsors full-credit courses that allow for innovation and experimentation" (Yale University colleges website, 10/28/98). Yale also fosters the relationship between students and visiting scholars by using the intimate environment of the colleges for interdisciplinary discussions on topical issues, after dinner discussions on current events, and other gatherings.

The environment and buildings of a college are intended to promote community. For example, most colleges have a courtyard (although some of the locked gates are giving way to concerns about access, safety, and student convenience). The courtyard is intended to be the site of college gatherings, both through happenstance and by design. Pick-up basketball, volleyball matches, and barbecues are typical activities. Although each of the colleges has a unique configuration of buildings and facilities, they all generally include a library, music practice rooms, seminar/meeting rooms, a computer lab, and a dining hall (students may eat meals at the other colleges if they so choose). Some of the colleges have dark rooms, pottery studios, letterpress print shops, or small theaters.

Each college has a governing council that oversees various social, administrative, and financial committees. In addition, two students from each college serve on the Yale College Council, where they represent their college with regard to issues affecting the entire Yale community.

The Living-Learning Center Program at the State University of New York-Stony Brook

Stony Brook, a Research I institution has implemented a program that consists of eight Living-Learning Centers (LLC) that emphasize different areas of study. The goal of the LLC program is to integrate the students' residential experiences with their academic interests.

The LLCs enable students to earn minors in areas such as Environmental Studies, Interdisciplinary Arts, Science and Engineering, International Studies, Health and Wellness, Human Sexual and Gender Development, and Service Learning for Community-Based Action Research. A four-year residential Honors program and a Women in Science and Engineering (WISE) program are also offered.

The LLCs are the product of a collaborative partnership between Student Affairs and Academic Affairs. They were developed to offer interdisciplinary academic programming (minors and concentrations) and enhanced faculty-student interaction. For example, the Environmental Studies LLC offers a minor in Environmental Science. It also organizes a variety of opportunities to address both social and scientific issues related to the overall field of Environmental Studies, such as campus beautification efforts and recycling projects. Students also have the opportunity to participate in field trips and internships.

Each LLC has a residence hall director and a faculty director. Faculty directors have a three-year appointment and they are given a half-time release from teaching as well as a 10% salary adjustment. Their duties include recruiting other faculty, designing courses, working with residence hall staff, and interacting with students.

Each LLC has credit and non-credit course offerings related to its field of interest. Courses are geared to the membership of the particular LLC; however all students are encouraged to attend. Similarly, other faculty and administrators are invited to participate in LLC events, seminar courses, and social activities. Each LLC has classroom space and ample areas for seminars and group projects. LLC courses are conducted throughout the university as well as in the various LLC residences. Courses generally taught in the residential setting include student orientation, freshman seminars, and capstone seminars (Stony Brook, 1998).

The University of Vermont Living/Learning Center

The University of Vermont Living/Learning Center (Center) recently celebrated its 25th anniversary. Its mission is "to create an environment for students to integrate their academic/artistic studies and their residential experiences, and to provide a venue for faculty and students to interact outside the classroom." The Center facilitates "innovative and interdisciplinary learning experiences [that] bring the intellectual life of the university in close alliance with the students' lives outside of the classroom" (Living/Learning Center, 1998-99).

To achieve their mission, 30 to 40 residentially-based academic programs are the foci of the Center. Students choose their interest and then live together in suite-style living arrangements. Each student-designed program is expected to encourage personal responsibility for learning. Each program covers the entire year and includes course work, seminars, independent study, and other theme-oriented activities. Some recent programs include Africa House, Art of Photography, Leadership, Documentary Photography, Folk and Celtic Music, The Holocaust, Women in Science, and Geology and Ecology of the Lake Champlain Basin.

The Center houses faculty and administrative offices, classrooms, faculty apartments, a reading room/conference library, a computer lab, a dining hall, an art gallery, a pottery cooperative, a photography cooperative, music practice rooms, and a central commons area with a fireplace. The Center also houses a staff and peer academic tutoring program, the campus Career Services Center, the Office of International Educational Services, and the Office of Integrated Professional Studies, which is part of the College of Education and Social Services.

A member of the faculty directs the Center and works closely with fellow faculty and students to develop the Center's programs. An assistant director is responsible for the daily operations of the Center and oversees recruitment and selection for the following year's programs. The director's staff includes the budget manager, a secretary, and a graduate assistant. The residential life staff consists of a complex coordinator, an assistant coordinator, and a staff of resident assistants.

Although members of the faculty live in apartments located in the Center, most student programming is presented or organized by residence life staff. However, a recent commitment to build "a new sense of cooperation between faculty and student affairs" has been initiated by the university leadership. This is evidenced by an overall positive attitude on the part of the faculty and the campus community as a whole regarding the learning potential of the residence hall environment (Henry & Bruce unpublished survey, 1998).

Residential Colleges

Residential Colleges at Northwestern University

Central to the undergraduate experience at Northwestern University is a system of eleven residential colleges ranging in size from 36 to 300 students. Five of the colleges began in 1972 as a result of a faculty committee's recommendation to establish "a community of scholars." Most of the colleges have a thematic focus. Some recent examples include themes such as the College of Community Studies, Philosophy and Religion (later refounded as Humanities), Commerce and Industry, and Communications.

Each college is headed by a faculty member who serves as the college master. Each college also has an assistant manager who is a graduate student. In addition, faculty associates are involved in the many activities of each college and often dine with the students. The Residential College Board (RCB) is an advisory board that consists of the presidents of each of the residential colleges. The RCB promotes community and sponsors a variety of cooperative programs.

The college system has created many traditions as it has evolved over the years. These traditions serve to distinguish the colleges from one another and help perpetuate a sense of community within each college. For example, Humanities Residential College is known for its "Faculty Frivolous Readings," coffeehouses, and the Helicon, a nationally known journal of the humanities and the arts. The Thomas G. Ayers residential College of Commerce and Industry sponsors an annual symposium on International Business and has an Investment Club for it members.

Some of Northwestern University's residential colleges also have special facilities. The Wayne V. and Elizabeth R. Jones Performing Arts Residential College showcases student talent. It includes a darkroom, art studios, ensemble rehearsal space, a dance studio, a seminar room, music practice rooms, and an advanced computer-arts station. Special equipment includes a MicroPro digital lightboard, a Kurzweil synthesizer, digital and analog recording facilities, a computer workstation for musical and visual productions, and seven pianos (including two grand pianos).

It should be noted that although most of the residential colleges at Northwestern University are structured around a theme for programing reasons, membership is open to all students regardless of their academic affiliation. Activities in the colleges are voluntary and they are not credit-bearing. However, various academic seminars (tutorials consisting of three to nine students) are offered for one credit (Northwestern University residential colleges website, 9/22/98).

James Madison College at Michigan State University

Michigan State University's James Madison College is another excellent example of a successful residential college. It was established in 1967 during a period in higher education when educational reformers were once again raising the question of what makes an appropriate education for undergraduates. It was a movement—often referred to as the cluster college movement—that was similar to the one that had occurred at the turn of the century; however it was a more intentional attempt to fuse a student's academic and social experiences into meaningful learning. (Another excellent example of a cluster college project is University of California at Santa Cruz whose evolution over the past 30 years is too complex to give it justice in a short description.

However, its development is interesting and informative, and should be more closely analyzed by those who wish to create their own residential colleges. Further information is available from Kliewer, 1999).

James Madison College (JMC) is an undergraduate liberal arts college of public affairs with a population of approximately 1,000 students. New students are required to live in the residential college, although there are many other students who voluntarily return to live there for additional years. The residential facility contains the college's administrative and faculty offices as well as several classrooms, a library, and seminar rooms. As a residence hall, it also provides a computer lab, a dining facility, a convenience store, and various recreational facilities.

The curriculum at James Madison College is multi-disciplinary. Its graduates seek careers and decision-making roles in such fields as law, politics, government service, the social services, business, and industry. First-year students enjoy small classes that have generally no more than 25 students. About half of the classes are offered in the college's own facilities; the remainder are offered throughout Michigan State University. Students pursue advanced course work in their junior and senior years including a field experience requirement and a senior capstone seminar in their respective areas of concentration.

As a residential college, life outside the classroom supplements the academic experience. Activities include guest speakers, career nights with alumni (e.g., Law School Night), panel discussions, a community service fair, and various social activities. Other programs and activities include the Madhouse, a coffeehouse for students and faculty; the Interfield Reading Group (faculty and students meeting weekly to discuss a variety of books); the JMC Student Senate; student organizations such as the International Relations Organization which coordinates model United Nations activities on and off campus and annually sends a model NATO team to compete in Washington D.C.; and the Madison Diplomats (student volunteers who serve as diplomats for the College.) Many Madison students serve in university-wide activities and leadership organizations.

All students in James Madison College are assigned an academic advisor by the College's Director of Academic and Student Affairs. The College's advising staff advise first-year students, whereas faculty in the Madison fields of concentrations advise upper-class students. Another initiative, SUCCESS (Students United to Create a Community of Excellence, Strength, and Support), is an effort supported by students, faculty, and staff to maximize the learning opportunities of the residential college environment. The Madison Writing Consultancy is an example of the SUCCESS initiative. It is a satellite writing center that provides tutoring as well as a variety of other workshops and presentations (James Madison College, 1998).

The Western College Program

Established in 1974, Miami University's Western College Program combines the individualized education of a small program (about 25 students) with the courses and opportunities of a major university. Home of the School of Interdisciplinary Studies, it is a bridge between the general and specialized education at Miami University. It combines an interdisciplinary core curriculum with a program that focuses on a student's individual career and educational goals. Toward this end, for example, students are encouraged to be actively involved in the development of meaningful internship opportunities.

Classes are small to allow for discussion and debate. Students live and learn together in a cluster of academic and residential buildings reminiscent of Western College for Women, the small, private liberal arts college that gave it its name and provided it with a mature yet intimate ready-made campus.

Research is encouraged in the Western College Program. Students can choose to work with any faculty member and they have full access to all of Miami University's facilities. They also participate in off-campus field trips of varying lengths that take them all over the world. The residence hall houses students, classrooms, and learning centers, a theater and lecture hall, faculty and administrative offices, and suites for visiting scholars. A variety of activities are provided ranging from the twice-monthly coffeehouses in the "cozy" Western Lodge to community dinners, intramural activities, movies, and discussion groups with professors (Miami University, 1997).

University of South Carolina

The University of South Carolina's first residential college, Ruttledge College, was established in 1805, four years after the founding of the university. Its intimate living and learning environment was typical of the colleges at the time. Initially, the college housed "students, faculty, staff, classrooms, library, and [a] chapel." Over the course of almost two centuries, the university followed the route of most universities in the United States, gradually moving away from the residential college ideal (Department of Housing, 1998).

In support of this goal, the university revisited the "residential college concept" in 1995. With the establishment of Preston College, the University of South Carolina renewed its historical "commitment to providing quality undergraduate education." The university sought to personalize the educational experience by creating "an intimate learning community where students [could] further develop the skills, knowledge, and attitudes associated with a liberal arts education" (University of South Carolina housing application, 1998).

The head of Preston College is the Principal, a senior member of the university faculty. The Principal reports to the Provost and serves a three-year term. A furnished apartment within the college, some meals, and reserved parking are provided to the Principal. These and other arrangements serve to facilitate increased involvement in the college community. The Principal's responsibilities include recruiting the college's 25 to 35 faculty associates, developing programming with faculty, advising the college Parliament, and assisting with the selection of residence life staff (Henry & Bruce, unpublished survey, 1998).

Faculty associates maintain office hours in the college, teach classes in the college seminar room, and take advantage of other opportunities to interact with the student residents, such as having dinner in the Preston College Dining Hall.

Selection to the college is competitive and committed to diversity. Student members are actively involved in reviewing new applicants. The college community includes 110 men and 110 women. It is a mixed group of students (freshman, transfer, returning) who live in alternating two-story style suites. Students who apply to live in Preston College must have at least a 2.3 GPA. They must also contribute $50 to the college activity fund, from which expenditures are approved by the student government and the Principal.

The Department of Housing reports that the University of South Carolina intentionally builds living and learning communities for its students. It characterizes its relationship with academic affairs and individual faculty members as "long-lasting partnerships," and states that there is a "shared commitment to sustained program development." The Department of Housing indicates that there is strong agreement across campus on the importance of an undergraduate focus and notes that this commitment is reflected in the goals and values expressed from the President on down (Henry & Bruce, unpublished survey, 1998).

University of Miami

In 1983, President Edward T. Foote II, announced that the University of Miami would develop and implement a system of residential colleges by 1988. This initiative was designed to enhance the undergraduate student experience as well as increase overall academic excellence. Five residence hall complexes were converted to include residences for faculty, classrooms, seminar rooms, and other facilities at a cost of $17 million.

Each residential college has a master who is a tenured faculty scholar who serves as an intellectual role model and sets the overall tone for the college. The master supervises two associate masters who also live in the residential college. These resident faculty members promote faculty-student interaction and coordinate the overall academic, recreational, and cultural programs that take place in the residential college.

A group of faculty fellows, who live outside the college, participate in the programming as well. A professional residence coordinator is responsible for the day-to-day operations of the residential college. His or her duties include supervising staff, coordinating judicial affairs, and performing the general administrative functions of the residential college. The residence coordinator also collaborates with the faculty on program development (University of Miami, 1996).

West Virginia University

West Virginia University (WVU) recently transformed its traditional residence hall system into seven residential learning communities, each of which houses approximately 450 undergraduate students. These new learning communities are part of a university-wide presidential initiative, Operation Jump-Start, designed to enhance the quality of the undergraduate experience.

Each Residential Learning Community (RLC) is viewed as a student's "home base" within the larger university campus and serves as the foundation upon which the undergraduate experience is initiated. It provides a point of access to student services and other university resources. It also facilitates learning connections among the academic, social, and civic areas of a student's life. Each of the residential learning communities has a general theme or focus that further serves to enhance the overall program. Most of these themes are quite broad such as community service, wellness, or the arts. Two residential learning communities have made informal affiliations with colleges—one with Arts and Sciences and another with Engineering. The university believes that "these connections will bring strength and breadth to *understanding*, spur creativity and ingenuity, and instill in a student a personal sense of meaning and purpose that will fuel a lifelong quest to learn, to lead, and to serve" (Department of Housing & Residence Life, 1997).

Each residential learning community has a resident faculty leader (RFL) who lives on campus in new or newly renovated homes next door to their residence halls. The houses are especially designed to accommodate the resident faculty leaders and their family, and provides an office/study and common gathering and entertainment areas to host student groups or possibly a special dinner.

The resident faculty leaders serve as intellectual and personal role models for the community. They coordinate special presentations and seminars presented by members of the university faculty and other guest speakers. Resident faculty leaders and residence hall coordinators, along with other members of the University community, teach a newly-designed orientation course in the residence halls. The resident faculty leader works closely with the professional live-in residence hall coordinator relative to the general administration of the residence hall and the overall student life. They work in partnership to intervene and provide guidance to students who may be having some academic or interpersonal difficulties. The RFLs (known by members of the campus community as "riffles") assume responsibility for program planning and implementation and manage a budget funded largely through a 1% allocation of room and board fees. Residence halls contain additional facilities such as computer labs, learning centers (tutoring and academic support services), fitness centers, and dining halls.

Now in its third year, the program reports enhanced retention, improved student academic success, enhanced relationships with parents and families, and a decrease in incidents. Other campus-wide programs are integrated with the residential experience and speak to the comprehensive nature of this initiative. WVU's Up-All-Night provides extensive programming in the student center on weekends to serve as an alternative to the local "bar scene." Near the end of the year, the Sophomore Launch celebration marks the students' successful conclusion to their freshman year. Given the nature of the learning communities, all of these activities and expectations are designed to support the personal growth and academic support of each student.

The Residential College at the University of Michigan

Every student admitted to the College of Literature, Science, and the Arts (LS&A) at the University of Michigan is eligible to join the Residential College (RC). This live-and-learn opportunity began in 1967 and currently enrolls about a thousand students. The RC is a small liberal arts degree-granting four-year college that has access to the full benefits of a major research university. Students graduate with a BA or BS degree from the University of Michigan, the College of Literature, Science and Arts, and the Residential College.

The RC requires freshman and sophomore students to live in, and as such, provides convenient access to faculty, academic advising, classrooms, a language lab, a computer center, and practice studios that are all located in the same quadrangle. RC students can choose from among 60 concentrations offered by LS&A or complete one of the residential college's six interdisciplinary concentrations. About 40% of students choose an RC concentration from among the following options: Arts and Ideas in the Humanities, Comparative Literature, Creative Writing and Literature, Drama, Social Science, and an Individualized Concentration.

Students of the RC have extensive contact with faculty that begins with the required First Year Seminar for all new students. Other distinguishing features of the RC include small classes, a required proficiency in a second language, and a great deal of student control over the design of personal academic programs. To assist in their planning, students receive detailed narrative evaluations in all RC courses so that they may fully assess their own performance (University of Michigan website, 1998).

St. Lawrence University

St. Lawrence's University's first-year students join one of 12 residential colleges, each of which comprises a live-and-learn community of approximately 45 students. Entering freshman are asked to take a year-long multi-disciplinary course that is team taught generally by three faculty. This course reflects the theme of their residential college. By living and studying together, discussions that begin in class can be continued at home. Students also have the opportunity to work collaboratively on assigned projects.

Typical college themes and course descriptions focus on social issues from women's voices, sports in society, popular culture, and spiritual traditions. The first-year students meet twice a week in a team-taught lecture format and twice a week in seminars. Members of the faculty have a minimum of four academic contacts per week with students, and thus are more able to advise students on academic and personal issues.

The First Year Program (FYP) is designed to provide its first-year students with a solid foundation upon which to base their four years of college. The FYP philosophy is that reading, writing, communications skills, and research are critical to a successful liberal arts education. By the end of the FYP experience, students are expected to demonstrate these skills through skilled oral and written argumentation. Journal writing is also a very important learning tool. It fuses communication and community service, encourages diligent research habits, and exercises critical thinking skills.

The residential life of the college is a critical part of the experience. The residential curriculum is organized by residence coordinators, college assistants, mentors, and faculty and consists of activities, community meetings, and discussions that allows students to reflect upon the connections between college themes and their personal experiences. For example, students are expected to resolve conflicts through negotiation and mediation; room changes are not authorized without first utilizing mediation, and students must be able to demonstrate that they have tried sincerely to make an effort to live together. The residence coordinator provides a community development workshop that helps students develop conflict resolution skills.

Piloted in 1987 and developed largely as a faculty initiative in response to their desire to make a more effective connection between teaching and learning, St.

Residential Colleges

Lawrence University's (1998) FYP has developed into a program that fully integrates the academic, the social, and the personal lives of its students.

Chadbourne Residential College at the University of Wisconsin-Madison

The fall of 1997 saw the opening of Chadbourne Residential College (CRC) at the University of Wisconsin-Madison. Developed from a traditional residence hall, the CRC is made up of a diverse, coeducational community that includes honors, first-year, and returning students. The CRC strives to be a learning community and it offers many opportunities for student interactions with each other and with faculty. The CRC aims to provide an environment and atmosphere for students who want to become actively involved in their life outside of the classroom and who desire the benefits and traditions of a small liberal arts education at a large research university.

The Chadbourne Residential College values student empowerment, leadership, inclusiveness, and involvement. The CRC Community Forum is a regular meeting where all community members are welcome to discuss issues and plan programs. The CRC Community Board is an elected body for the hall and serves as the Community Forum's executive committee. Four mission groups or executive committees address issues of concern for the entire community: Diversity, Facstaff, Community Outreach, and the Coffeehouse.

Students pay an additional $300 per year to live at the CRC. This fee provides for a student-controlled $18,000 programming budget. A faculty director and a residence life coordinator work together to administer the daily functions of the CRC. In addition, a network of fellows consisting of interested faculty and staff participate in the CRC life by taking an occasional meal in the college, leading informal discussions, attending field trips, and participating in community service and recreational activities.

The CRC program continues to grow relative to student interest and faculty involvement. In the fall semester of 1996, Chadbourne presented 109 programs with a total attendance of 2,747, which included 20 faculty visits. The fall semester of 1997 saw 238 activities attended by 10,563 students. Faculty and staff visits numbered 361 (Rhem, May/June 1998).

Some Important Considerations

As we approach the next century, the residential college movement is riding a wave of popularity for a third time this century, and it is difficult to resist the desire to jump in with everyone else. However, it is important to look past the familiar, inviting call of Alex Duke's Oxbridge image. University administrators who wish to develop a residential college model of their own must consider whether their institutions truly are prepared to make the commitment necessary to develop and sustain a viable, meaningful program. Such a commitment means more than assigning people and money to the project.

If the project is to work well, it will require, at the very least, a productive partnership between professional residence life staff and members of the faculty based on mutual respect and trust. Administrators are advised to encourage open and ongoing communication between academic affairs and student affairs early in the planning stages so that the influence of territorial inclinations and stereotypes may be diminished. To truly support the ideal of a learning community, traditional boundaries must be traversed often enough to blur the line.

Students also need to be involved in the design and control of any live and learn program. Self-governance relative to the community and personal responsibility relative to the individual are fundamental tenets of a learning community. Students who are denied ownership in a new project will invest in something else. Their full participation is necessary to breathe life into the project, to ensure its continued relevance, and to carry traditions forward to future generations of students.

Finally, a learning community can be an exciting laboratory for faculty, staff, and students. The university president must set and maintain this tone by encouraging experimentation and rewarding ingenuity. It can be messy. It can be risky. It can be absolutely frightening to give such free rein. But no matter what the disruption, a strong, healthy community will always settle back into itself, incorporate what it has learned, and move on to the next unknown. This is how it grows; it is how its members grow. This is what a learning community is all about.

A Final Word

This chapter discussed the residential college movement in the United States and traced its historical roots in the colleges of Oxford and Cambridge, England, as well as its earlier adaptations in the United States at the turn of the twentieth century.

Presented herein are the essential elements of the live and learn philosophy, such as out-of-class student interactions with faculty, community-building traditions, and an opportunity to connect academic learning with real life experiences. Included was a detailed description of the evolving relationship between the undergraduate and the tutor at Oxford and Cambridge, as well as a discussion of various educational philosophies and social changes that influenced higher education in England and the United States.

It concluded by outlining the wide range of live-and-learn initiatives, such as special interest housing and freshman year experience programs, and several examples of successful residential learning communities, including a few residential college programs.

In his book, *College: The Undergraduate Experience in America*, Ernest L. Boyer (1987) points out that the concept of "matriculation" has lost its connotation of fellowship (p. 43). Sprawling and eclectic universities—especially those whose gates have long been flung wide to accommodate an increasingly diverse student body—may have not consciously traded expectation for access or tradition for inclusion, but the result is the same: many universities are so porous that students flow in and out (and often back again) unnoticed, untouched, and uninitiated into a universitas of scholars. A small, intentional living and learning environment is viewed as a means by which to mitigate this effect. It scales down and personalizes an overwhelming university presence by establishing a home base for its members and a focal point for their experiences. Even today in the United States, the residential colleges of Oxford and Cambridge are often held up as the epitome of a living and learning environment; however it is the many modifications of this model that ensure the perpetuation of its ideals over time.

References

American College Personnel Association. (1996). The student learning imperative [Special issue]. *Journal of College Student Development, 37*(2).

Branford College. (9/21/98) [On-line]: Available: http://www.yale.edu/branford/rescol.htm

Boyer Commision on Educating Undergraduates in the Research University. (1998). *Reinventing undergraduate education: a blueprint for America's research universities.* State University of New York at Stony Brook: Author.

Boyer, E. L. (1987). *College: The undergraduate experience in america.* New York: Harper & Row.

Cambridge University. (12/15/98). [On-line]. Available: http://users.cam.ac.uk/

Cambridge University. (9/22/98). *A short history* [On-line]. Available: http://www.cam.ac.uk/CambUniv/pubs/history/

Cambridge University. (10/17/98). *The way it works* [On-line]. Available: http://www.cam.ac.uk/CambUniv/pubs/works.html

Department of Housing. (1998). *Preston new/transfer students application* [application form]. Columbia, SC: University of South Carolina.

Department of Housing & Residence Life. (1997/February). *Operation Jump-Start: An experience like no other* [duplication]. Morgantown, WV: Author.

The Division of Campus Residences. (No date). *Living Learning Centers* [Brochure]. Stony Brook, NY: University at Stony Brook.

Duke, A. (1996). *Importing oxbridge.* New Haven: Yale University Press.

Girton College. (10/15/98). [On-line]. Available: http://www.girton.cam.ac.uk/

Haskins, C. H. (1957). *The rise of universities* (13th ed.). Ithaca, NY: Cornell University Press.

Henry, C. S., & Bruce, S. (1998). [Living and learning programs in american colleges and universities]. Unpublished survey responses.

James Madison College. (1998). *1998-99 Academic year student handbook.* East Lansing, MI: Michigan State University.

Kennedy, D. (1997). *Academic duty.* Cambridge, MA: Harvard University Press.

Kliewer, J. R. (1999). *The innovative campus: nurturing the distinctive learning environment.* Phoenix, AZ: Oryx Press.

Leslie, W. B. (1992). *Gentlemen and scholars.* College and Community in The "Age of the University," 1865-1917. University Park, PA: The Pennsylvania State University Press.

Little & Associates Architects. (1998). *Campus design* [Brochure]. Charlotte, NC: Author.

Matthews, A. (1997). *Bright college years.* New York: Simon & Schuster.

Merton College website. (12/15/98). [On-line]. Available: http://www.merton.ox.ac.uk/

Miami University. (1997). *The school of interdisciplinary studies: Western College program* [Brochure]. Oxford, OH: Author.

Midgely, G. (1996). *University life in eighteenth century oxford.* New Haven: Yale University Press.

Murray State University. (2/1/98). *Houses* [On-line]. Available: http://www.mursuky.edu/secsv/hous/res.html

Northwestern University. (9/22/98). *Residential colleges.* [On-line]. Available: http://stuaff.nwu.edu/rescoll/list.html

Oxford University. (12/15/98). [On-line]. Available: http://users.ox.ac.uk/

Princeton University. (10/19/98) *Forbes college* [On-line]. Available: http://www.princeton.edu/~fpage/info.html

Princeton University. (10/22/98) *Wilson college* [On-line]. Available: http://www.princeton.edu/~wilsonco/info.html

The residential nexus: A focus on student learning. (1996, April). *ACUHO-I Talking Stick,* 6-8.

Rhem, J. (1998, May/June). *Living as learning: A look at chadbourne residential college.* On Wisconsin, 22-26.

Rothblatt, S. (1968). *The revolution of the dons: Cambridge and society in victorian England.* New York: Basic Books.

St. Lawrence University (1998, January). First year program (FYP). Canton, NY: Author.

Study Group on the Conditions of Excellence in American Higher Education. (1984, October). *Involvement in learning: realizing the potential of American higher education.* Washington, DC: National Institute of Education.

Residential Colleges

University of Miami. (1996) Position description: Residence coordinator. Author.

University of Michigan. (9/17/98). *About the RC* [On-line]. Available: http://www.rc.lsa.umich.edu/aboutrc/index.html

University of Vermont. (1998). *Living/Learning Center Information 1998-1999* [Brochure]. Burlington VT: University of Vermont.

University of Virginia. (1991). *Monroe Hill College annual report.* [No location]: Author.

Veysey, L. R. (1965). *The emergence of the American university.* Chicago: University of Chicago Press.

Westmeyer, P. (1997). *An analytical history of american higher education.* Springfield, Illinois: Charles C. Thomas Publisher, Ltd.

Wingspread Group on Higher Education. (1993). *An American imperative: higher expectations for higher education.* Racine, WI: The Johnson Foundation.

Yale University. (9/21/98). *Branford college history* [On-line]. Available: http://www.yale.edu/branford/history.html

Yale University. (2/5/98). *Academics* [On-line]. Available: http://www.cis.yale.edu/admit/academics.html

Yale University. (10/28/98) *The faculty* [On-line]. Available: http://www.yale.edu/admit/faculty.htm

Yale University. (9/21/98). *The residential colleges* [On-line]. Available: http://www.yale.edu/admit/colleges.html

Academically Sponsored
Residential Learning Programs

William J. Zeller
Director of Housing

Mary L. Hummel
Associate Director of Housing-Learning Initiatives

University of Michigan

Academically Sponsored Residential Learning ─────────

Reform initiatives in undergraduate education over the past decade have created a renewed sense of commitment among faculty and student affairs professionals toward the development of improved student learning experiences. In particular, significant attention has been placed on the importance of establishing coherence between curricular and co-curricular educational outcomes. Recent research findings indicate that undergraduate learning can be significantly enhanced when activities outside the classroom complement formal classroom instruction (Astin, 1993; Kuh, Schuh, and Whitt, 1991; Light, 1992; Terenzini & Pascarella, 1994).

Campus educators who have pursued these initiatives often have found that the most effective means for achieving their goals has been through the development of residentially-based learning communities. In essence, the student living community has been found to be the setting where innovative curricular and pedagogical practices can be implemented by creating connections between students' in-class and out-of-class experiences.

An additional benefit achieved through the development of these programs has been the attainment of a renewed sense of community on campus. In particular, this is being achieved as academic affairs and student affairs staffs have collaborated—often for the first time—in an effort to achieve common educational goals.

These new partnerships have resulted not only in the development of many exciting new educational offerings, but quite often they have also created a sense of collegiality on campus that has not existed previously. Parallel reform initiatives in academic affairs and student affairs over the past decade have allowed these two areas to find common ground where historically it did not exist. In general, this common ground has been found through mutual commitments to enhance teaching and learning.

Campus residence halls have thus fortuitously become the setting where innovation and educational synergy is being achieved on many campuses. This newfound attention and subsequent credibility is dramatically changing the role of campus residence halls. Although Housing and Residence Life professionals historically touted the educational importance of the residential experience, this concept was not shared among faculty, administrators, and students until very recently. On many campuses, the reform movement in undergraduate education has solidified the importance of the potential contribution residence halls can make toward fulfilling curricular and educational goals.

It is also interesting to note that as campus partnerships have formed in the pursuit of developing new residential learning communities, this collaboration has produced programs which are uniquely designed to address the educational needs and outcomes of a particular institution. Different campuses produce different learning community programs. Likewise, different campuses produce different types of partnerships between academic and student affairs staff. This uniqueness occurs primarily because the resources, energies, and educational goals vary greatly from campus to campus. As these campus characteristics blend and merge with one another, new and unique campus-based learning opportunities are emerging that are not being duplicated anywhere else. It seems, therefore, that the process is equally as important as the final product in determining the overall design of these programs. In addition, the nature of the student affairs/academic affairs partnership is influenced greatly by the initial source of sponsorship, the personalities involved, and the political dynamics of a particular campus.

To maximize the potential of these programs and partnerships, it is important for residence hall professionals to function effectively in collaboration with academic colleagues. Healthy partnerships are the key to the success of these programs. Unfortunately, many campuses have experienced difficulty in developing these partnerships as colleagues have attempted to find common ground among the previously disconnected cultures of academic and student affairs.

This chapter provides insights for developing sustainable partnerships, particularly when sponsorship emerges from academic affairs.

Campus Models For Developing Residential Learning Programs

A Brief History

Although the residential college model was adopted as the primary model for the first institutions of higher education in the United States, commitment to this concept has waivered throughout our history (Ryan, 1992). Over the past thirty years, interest and commitment toward the development of residential learning programs has continued to be sporadic on many campuses. During the 1960s, residential colleges in particular saw a resurgence of interest on many campuses as faculty explored new ways to teach and to learn. This was in response to issues campuses were facing as they were growing in size and becoming more impersonal (Newcomb, 1961). Many faculty during this time felt that educating the whole student, inside and outside of the classroom, was their responsibility and thus took responsibility for the development of these programs.

In addition, on many campuses the 1960s and early 70s also saw the development of a number of theme-based living-learning centers that focused on developmental non-curricular interest areas. These programs were often implemented by the institution's Housing or Student Affairs offices. Collaboration between academic and student affairs during this time was essentially non-existent, and thus these new programs were developed as self-contained enterprises tangential to the institutional mission.

By the late 1970s, interest in these types of educational opportunities waned. Since the end of World War II, faculty reward systems had moved away from valuing teaching and learning to the recognition of research and scholarship. Subsequently, the student affairs profession gained more responsibility for out-of-class environments and embraced Student Development Theory as a theoretical foundation. Consequently, the gap between in-class and out-of-class activities grew substantially. During this time, interest in residential learning programs and finding connections between the curriculum and co-curriculum dissipated.

The mid-1980s brought renewed attention to these issues (Astin, 1993; Boyer, 1987; Study Group, 1984;) as significant deficiencies were found in the undergraduate experience on campuses across the country. Since the mid-1980s, campus leaders have worked diligently to respond to the calls for reform that were brought forward. These calls were coming from several sources. National and state governments began to call for accountability in the face of rapidly rising costs and perceived diminished quality in an undergraduate education. Institutional leaders were faced with responsibilities to enhance retention, increase success rates of underrepresented students, to be highly competitive for students in a declining traditional student demographic market, and to manage the concerns of an increasingly diverse student population.

Academic leaders were pressed to place greater importance on teaching and learning in undergraduate education, particularly with the need to address educational outcomes. Pedagogical reform, general education reform, the utilization of technology, and curricular reform were manifestations of this trend.

Student affairs leaders began to move away from viewing Student Development Theory as a foundation for the profession and embraced student learning as a new construct. Although Student Development Theory is an important tool for anyone working with traditional-aged college students, student learning theories are now viewed as more encompassing of a broader role within the institution.

These events also brought opportunities for the development of collaborative partnerships and restructuring opportunities between academic and student affairs. Previous organizational structures had created parallel organizations with minimal formal collaboration. Terenzini and Pascarella stated, "Academic Affairs and Student Affairs functions of most institutions have been running essentially on parallel, but separate tracks: Academic Affairs tends to students' cognitive development, while Student Affairs ministers their affective growth" (1994, p. 32). From these findings, new opportunities for informal and formal collaboration had begun to emerge.

Three Areas of Sponsorship

During the 1990s, campus leaders, faculty, and student affairs professionals have responded to the calls for reform with initiatives designed to create coherence between in-class and out-of-class experiences and to redefine campus community.

One response that has come from both the academic and student affairs areas has been the development of residentially-based learning communities. Although different types of partnerships have been created on different campuses, three primary sources of sponsorship have emerged.

1. *Programs where primary sponsorship has come from academic affairs:*

On many campuses, the catalyst for the development of these learning programs has come from individual faculty members, academic departments and/or schools or colleges. Their interests are in enhancing pedagogy, the fulfillment of curricular and educational outcomes, and research and grant opportunities.

2. *Programs where primary sponsorship has come from student affairs:*

The primary interest of student affairs staff is to enhance the intellectual climate of student life outside of the classroom, strengthen campus community, and create connections for students between their in-class and out-of-classroom experiences. A secondary interest is making student affairs an integral part of the educational mission of the institution.

3. *Programs where primary sponsorship has come from institutional leaders:*

Institutional leaders who have sponsored these programs have done so primarily in response to critics of higher education who have questioned the value of undergraduate education and called for greater accountability. As a part of addressing these concerns, institutional leaders are interested in enhancing campus culture and improving recruitment and retention initiatives.

This chapter discusses the issues, opportunities, and benefits for programs that are primarily sponsored by academic affairs, as well as the responsibilities of student affairs and residential life professionals as partners in these programs.

Academically-Based Residential Programs—Motivating Factors

Over the past decade, individual academic faculty, academic schools and colleges, and academic executive officers have pursued the development of residential learning communities actively on many campuses. Academic sponsors of Residential Learning Programs have been motivated by three primary factors: enhancing and measuring the attainment of curricular objectives, improving pedagogical practices, and pursuing research opportunities.

Examples of curricular objectives that have been addressed by these programs include first year experience initiatives; general education initiatives; Math, Science and Engineering curricular enhancements; internationalization; diversity and intergroup relations; development of technological skills; service learning; and leadership education.

Examples of pedagogical initiatives include collaborative learning, learning community models, supplemental instruction, and experiential learning.

The calls for educational accountability have come from both inside and outside of the institution. Students and institutional administrators have urged faculty and academic departments to have greater accountability for the educational value of their classes. In addition, external constituents—including parents, the media, state and federal legislators, and national Higher Education leaders—have called upon colleges and universities to be more accountable in terms of addressing educational outcomes, providing more personal attention, and being more affordable.

A secondary objective of the academic sponsor is often to create a setting where new educational theories and research can be accomplished. The Residential College and the 21st Century Program at the University of Michigan were established with the intent of testing particular theoretical models created by the faculty sponsors.

The Residential College was created in 1967 to address the growing concern among faculty about the growing disconnection between students' in-class and out-of-class experiences. Professor Ted Newcomb (1961) believed that students' educational experiences should be evaluated based not only on their acquisition of academic skills and knowledge, but also on their development of what he called "intellectual values"— tolerance for new ideas, intellectual curiosity, and enhanced aesthetic sensitivities. He felt these values might be overlooked as the University was expanding and becoming more impersonal. To counter this sense of isolation, he proposed a living-learning community of students and faculty that would develop students both in and out of the classroom. Thirty years later, this alternative is still thriving.

Academically Sponsored Residential Learning ─────────

Professor Claude Steele initiated another example of a faculty member testing a new theoretical framework by developing a living-learning program in 1991. Steele was interested in exploring the reasons for differences in achievement and retention between African-American students and Caucasian students on university campuses. His work describing stereotype vulnerability and dis-identification with education became the conceptual basis of the 21st Century Program (Steele & Aronson, 1995). Based on this theory and national concern about achievement, the 21st Century Program was developed to address issues of academic achievement and retention of students.

Cultures of Student and Academic Affairs

As collaborative partnerships between academic and student affairs have formed in recent years, the distinctive characteristics of each culture have become more and more apparent. The two sets of professional beliefs, values, and behaviors that have separately evolved for over half a century have been accentuated by attempts to collaborate.

One major area of cultural difference is in regard to professional belief systems. Faculty differentiate between formal learning (within the classroom) and the various other kinds of learning. Faculty clearly value formal learning most highly. Student affairs staff have based their professional beliefs on Student Development Theory as a body of knowledge for their work. Faculty have often viewed these theoretical applications as a "pseudo discipline" (Zeller, 1997). In addition, faculty perceive student affairs work as having little to do with the formal classroom or discipline-based learning they value. In formal learning, students are moving from their known experience to generalized concepts. In the more informal learning experiences, it is the other way around (Blake, 1996). Hence, a philosophical difference exists between the two cultures in approaches to learning itself.

Another contrast between these two cultures is in the area of values. Faculty work within a discipline, often on isolated projects, questioning and challenging existing knowledge. Student affairs staff, however, are working within a more structured setting, looking at a broader view of the community and how the parts interact. Rarely does student affairs staff operate in isolation from the larger community. Little value is placed on the other's world of work (Zeller, 1997).

Given the contrast in professional beliefs and values, it is not surprising that the behaviors between these two cultures are different. In general, faculty's individualized approach to work results in a perceived focus on research and an allegiance to one's discipline; whereas the community-based approach of student affairs is perceived to foster collaboration, outreach, and an allegiance to the institution.

Given these distinct cultures, efforts for collaboration may seem futile. However, there are successful examples of collaboration which illustrate the strength of the end result when the two cultures do work together. Much of this successful collaboration is being achieved through mutual attempts to respond to calls for improving undergraduate education.

In the development and management of residential learning programs, roles and expectations may need to be clearly defined and articulated. At the University of Michigan, a set of written protocols has been developed between University Housing and the College of Literature, Science, and the Arts. These protocols grew out of the need to establish guidelines for living-learning programs as the programs have increased in size and complexity and have created a broader network of collaboration across the campus. Staff turnover and increased staff size have also contributed to the need for these protocols.

The protocols were developed jointly by academic program directors and University Housing professional staff. For each point of interest there is a guiding principle and also several practical examples of how such a principle would be implemented.

One example of a common point of interest is "Joint Communications." The Guiding Principle is that both the Academic Director and the Residence Hall Staff member must review and approve joint communications and letters before releasing them to the public.

Here is an example of this principle in practice. The Housing staff member and the Academic Director want to send out a joint letter to articulate community expectations. The Housing staff member drafts a letter. The Academic Director reviews the letter, edits it, and talks with the Housing staff member. Both parties obtain approval from higher authority in their own units as needed. The Housing staff member revises the letter and both sign it. The letter is sent out to students.

Although this seems to represent very basic administrative practices, these types of written principles can clarify expectations and avoid potential problems as the two groups work together, often for the first time.

Types of Academically Sponsored Programs

In an effort to fulfill college or departmental curricular and pedagogical objectives, academic affairs faculty and administrators have, with increased frequency, initiated residential learning programs. The types of residential programs with an academic base of sponsorship range from the degree-granting immersive experience of the Residential College to the less intensive.

The strictest definition of a Residential College is a four-year degree-granting program around which a student makes a commitment to center their academic experience. It often combines opportunities to develop unique interdisciplinary majors with smaller faculty-to-student ratios. The Residential College at the University of Michigan is an example of this model. Some residential colleges offer a variety of majors, while others focus specifically on one discipline such as science or the humanities. Murray State University is an example of a large scale conversion of the undergraduate experience to residential colleges; Michigan State University offers examples of residential colleges such as Lyman-Briggs, which is focused on specific academic disciplines.

The less intensive academically-sponsored programs are usually centered on the first-year experience and include programs such as transition programs (freshmen experience), linked course models Freshmen Interest Groups (FIGs), and other types of one-year offerings. Transition programs focus on helping students navigate the transition from high school to college and may include a seminar that introduces students to university life, resources and skills such as the Freshmen Seminar Program at Washington State University. The University of Missouri, Columbia is an example of a program that offers "linked" courses that combine students who live together and take classes in several disciplines as a single cohort. Other programs may focus on course offerings, seminars, and common experiences based on interest areas such as multiculturalism or women's studies, as illustrated by the College Park Scholars Program at the University of Maryland.

On many campuses, the residential living-learning programs often have first-year students as their primary focus. Other learning community initiatives, both residential and non-residential, have often addressed educational outcomes and needs for juniors and seniors. An example of such a program is the Stonehill College Senior Transitions Conference. These programs are generally connected to students' majors and are sponsored through a particular academic department. Other offerings for upper-level students include capstone courses designed to help students find coherence within their entire undergraduate curriculum. Research opportunities, practicums, and internships also provide upper-level students with small group experiences.

It seems that a significant void exists on many campuses in addressing the needs of sophomores, who often wish to continue their learning community experiences but find few opportunities available to them. The sophomore year offers thus another significant opportunity for Housing professionals to form new partnerships with academic colleagues. These opportunities might include sophomore mentorship and leadership programs in first-year student living-learning programs, or work with faculty to develop whole new offerings for sophmore students.

This depiction illustrates the numbers of programs available by class year.

First Year*

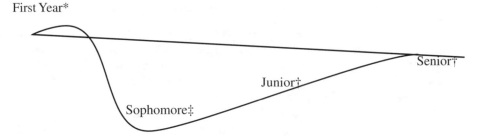

* consists primarily of residential learning programs
† examples include: • capstone • major-based learning communities • research and experiences
‡ • mentorship • leadership • potential for new sophomore programs

Pedagogical Innovation in Residential Learning Programs

The desire to improve classroom teaching methods also has been a primary catalyst for academic affairs in the development of residential learning programs. New pedagogical innovations that are more active and interactive provide rich opportunities for transcending traditional classroom boundaries. By incorporating co-curricular opportunities into the curriculum, these new pedagogies open the door for substantial partnerships to be created between academic and student affairs.

Over the past decade, traditional classroom instruction models generally have been found to be ineffective in fulfilling new learning outcomes. New pedagogies are moving away from traditional lecture formats to embrace more active and experiential learning models.

These non-traditional teaching practices include:

- Collaborative and cooperative learning models that group students in a variety of active learning formats;
- Practical and service-learning components that provide experiential learning opportunities;
- Learning community models that link student groups with several different courses;
- Freshman Interest Groups that develop learning communities that support first-year transitions;
- Study groups that guide students through course lectures;
- Self-directed learning modules that allow students to learn in their own time-frame and at their own pace;
- Peer teaching opportunities that enrich learning by allowing students to teach other students;
- Supplemental Instruction Models that allow lecture materials to be reintro-duced to small groups by upper-level peer instructors.

Opportunities for collaboration between academic and student affairs colleagues exist in each of these models. Each model transcends traditional classroom boundaries, thus creating a setting for student affairs staff to viably contribute to the educational outcomes of the class.

An untested construct that might help structure the partnership between academic and student affairs can be found in the model of Confluent Education shown below (Brown, 1971). This model was developed in the 1950s in an attempt to merge cognitive and affective learning elements in individual and group learning. Cognitive refers to the activity of the mind in *knowing* an object and intellectual functioning. The affective refers to the *feeling* or emotional aspect of experience and learning.

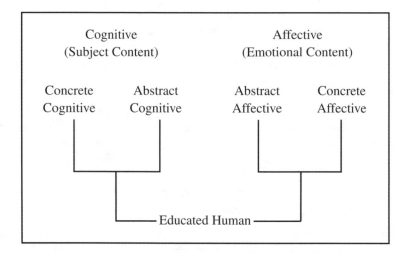

In essence, Confluent Education argues that no intellectual learning takes place without some sort of feeling, and there are no feelings without the mind being somehow involved. Without both dimensions interacting with one another, deep learning cannot occur.

Brown (1971) states, "for a long time we have known the importance of personal involvement in learning. Educational psychologists state that if learning has no personal meaning, it will not change behavior. Seldom has the converse been stated: If we add an emotional dimension to learning, the learner will become personally involved, and as a consequence, there will be change in the learner's behavior."

Residential Learning Communities provide many opportunities for the cognitive and affective to interact with one another, and are thus an opportunity to use this model. In many ways, this model could be used by residential life staff to structure dialogues with faculty and to coordinate curricular and co-curricular opportunities for specific classes. These efforts would be coordinated to maximize the potential for "deep learning" to occur.

As an example, suppose a Political Science course was being offered to members of a particular living-learning community. Within the course, the faculty member was introducing concepts of electoral processes and voter apathy. Using the Confluent Education model, an academic affairs/student affairs collaboration might provide the following opportunities:

Concrete Cognitive: Presentation of demographic data on voting trends. Pertinent theories and research findings would be presented.

Abstract Cognitive: Classroom discussion on the future implications of research findings regarding national voting trends.

Abstract Affective: Observations could be made of a Hall Council election and voter response to candidates. Class members could interview and lead discussions with hall community members who ran for office, who voted, and who did not participate. Summaries of the interviews would be shared in class.

Concrete Affective: A service learning project could be coordinated by hall staff to promote voter registration in a disadvantaged neighborhood. Subsequent processing would occur regarding the feelings students had about their experiences.

The full collaboration of both academic faculty and residential life staff would be needed to allow the cognitive and affective experiences to connect with one another. Thus, Confluent Education helps enrich the learning process, and curricular and cocurricular opportunities must exist in order to allow "deep learning" to occur.

A New Role for Housing Professionals—
Creating Cocurricular Learning Environments

As quality partnerships are initiated between academic and student affairs, an important role of Housing professionals will emerge in the development of residential environments that support student learning. The research findings of Alexander Astin

(1993) provide a structure for the types of environmental characteristics that should be incorporated into a residential facility to best promote student learning. If these characteristics were incorporated actively into the living-learning program environment, the potential for providing a quality learning experience would be greatly enhanced.

Astin (1993) identified the following environmental factors that enhance educational outcomes:

- Quality student-to-student interaction;
- Quality student-to-faculty interaction;
- A faculty that is very student-oriented;
- Discussing racial/ethnic issues with other students;
- Hours devoted to studying;
- Tutoring other students;
- Socializing with other students;
- A student body that has high socio-economic status;
- An institutional emphasis on diversity;
- A faculty that is positive about the general education program;
- A student body that values altruism and social activism.

If used creatively, Astin's research findings can serve as a means for structuring residence hall facility design, staffing patterns, program objectives, and budget structures.

Facility Design

Taking Astin's findings into consideration, decisions regarding space utilization, interior design, facility remodeling, and new construction could be greatly influenced. If the role of the residential facility is to support student learning, then design characteristics must promote quality student-to-student and student-to-faculty interactions. The facility must provide quality space for students to study, to mentor and tutor one another, to socialize with one another, and to experience community service opportunities. The facility must allow students from different backgrounds to live and learn together in a comfortable but highly interactive environment.

Staffing Patterns

Residence hall staffing patterns could be restructured to allow Astin's environmental characteristics to be more substantially provided. Professional and paraprofessional positions could be introduced into the residential environments that would promote student interactions around academic subject matter. In addition, staff could facilitate quality interactions between students and faculty. Staff could also create dialogues around diversity issues and maximize "teachable moments" that might arise in the residential setting. Staff also could be introduced who would support studying and tutoring other students. Specialized staff who would coordinate service projects and altruistic activities also could be provided.

A recommended approach for exploring new residence hall staffing patterns with faculty colleagues would be to initiate a "zero-based" staffing exercise. By creatively rethinking staff functions from the ground up, student affairs/academic affairs partners could maximize staffing resources in the fulfillment of stated learning outcomes for a particular program. Thus, traditional RA and Hall Director positions might be replaced by peer tutors, academic advisors, diversity educators, faculty assistants, and so on. Obviously, administrative and security functions would need to be addressed, but opportunities abound for new approaches to residence hall staffing.

Program Models

Traditional residence hall programming models should be challenged to ensure that programming activities maximize student learning, particularly in residential learning programs that are sponsored by an academic unit. In order to enhance learning and fulfill stated curricular outcomes, co-curricular programming must promote quality student/faculty interactions, complement diversity initiatives, provide for community service and altruism, and ultimately support academic success. How this is achieved can vary from program to program and from campus to campus, yet the essential components of a quality programming model can be found in Astin's model.

Budget Structures and Financial Decision Making

Quality living environments must meet certain standards of acceptability for cleanliness, repair and maintenance, accessibility, and appearance. These areas must have the highest priority for budget allocations to ensure short- and long-term facility viability. However, as funding decisions are made regarding facility renewal, staffing, programming, and other areas, the findings of Astin can serve as a decision-making guide for establishing budget priorities. The development of residential environments that support student learning should be the foundation of all budget decisions, and certainly these characteristics should be given the highest priority.

The effective and comprehensive use of Astin's characteristics can help shape the role of the Residence Life and Housing professional as they form partnerships with academic faculty in the development of Residential Learning communities.

It is hoped that the information provided above will be an effective tool for Housing professionals in forming partnerships with academic colleagues. In addition, the following tips can also serve as a foundation to help Housing professionals develop connections with academic departments and individual faculty.

Practical Tips for Building Faculty Partnerships

1. *Assess Academic Departmental Priorities and Develop a Residential Life Response.* Areas ripe for forging partnerships include: Internationalization, Diversity Education, Service Learning, Information Technologies, Leadership Education, and General Education Reform. In addition, academic support services can be incorporated into the residential setting that support academic goals (academic advising, tutoring, academic outreach, faculty office hours, study groups, etc.) and can all be developed in collaboration with faculty.

2. *Assess Individual Faculty Attitudes Toward Residential Life and Develop a Residential Response.* Compiling data on the perceptions faculty have toward campus

living groups can help structure departmental responses from Housing to faculty and academic departments.

3. *Become Aware of Innovative Pedagogical Initiatives:* Determine how residential staff, facilities, and student contact opportunities can be used to help faculty achieve their teaching goals with students.

4. *Study Faculty Reward Systems and the Academic Culture:* Be astute in framing proposals so as to support faculty promotion and tenure initiatives. Research and service opportunities abound in residential learning programs. For institutions that reward innovation in teaching, residential learning programs provide a rich resource for developing a teaching portfolio.

5. *Use Residentially-Based Technologies as Instructional Support Technologies:* In-room connectivity, residential computer labs, television and radio stations, and computer training and support resources can all be used to support instruction and faculty interests. By framing these resources as Instructional Support Technologies, new partnerships can be formed.

6. *Be Entrepreneurial with Housing Funds:* Although the need to be advocates and stewards of room and board fees is paramount, new funding sources can be cultivated by using Housing funds as "seed monies" for new projects. In particular, external-funding opportunities from grants and other sources can create meaningful and sustainable partnerships. Jointly seeking the attainment of other institutional resources can create opportunities for new funding and partnerships.

7. *Research and Assessment Opportunities:* Develop research and assessment opportunities of living-learning programs and other initiatives in partnership with faculty.

8. *Conference Presentation:* Develop a conference presentation with a faculty member which involves a collaborative initiative. Host the faculty member (and pay for their attendance) at a student affairs conference.

9. *Cultivate Connections Through Students:* Create opportunities for enhancing residential programs by having student paraprofessionals and other student leaders connect and form partnerships with faculty.

10. *Provide Opportunities:* Provide viable opportunities for faculty to eat and meet with students from their own classes. Special group dinners, providing lounge space for group meetings, helping sponsor field trips, service learning opportunities, or recreational activities between faculty and their students are means for forming quality partnerships.

11. *Faculty Profiles:* Learn the profiles of faculty who have the greatest likelihood for becoming partners:

    a) New faculty who have a love of teaching and working with students;

    b) Mid-career faculty who see a professional advancement opportunity in the formation of partnerships;

    c) Senior faculty who want to reconnect with teaching undergraduates at the end of their careers.

Assessment

Assessments is covered thoroughly in chapter 2. Nevertheless, it is important to talk about assessment in the context of residentially-sponsored learning programs to emphasize the importance of this activity. In the previous section, one of the "tips" stated the importance of collaboration between faculty and student affairs staff in the development of research and assessment opportunities. The assessment instrument and process discussed in this section is an example of how to put this suggestion into practice.

Faculty and administrators have long bemoaned the fact that while residential learning communities have existed for a long period of time, very few evaluations of the effects of the living-learning experience have been published (Terenzini, Pascarella, & Blimling, 1994). At the University of Michigan, a need has been identified by campus administrators to assess their learning communities for the possibility of future growth and improvement. The combination of these two circumstances—the lack of an assessment model on the national level and the local need to evaluate programs—led to the development of a new instrument through a collaborative model.

The collaboration began with two higher education faculty members (Sylvia Hurtado and Eric Dey), a living-learning program director (Director of the 21st Century Program, Mary Hummel), Housing staff member (William Zeller), and two graduate students (Gertrude Arnold and Joe Gutowski). The process began with an extensive review of all conceivably related survey instruments. A new instrument was developed based on sets of questions from a variety of sources and using original questions.

The instrument that was designed in this process is unique as it is useful to both practitioners and researchers. In addition, although it was designed for use among the different programs at University of Michigan, it is flexible enough to be used by programs on other campuses as well. Input and consultation with other University constituencies such as other living-learning directors, academic administrators, students, and residence hall staff were solicited and a draft instrument was developed that incorporated key areas of students' college experience.

The instrument incorporates questions that address the following themes: transitions to college, interactions with faculty members, interactions with peers, abilities in making in-class and out-of-class connections, growth and development, perceptions of the residence and living-learning environment, living-learning participation and use of programs/services, satisfaction with living-learning programs, and communication systems in living-learning program. Following the initial development of the instrument, collaboration with an existing living-learning program was sought in order to pilot test the survey.

The instrument was pilot tested in Winter 1998 in one of the residence halls that included a living-learning program on campus. Both participants and non-participants received the survey. The results included here are from the pilot test with a 27 % response rate. While the response rate may be low, the demographics were diverse by several attributes including gender and ethnicity. The response rate was similar to other response rates in surveys using the undergraduate population at this institution.

The findings from the study indicate that living-learning participants found their living environments to be highly satisfactory on a number of academic measures: support for academic achievement, adequate peer support to achieve, adequate study space, conducive to forming study groups, and intellectually stimulating. Another important finding was that living-learning participants indicated that their peers supported their academic achievement by providing support to succeed academically, supporting positive study habits, being aware of campus support services, and thinking that academic support was important. In addition, the program participants indicated that they appreciated diversity and interacted often with students of different backgrounds.

Little-to-no difference between living-learning participants and non-participants was found in terms of ease of transition to college, interactions with faculty, academic and social connections, and perceptions of growth or development.

It is important to note these results are from a very preliminary study and that in Winter 1999 a modified survey (based on feedback from the pilot) will be distributed to all the living-learning program participants on campus. In addition, consideration is being given to a mixed methodological design, both quantitative and qualitative, to add breadth and depth to the information gathered.

Perhaps the key issue to come from this survey instrument is the practicality of use that allows the program and residence hall staff to not only assess outcomes but also to use the instrument to make specific programmatic changes. The second key issue is its applicability across a variety of programs not only at the University of Michigan, but on a national scale as well, which will allow for future research and assessment to address the current gap in the literature with regard to these programs. In addition, it is an excellent example of the kind of outcome that can be achieved in a true collaboration between academic and student affairs.

References

Astin, A. W. (1993). *What matters in college?* San Francisco: Jossey-Bass.

Blake, E. (1996, September-October). The yin & yang of student learning in college. *About Campus.*

Boyer, E. L. (1987). *College: The undergraduate experience in America.* Princeton, NJ: Carnegie Foundation for the Advancement of Teaching. New York: Harper & Row.

Brown, G. I. (1971). *Human teaching for human learning: An introduction to confluent education.* New York, NY: The Viking Press.

Kuh, G. D., Schuh, J. H., Whitt, E. J., & Associates. (1991). *Involving colleges: Successful approaches to fostering student learning and development outside the classroom.* San Francisco: Jossey-Bass.

Light, R. L. (1992). Explorations with students and faculty about teaching, learning, and student life. *The Harvard Assessment Seminars: Second Report.* Cambridge, MA: Graduate School of Education, Harvard University.

Newcomb, T. (1961). *A Modest Proposal.* Ann Arbor, MI: University of Michigan.

Academically Sponsored Residential Learning ─────────

Ryan, M. B. (1992, September/October). Residential colleges: A legacy of living & learning together. *Change*.

Steele, C., & Aronson, J. (1995). Stereotype threat and the intellectual test performance of african americans. *Journal of Personality and Social Psychology. 69*(5).

Study Group on the Conditions of Excellence in Higher education. (1984). *Involvement in learning realizing the potential of higher education.* Washington, DC: National Institute of Education.

Terenzini, P. T., & Pascarella, E. T. (1994, January/February). Living with myths: Undergraduate education in America. *Change*.

Terenzini, P. T., Pascarella, E. T., & Blimling, G. S. (1996). Students' out-of-class experiences and their influence on learning and cognitive development: A literature review. *College Student Development, 37*(2), 149-162.

Zeller, W. J. (1997). Two cultures united: Residential programs of the 21st century. *The Journal of College and University Student Housing. 26*(2), 7-13.

Chapter Six

Community Development

Frankie Minor
Director of Residence Life
University of Missouri-Columbia

Community Development

A review of most housing/residential life program mission statements reveals community development, either explicity or implicitly stated, as a primary goal. However, the formation of community often has been viewed as the end itself, and not as a means to the greater end of student learning and development. Residence life professionals have focused on developing cohesive, integrated, and effective communities assuming that students share that same commitment. However, in our fast-paced and increasingly disjointed society, it is much more likely that students have not enjoyed the benefits of the type of community we seek to develop, and thus have a limited point of reference. Similarly, the communities that we traditionally have sought to develop in residence halls have focused on the shared living experience and failed to capitalize on and integrate the larger community in which the students interact daily—the academic community. This chapter discusses, from a learning community perspective, the value of a community and the ingredients for a cohesive community, a process by which to develop that community and the learning outcomes that will accrue for its members.

The Value of Community

The emphasis on community development in residential life programs has grown from the recognition of the multiple benefits that an effective and cohesive community can have for individual community members, for the collective community itself, and for the institution. From the beginning, when a new member joins a community or the community itself is assembled as a group of individuals, the initial value often is couched in terms of providing a "home base" for each individual. Schlossberg (1989) and others have discussed the importance that an individual feel that he or she "matters" and the negative impact when an individual, and in some cases a group, is marginalized. This degree of inclusion or alienation can have a significant influence on the individual's eventual success and retention at the institution. Beyond the initial transition and assimilation into the community and institutional culture, the peer influences within a community that can provide a positive influence on a student's academic achievement and personal development on a variety of dimensions have been well documented (Astin, 1973, 1977; Chickering, 1974; DeCoster & Mable, 1980; Pascarella & Terenzini, 1991).

Crookston (1974) aptly describes the symbiosis between individual and community—as the individual contributes to the enrichment of the community, so the community is able to enrich the individual. Whether a residence life program chooses to focus on the development of the individual by virtue of his or her participation in the community, or the education and development of the community, albeit as a collective of individuals, is not as relevant as the understanding that the two are frequently intertwined. Initiatives that sought to promote the ethical, moral, or intellectual development of residence hall communities—such as the Sierra Project (Whitley & Associates, 1982), the Evans Hall Democratic Community (Ignelzi, 1990), or even Crookston's intentional democratic community (1974)—were just as concerned about the development of the individual. In these circumstances, the individuals in a collective format demonstrated their own development as part of the community identity.

Ideally, residence life programs that focus on community development have the students' educational and personal development needs as their highest priority. The institution and its staff also benefit when residence halls are a series of cohesive communities. Fully-functioning communities frequently diminish the negative workload of staff and allow them to work on more productive educational and developmental tasks, whether it be reduced incidences of student conduct cases or damage to facilities, more involved or satisfied students, or actual circumstances where community self-governance is achieved. Additionally, student members of these communities exhibit a greater level of institutional identification, and commitment, and overall satisfaction with the institutions (Pike, 1996; Schroeder & Mable, 1994; Winston & Anchors, 1993). Institutions, in turn, can redirect human and financial resource savings to other initiatives that promote their overall goals.

Whether for the benefit of the individual member, the community, or the institution itself, emphasizing community development as a primary goal for a residence life program can be viewed as a wise choice. All too frequently, as mentioned earlier, it is seen as the desired outcome or end point for the combination of residence hall staff, resources and programs—the end rather than the means. Student affairs educators would be wise to remember that learning is the core enterprise at educational institutions and that our efforts must always support this mission. Therefore, while we may focus our attention on the formation of effective, cohesive communities in our residence halls, we must link them closely with the academic mission of the institution, so that "student learning and development are inextricably intertwined" (American College Personnel Association, 1996, p. 118). We must expand our view, our horizons, and our ambitions beyond our traditional orientation, and even our training and experience, to begin to examine the components, processes, and goals of community development from a student learning perspective.

Essential Elements of Community Development

A group of individuals alone does not constitute a community. Essential elements and even processes need to be present for the formation, maintenance, and enhancement of an effective community. Crookston (1980), through his work at the University of Connecticut, identified some of the essential elements to include primary groups, shared goals and values, social contracts, boundaries, power, commitment, communion, and meaningful processes. Boyer's (1990) reflections on community identified six fundamental characteristics of a true community—Caring, Just, Open, Purposeful, Disciplined, and Celebrative. Consistent with both Boyer and Crookston, and for the purposes of our discussion on the formation of communities that emphasize both student learning and development, the following set of essential elements have been identified.

1. *Common Purpose and Core Values*: What is the primary focus of this community and the commonality of purpose of its members? What are the core values of the community and the degree to which they are reflected in the behavior of members and the activities of the group?

2. *Membership and Relationships*: Who constitutes the members of the community; how are they identified? What defines the nature of their interaction and relationship to one another? Is there a recognition, understanding, and eventual appreciation of the interdependence upon one another?

3. *Proximity, Territory, and Boundaries:* What is the physical proximity of the members and the frequency of their interaction? Is there a defined territory that they call their own, and are its boundaries clearly marked or recognizable?

4. *Shared Standards and Expectations:* Are the standards of conduct for members clearly defined, and how were they determined? Are there expectations members have of one another, and how are they articulated, either explicitly or implicitly? Are the standards and expectations consistent with the common purpose and core values?

5. *Communication and Decision-making:* How does the community identify issues, share information, and make decisions? How well do members know each other and believe that they are "in touch" with what is happening within the community? Are there opportunities for members to reflect on experiences or issues?

6. *Active Involvement in Shared Experiences:* Are there common experiences in which members routinely participate? Do members develop and coordinate these experiences? Is there substantial participation by an appropriate number of members in the activities? Do the shared experiences reflect the common purpose and core values?

7. *Customs, Traditions, and Celebrations:* Does the community have identifiable customs or practices for its members and, in particular, for new members? Are there traditions or reoccurring programs that are part of the common experiences? Are there methods to recognize or celebrate the achievements of the community or its individual members?

8. *Identity and Commitment:* Does the community have a recognizable identity that is distinguishable from other communities? Do the members have an individual identity, such as a role or nickname, that is tied to the group identity? How do individuals express their commitment to the community and vice versa?

The elements identified above characterize most of the essential building blocks to form an effective community. However, it is also critical that we assist community members in understanding not just the interrelationship between members, but also in understanding the different levels of community and the interrelationship between them. In other words, a residence hall floor community is part of a slightly larger hall community, which in turn may be part of a residence area community, the residence hall/housing community, the campus community, and the city/town community. This relationship may be characterized by the concentric circles of community metaphor, wherein each level of community has its own identity, shared values, and the other elements listed above. Members need to understand and appreciate that they are members of all other communities beyond their primary level of community. While this may imbue certain privileges and opportunities, it also comes with particular responsibilities.

Stimulating or Promoting Community Development

Understanding the important elements of a community is one step; putting the pieces together into a coherent process is another. Occasionally, individual residence life programs will develop a framework for guiding staff efforts and supporting specific programs or initiatives. More frequently, there is a reliance on individual staff members in a residence hall or area to implement their own strategy based upon their professional education, development, and/or prior experience. All too often this results in an eclectic series of experiences, programs, and initiatives, each with their own value, but not blended in a coherent fashion with a clear set of objectives and outcomes in mind. In other situations, a residence life program or staff member will seek to implement a framework that has been used or developed successfully at another institution. An example is Tuckman's (1965) observations of the four stages of community development: forming, storming, norming, and performing. Similarly, Peck (1987) described four stages as pseudo-community, chaos, emptiness, and community. Student affairs professionals have used these models, translating the observations on stages and developing strategies to either stimulate development or progress to the next stage, or respond to challenges experienced in that stage.

Six I's model. Another model was developed at Saint Louis University as part of the residence life program focused on community development through high levels of student involvement and self-governance. Schroeder (1993) described some aspects of this model, which uses an alliterative device to help professional and paraprofessional staff remember the framework. The full Six I's model, more clearly outlined in a handbook developed for residence life staff (Kahmi & Thompson, 1996), describes a series of progressive, overlapping stages.

1. *Introduction:* New members are welcomed to the community by current members. Community stories, traditions, values, standards, expectations, and norms are shared. Rituals of initiation and orientation occur. "Tribal elders" or more experienced community members are recognized. Opportunities for new members to become more active in the community are identified, through both formal and informal roles.

2. *Interaction:* A wide variety of planned and spontaneous activities occur to foster new or strengthen existing relationships among community members. Many opportunities for interpersonal bonding among individual members and larger clusters of members within the community are available. Further exploration of roles and responsibilities occurs as the community begins to function. New myths, stories, or expectations may begin to evolve.

3. *Involvement:* Members are incorporated more fully into the community, and begin to understand their impact on each other and how individual actions affect the community. Cultural norms that incorporate both the new and experienced members emerge. Formal roles (those with a title) possess some level of authority and responsibility, but validation is often sought from external sources (staff). Conflicts begin to occur, and the community responds usually at the surface level. Initial emergence of community identity.

4. *Investment:* Members begin to exhibit concern about the welfare of the community and other members, particularly from perceived threats. They begin to recognize that at times the community's needs may supersede those of an individual. More effective conflict resolution techniques are identified and implemented. There is a high degree of association with community members and community boundaries; nicknames and language are identifiable. Community identity strengthens.

5. *Influence:* The community expresses a desire for control of, or minimally to have input into, decisions which will affect the community. Members reflect on what they value about the community and seek to maintain and improve it. Members exhibit a sense of accomplishment and pride, and value self-governance. The diversity and

similarities of community members are appreciated, and roles, both formal and informal, are clearly defined. Members are able to clearly express the community.

6. *Identity:* The members of the community know what their community stands for and what it means to be a member of this community. Members describe themselves using we or us, not I or they. A person's identity (membership/role/status) within the community plays a significant role in their current personal self-identity. Members take an active interest in maintaining and preserving the community identity, including the recruitment of new members to the community.

Linking & Aligning Community Development and Learning Outcomes

Although membership and active participation in an effective community offers many benefits to a student, it may not necessarily promote or support their learning and academic objectives. A community with many of the above traits can play a neutral role in a student's success, or even potentially inhibit personal and academic success, if it does not reinforce these as shared values supported by the community activities. The Delta House fraternity in the movie Animal House displayed many of the characteristics of a community that were described previously, including a high degree of member allegiance, but was the antithesis of the values of its imaginary academic home, Faber College. While this example thankfully is fictitious and comic, real-life examples of communities that do not actively or intentionally support students' personal and academic success are all too common and serious. Therefore, it is essential that residence life professionals and paraprofessionals, in conjunction with faculty and academic affairs partners, integrate academic and learning objectives into their community development efforts. The categories will be examined in the context of linking traditional community development goals with learning outcomes, which more explicitly support students' academic success.

The Benefits of Community Development.

Students, and in particular freshman students who comprise the majority of residence hall students on most campuses, are in social and academic transition. Traditional efforts promoting communities address many of their social and interpersonal concerns. Providing students with opportunities to live in communities that have a clear, learning-centered focus, or that are related to particular academic majors or themes, increases the likelihood that they will be successful academically and interpersonally (Pascarella & Terenzini, 1991; Pascarella, Terenzini, & Blimling, 1996; Schroeder & Mable, 1994). Students at the University of Missouri-Columbia (MU) who participated in Freshman Interest Groups (FIGs), wherein students are co-enrolled in classes and live together, and other academic theme-oriented learning communities experienced higher levels of academic achievement and gains in other measures related to their satisfaction and success, even after controlling for entering academic ability (Pike, 1997). A community that reinforces strong academic expectations can convey to new students, early enough to make adjustments, that this differs from high school. Likewise, it can begin to create their sense of academic identity that will be reinforced by their affiliation with a particular academic program.

These same students have been retained in the residence halls at much higher rates than their non-participating colleagues (up to 15% greater), which provides a greater level of stability for communities, and the presence of experienced and successful role models for new members. These students report greater levels of involvement in community activities and more time dedicated to academic activities (Johnson, 1998). Faculty at the University of Missouri-Columbia have reported that students in the FIGs attend class more regularly and participate more in class than students who do not live in these communities, presumably because they feel the additional level of support in class and are less concerned about taking risks in class among their friends. Additionally, these students are retained at the institution in greater percentages than non-participants and exhibit greater levels of institutional commitment (Pike, 1996). Data is not yet available for graduation rates for these programs, but a three-year longitudinal study of an original cohort shows an 11% greater retention rate than non-participants, which bodes well for graduation rates (Pike, 1996). Similar positive results in different dimensions were experienced in initiatives cited above.

Ingredients of Community Development

A number of ingredients are essential to the development of community. This section discusses these ingredients in detail.

Common Purpose and Core Values

Residence hall staff frequently face an uphill battle in trying to establish a community because insufficient attention has been given to the foundation of the community. Students assigned to a residence hall community most often have nothing in common other than enrollment at the same institution and that they may have requested a specific hall for a wide variety of reasons that have nothing to do with the purpose of that community. Staff trying to promote community development and students seeking to find something in common with their peers have to work much harder than should be necessary. Residence life programs should provide students and staff an opportunity to live in communities that have an explicitly stated theme or purpose based on the characteristics of their students and institutions.

Many institutions provide "theme" floors or halls that are focused on common experiences or interest areas. These include wellness floors, freshman housing, or housing that pairs international and domestic students or students from a variety of cultures. Unfortunately, with the exception of some honors housing, or communities focused on the natural sciences and engineering, many of these efforts lack an academic or a learning-centered focus. Those that are related to academic majors are often developed by student affairs staff without clear learning objectives developed in partnership with faculty.

Residence life staff roles. Residence life staff need to examine enrollment trends at their respective institutions and meet with deans, department chairs, and faculty in those areas that are either experiencing high enrollment, or are seeking to attract and retain higher numbers of students in their programs. Faculty and academic administrative staff, particularly advisors and those involved in recruitment and retention efforts, can help identify focus areas that will have a critical mass of students that could populate an entire wing, floor, or even a hall. Opportunities may be available for students to co-enroll in courses, receive educational assistance in the form of tutors or study groups in the hall, and have advisors meet with them to discuss major and career options in addition to course planning. Currently enrolled students can play an important role in identifying features and elements of the learning community that would be attractive to them. Reformatting reports to sort the names of residents by major, course enrollments, and where they live can provide valuable data on where clusters of students may already be.

Common experiences or academic interests. While providing common living and learning experiences by academic major can be a successful initiative, institutions need not limit themselves to this area. Students also may be given the opportunity to live in communities with students who share a common academic interest, but perhaps not a major. The Fine Arts Residential College and language houses (Spanish and French) at the University of Missouri-Columbia house very few Fine Arts or Romance Language majors, respectively. Rather, students who live in these communities share a common interest in the arts, or establishing a proficiency in another language, respectively. Yet each program has links with the faculty and department chairs in these academic departments, and provides resources, programs, and services that help students set and achieve academic or learning goals. Similarly, the College Park Scholars program at the University of Maryland seeks to provide students with broad areas of academic interest with interdisciplinary and experiential learning opportunities that expand and deepen their understanding of an issue or academic theme, and not just an academic major.

For those communities that are based on common experiences, such as first-year student programs, international houses, honors communities, or common interests such as wellness or community service, an opportunity to link them more explicitly with academic resources is possible. After reading about the success of these programs, many institutions offer freshman only housing, or programs focused on first-year students (Upcraft, Gardner, & Associates, 1989). All too common, well-intentioned residence life staff focus mainly on the transition, identification, and interpersonal issues that these students face and do not as often take into account the academic issues, beyond time management programs, these students face. Are these students in high-risk courses? Can staff identify high-risk courses, and if so, what resources are or should be made available to students? Have staff worked with students in setting academic goals, and do they follow up with students to assess their progress during the semester? Can academic advising or even registration assistance be provided in the residence halls?

Study abroad. Another alternative is to offer housing options that focus on bringing together students from different countries and cultures or that promote an appreciation of diversity. As we move towards a greater realization of more diverse college campuses and a true global community, it is likely that the interest in these programs will rise. It would be a missed opportunity if these living arrangements were not developed or closely aligned with either academic departments such as Asian, Middle Eastern, or Latin American Studies; faculty members with expertise in these fields; or even the International office. Opportunities for students to study abroad should be actively promoted in these communities. These communities could even serve as a precursor to study abroad experiences and a "re-entry point" for students returning from these experiences. Similarly, opportunities exist on a campus with a Wellness floor to create active links with Nursing, Physical Therapy, Nutrition, Physical Education, Religious Studies, or other academic departments that share common goals. Students interested in these fields of study could live in these communities, and also interact with faculty from varied disciplines that compliment their own academic area.

Emphasize learning. Even if a residential community does not have a clear link with a specific academic program, common interest, or experience, nevertheless it can still reinforce student learning. When students move into the community, they should encounter visual cues that learning is important. Bulletin boards can outline academic support services and sign-up sheets for study groups. At initial floor meetings, paraprofessional staff and returning students should discuss goals and expectations for floor grade point averages, quiet hours, and use of public space to support studying. Staff should develop mechanisms to recognize achievement on tests, quizzes, or reports that celebrate academic success, both publicly and privately. Information on advising and registration including checklists, materials, and deadlines should be readily available and promoted on the floor. Staff can request students to share their schedules or request this information from the registrar to identify students on the floor, or even in the hall, that share common classes as a precursor to forming study groups.

Develop a learning curriculum. Regardless of the particular focus, a community that seeks to promote student learning needs to develop a residential learning curriculum. The curriculum should explicitly state the purpose of the community, the intended outcomes of residents' participation, and the experiences that will lead to that outcome. The curriculum should be closely linked and aligned with institutional goals so that even the casual reader will understand the connection. An institution's mission statement, General Education curriculum, or current strategic plan can serve as outstanding source materials on which to build the curriculum. The experiences should be developed through active collaboration between residence life staff and faculty/academic staff. Each group must be invested in these outcomes and must be active participants in these experiences.

Membership and Relationships

In most circumstances, students are assigned to residence hall communities by virtue of preferences expressed on application or assignment forms and their date of application. Descriptions of living options most often emphasize the amenities the facility provides, the physical structure (suite style, double-loaded corridor), the size of the facility, gender breakdown, and its location on campus. Much less frequently do students have the opportunity to discover or request a community by virtue of its stated purpose, values, or explicitly stated goals. Are we then surprised that they arrive with no real understanding of what is expected of them or of the community and what it strives for? Why not provide prospective members with information on what it means to be a member of this community?

Faculty and staff working to build a learning community have an idea of the type of student who would ideally be interested in or benefit from this experience. For communities dedicated to particular majors or career interests, this is fairly straightforward. Communities with a broader focus (fine arts, the environment, wellness, honors, etc.), can identify students who have participated in high school or college activities that are related or have common goals. Students who meet this profile, who are either currently enrolled or are prospective students, can receive materials jointly developed and promoted by faculty and staff. Ideally, current members of the community will contact prospective members to recruit them. Admissions staff and academic advisors must be kept informed about learning communities given their critical role in recruiting and advising students. Admissions staff can identify "feeder" high schools whose graduates attend the institution. Teachers in subject areas can also be sent information on these communities to either identify possible community members or to share with interested students. All of these activities work to increase the strength of commitment and commonality that members will have in the community as they begin their association with it.

Criteria for membership. Community members, faculty, and staff also need to determine whether new members will be required to complete a separate application process or meet additional criteria beyond what is normally required for housing. New members of MU's Language Houses must submit a separate application that is mailed to them by current members of the community. It seeks to identify their interest in living in the community, and also expresses the expectation that members speak the language a certain number of hours per week at certain events and locations, as well as participate in house activities. Returning members to MU's Fine Arts Residential College must re-apply to their student governing council, which evaluates among other factors their participation in community events. At Saint Louis University a few years ago, members who sought admission to Scholars House did not have to have a certain grade point average or major, but did have to express in an interview and application their commitment to succeed academically and participate in community events. Applications can convey to new members that there are clear expectations for members, that not everyone may qualify, and that by being selected a new member has already demonstrated a small commitment to the community.

Behavioral guidelines. Members need to have a clear understanding of the nature of their relationship to one another. While that which they share in common may be easy to identify, less clear are the governing principles that dictate their interactions. Typically complicating the situation is the presence of a large number of new students who are not only adjusting to this community, but their own independence for the first time. Therefore, it is essential that the community leaders, both appointed and emergent, be able to articulate certain fundamental guidelines for behavior of new members. Community members must be able to discuss their expectations in a process wherein all members have the opportunity to express themselves and at which a clear consensus on expectations is reached. However, new members first must be given a starting set of guidelines. Most often, this comes from the paraprofessional staff member in the form of rules and policies. More powerful is when the more informal guidelines of how members should treat one another, or what it "means" to be a member of this community, are explained by peers who are paid by the institution, or even faculty partners in the community. Expectations for academic conduct, studying, and maintaining an academically supportive living environment must be included in this discussion.

Proximity, Territory, and Boundaries

A common exercise used by residence life professional staff to determine how well floor members know each other, or how well resident assistants know their residents, is to have students complete a blank floor roster. A similar exercise is used to demonstrate cognitive mapping in which participants are asked to sketch out the details around their neighborhoods, place of work, etc. Most often residents can more accurately list the names of the residents closest in proximity to their own rooms, much the same as any of us will sketch with greater accuracy the details closest to our homes. However, the further people move from their frame of reference, the less clear the details or names of community members become. It is not only commonality, but also proximity, and in turn, frequency of interaction, that help define a community.

Whenever possible, members of a community should be placed in close physical proximity to each other in order to foster greater familiarity and understanding of each other. This is particularly important on large campuses, or even in larger residence halls, which can promote a feeling of isolation and anonymity among students. Unfortunately, in many circumstances residence life staff can do little to shape the physical environment that they inherit, which sometimes can be an inhibitor to community development. However, the social and interpersonal dimensions of a community can overcome these factors, particularly if there is a sense of common purpose.

Room assignments. The room assignment process can play a critical role in the success of a community. This may, however, warrant a return to a process of "hand assignments" done by a staff member familiar with the community, its goals, information about new and current members, and even the physical layout and its influence on behavior. More common today are computerized assignment processes or manual assignments done by a staff person in a central office. Whenever possible, the staff person responsible for the community, with the most knowledge about it and its members, should make the assignments.

In making the assignments, there are other criteria, such as those mentioned previously under Membership, which might dictate who is eligible for assignment or the order in which they are assigned. Information on co-curricular experiences, interests, or even personality type (e.g., Myers-Briggs Type Inventory) can be used not only to assign students to the community, but even where on the floor they are assigned. Rather than placing common personality types or those with similar backgrounds together or right next to each other, staff should consider spacing them apart but still close enough where they might find each other, thus avoiding pockets of interest and expanding the boundaries of those students get to know quickly. Kalsbeek, Rodgers, Marshall, Denny, and Nichols (1982), and Schroeder and Jackson (1987) found that, in using the Myers Briggs personality indicator, the most effective and satisfied roommates were those with complimentary, not identical personality types. In a learning community focused on math and science, or in an honors community with a wide range of academic majors, placing students with common majors a few doors apart or on an adjacent wing will allow them to not only get to know their peers next to them, but also those with the same major.

Campus location. When developing a learning community, its location on campus, assuming there are multiple residence halls, can also be important. If there is a link to an academic department, staff should give serious consideration to locating the community in close proximity to that department. Students frequently look at the placement of a residence hall on the campus within the framework of where they plan to spend time. Likewise, if staff can shorten the distance faculty must travel to visit the hall from their offices or classrooms, they are more likely to visit for meals or programs, or to provide support services in the halls.

Personal space. Personal space for individual members is important. However, some common space other than hallways is also important. Recognizing this, most architects designed residence halls with hall or floor lounges. However, it is important that the community defines the purpose of this space and sets guidelines for it use. Staff should respond by placing appropriate furnishings and fixtures. Is it primarily social space calling for dimmer lighting, comfortable chairs and couches, and a television; or is it primarily a study space in which good lighting, flat writing surfaces, and other features are desirable?

Less expensive than furnishing a space is allowing the community to clearly demarcate its territory. This can be accomplished with little effort using a few signs or gallons of paint, much as cities post city limit signs to identify to visitors that they have entered the community or to welcome members back home. Residence hall staff should not just permit, but actually promote, this activity not only for the positive effect on forming community, but to decrease vandalism and damage (Schroeder, 1980, 1981). Procedures for communities to mark or decorate their community should be designed for ease of use. The use of symbols or logos related to academic majors should be encouraged. If possible, allowing floors to name their community after distinguished leaders in that field or successful alumni will strengthen their sense of identity. Years ago at Auburn University, floors within the Magnolia Dormitory—previously characterized by low retention, average academic performance, and high vandalism—renamed themselves after successful living alumni. Not only did the behavior and performance of these students improve, but these alumni visited the communities and offered financial support and resources for the students (Schroeder & Grant, 1978).

Shared Standards and Expectations

The strength of a community can be the diversity of its members who share a common purpose. This diversity may be reflected in a variety of personal habits, personality traits, background experiences, and a host of other behavioral factors that influence how individuals conduct themselves in pursuit of that purpose or goal. Just because members of a community might share a common goal or interest, it does not mean that their habits, behaviors, and customs in pursuit of that goal will also be identical. It is therefore essential that a community discusses and establishes a shared set of standards and expectations for values, practices, and conduct to which they can agree. If a common purpose within a community represents the end, then a shared set of standards and expectations for the members represents the means.

Staff members who promote, support, and sometimes even guide these discussions of community standards must recognize that it is not only the outcomes of these efforts, but the discussions themselves that have tremendous value. All too often today, we seek avoidance of conflict and debate, or use the impersonal or anonymous confrontation that electronic technology allows. The community instead must actively discuss those issues that will influence member conduct on a daily basis, sometimes very simply, others much more profoundly. These topics should include basic conduct issues ranging from quiet/noisy activity, cleanliness, visitation and safety issues, to the use of public space and funds, expectations for group activity including intramural sports, community service, and study groups to meeting community goals such as a desired floor grade point average.

Piper (1997) and others have discussed the value and methods for establishing community standards, primarily for the benefit of the community. Asking individuals to own a set of beliefs and values, and then to express them publicly among their peers, is understandably challenging, yet also reaps tremendous rewards for the individual and the community. Recognizing that this will be a novel and sometimes difficult experience for many members of the community, staff must provide the appropriate amount of support, or promote guidelines within the community, to minimize the risk for individuals. Depending on the number of new members in a community, staff—or ideally a cohort of continuing community members—should develop a set of guidelines outlining the initial areas for discussion as well as ground rules for debate and discussion. The common or core values upon which the community has been developed or have agreed on should serve as a template for the issues to be discussed and a guideline for decisions.

Emphasis on academic achievement. In trying to create a learning-supportive community, it is essential that the community publicly and explicitly reinforce the value they place on academic success, achievement of academically related goals, and learning in a broad sense. If the community has an academic theme, such as engineering or health sciences, then the members ideally should express a set of expectations that are related to success within this field. Faculty or academic stakeholders in the community can become active participants in this discussion. Likewise, if the field of study has a code of ethics or governing principles that have been adopted, this information should be shared with students to be incorporated into their discussion. Minimally, the curricular guidelines should be understood and incorporated into the process whenever possible. For example, if there is a particularly challenging course within an academic program, do members in the community want to co-enroll in the same section during the same semester for support, or are members who have successfully completed that course willing to serve as study aides?

However, if members of the community do not share a common academic major or interest, academic themes should also be part of the discussion on community standards. If a community values academic success by its members, what quiet hours or visitation guidelines are necessary to support a learning-conducive environment? Likewise, should use of public space be dedicated to studying, or should that be the first priority over social activities? Does the community want to establish a target grade point average for members; do individuals want to establish a set of academic goals for themselves that they may or may not share with the community at large? If there are study groups available, does the community subtly reinforce that participation is encouraged or even expected? When guest lecturers or special programs are offered, do members of the community participate as a group?

Staff Roles. Staff members can reinforce these standards or expectations as well. First, they need to make sure their own conduct is consistent with community expectations. Additionally, they can create or support efforts that publicly acknowledge the academic success of individuals within the community. Paraprofessionals can create bulletin boards or door decorations that celebrate the success of a community member on a quiz, paper, or project. Professional staff can send letters, make personal visits to students who also meet certain academic objectives, or host special programs to celebrate their success.

Written Affirmation of Students. Once a community has established a set of community standards or expectations, it is encouraged whenever possible to articulate these publicly in written form. Some communities create large posters for bulletin boards or walls and have all members sign the poster. Others create individual sheets or cards that are distributed to all members of the community. Public presentation of the standards reinforces the expectation for compliance; it also informs guests what the standards of conduct and values are within this community.

Two caveats must be considered when discussing community standards. First, this is an ongoing process, not an outcome. In other words, once a community has established their standards, it should be publicly noted that it will likely be necessary to revisit the standards as situations arise or community sentiment changes. A method of how the community might discuss new standards is a topic members are encouraged to discuss. Secondly, at some point during the year, a member or members will not adhere to the standards. Before this occurs, the community should discuss how these situations are to be confronted, by whom and in what manner, and if not successfully resolved, what are the appropriate "next steps" or consequences. At the start of an academic year, optimism and some naiveté may cloud new members' beliefs that this will occur. Returning members to the community can be a valuable source of "lessons learned" at this point.

Communications and Decision Making

Within individual languages, dialects emerge where communities interact frequently with each other, developing their own idioms, jargon, and local vernacular. While it may be possible to have multiple languages present within a residence hall community, more likely a common language exists through which members communicate. However, the meaning that the community places on words, phrases, and idioms serves both as a unifying feature of the community and one that distinguishes it from other groups. As part of their standards process, communities should discuss what "quiet," "respect," "clean," "involved," and "academically successful" means. In one residence hall community, members did not consider it "vandalism" if a piece of property that had no direct impact on residents was damaged, such as an "EXIT" sign, because residents knew where the exit was. However, they did consider it vandalism if the damage affected residents, as when a damaged water fountain caused leaks in a resident's room and deprived them of the water fountain. Likewise, staff should be alert to the evolution of idioms or "in" phrases within a community as indicators of language and community development, and should also be aware of their meanings.

Developing communications skills. A viable community must offer its residents a variety of opportunities to interact and develop effective communication skills. These include formal means, such as house or floor meetings; focused programs that promote learning and debate, such as diversity, sex roles, and political issues; and impromptu discussions and debates over meals, in lounges, or hallways. Staff members or older members of the community can promote these activities at the start of the academic year to introduce members to each other and promote discussion on common interests, both individual and for the community, such as standards and expectations. Likewise, guidelines or expectations about communication when conflict or disagreement occurs need to be discussed. It cannot be assumed that all members will respond in the same manner without an explicit statement or agreement of how conflict should be handled. Floor meetings should occur on a regular basis, and not just during times when staff need to convene them (such as after opening or prior to closing), or when conflict arises. Regularly occurring meetings allow members the ability to reflect in a group setting on initial plans and goals, and to assess their progress towards those goals. It also allows members whose daily routines may not bring them in contact with others an opportunity to "catch up" with each other, or for the community to discuss issues before they reach a "flash point."

Decision making. While a common language and opportunities for communication are essential, a community cannot be truly viable if the members do not have the ability to exercise communal decision-making, particularly over matters of relative importance to its members. These matters can be routine, such as participation in group activities like intramural sports or campus events, use of common space, or expenditure of floor funds. However, it is possible for communities to determine more profound issues, such as policies for their community, sanctions for individuals who violate community or institution policies, or even membership within the community. Until a few years ago at Saint Louis University, residents on a floor determined who obtained the coveted single or preferred rooms, who moved onto the floor, and even made the room assignments. Frequently, it is the department or institution, not the community, that places limitations on what it permits students to decide. The model "Involving Colleges" identified by Kuh, Schuh, Whitt, and Associates (1991) is distinguished by the trust placed in students, allowing them to make these types of decisions.

While the encouragement of effective communication and decision-making has clear benefits for community development, it can also support the learning goals of the institution. There are very few, if any, general education curricula that do not have strong oral and written communication skills development as a goal for students. Critical thinking skills is also another common goal, frequently at the heart of many liberal arts programs. Other than with writing, there is always no clear connection between classroom experiences and development of these skills. There are some noteworthy exceptions, such as Alverno College, that infuse the development and assessment of these skills into the students' curricular and co-curricular experiences. Residence life staff should identify opportunities in which they can create in-hall experiences that achieve both the objectives of community development and skill development sought by the institutions.

Staffing issues. Staff must first become familiar with institutional goals and specific curricular objectives for oral communication, writing, and critical-thinking skills, and then, whenever possible, create experiences that reinforce these skills directly or indirectly. Applications for student positions or staff roles could require a written application in which students must explore a topic relevant to the position. If the roles involve public interaction, the interviewing process could involve an oral presentation. Similarly, requests for operational changes in the hall, or expenditure of community funds could also require a written or oral presentation. Staff, either independently or in conjunction with academic support staff, could offer skill or review sessions prior to these processes to assist students in developing written or oral presentations. Upperclassmen or residents with strong written skills could be encouraged to serve as editors or readers for papers written by other community members. Similarly, the aforementioned discussions on community standards, expectations for involvement, and decisions on issues relative to the students' experiences or the communities' interests present a rich opportunity for critical thinking and decision-making skills. This exercise of civic involvement and responsibility will also prepare students to become active citizens within their communities after graduation.

Active Involvement in Shared Experiences

Perhaps the most easily understood essential element of a community is that members spend time doing things together. Student and professional staff spend time and effort creating these experiences or providing the incentives and opportunities for students to create their own activities. However, of all the elements, it is also the one that will likely occur most spontaneously without direct staff encouragement or intervention. It is no mystery that students, by and large, seek to involve themselves in activities as broad as joining clubs and organizations, and as mundane as doing laundry and eating. Not surprisingly, as the social beings they are, students will most often do these things with other people, frequently those in the closest physical proximity to themselves. However, as grades are issued for individual effort and most students have developed habits of studying alone at home during high school, we should also not be surprised if students participate in social activities in groups, but academic activities individually. Therefore, it is essential that residence life staff, in conjunction with faculty and academic support staff, also create opportunities for students to interact socially around academic or learning-supported initiatives.

Expectations. The expectation that community members engage in learning activities together should be communicated clearly and early. Promotional materials need to build this anticipation in new members. Current and continuing members of the community can play a vital role in building this expectation through their involvement in the recruitment process, by contacting new members prior to their arrival on campus, and reassuring them that they are entering a supportive social and academic environment. These experienced community members also will set the tone early in the semester through their own conduct and participation in floor meetings. Student staff should meet with these members in late spring and early fall to discuss expectations.

Shared academic experiences. If coenrollment through various programs (for example, Freshman Interest Groups or Learning Communities) exists on campus, a residential component should be added if it does not already exist. If this is not an option, residents who have similar academic programs or who must meet the same general education program requirements can coordinate efforts to coenroll with community members through add/drop or early registration periods. Even if residents are enrolled in different sections or levels of the same course or subject matter, the formation of study groups should be actively encouraged. A volunteer "academic coordinator" on the floor can collect everyone's schedule if a common listing by course cannot be obtained from the registrar. When this is not feasible, "study buddies" can be assigned as a support system to promote appropriate time spent studying, even if it is on different content. A student staff member can always take on the duties of coordinating these initiatives, yet it is more powerful if a member of the community or volunteers can be enlisted.

Educational events. In addition to social or recreational events on campus, communities can participate in educational events together such as visiting speakers, theater productions, or even campus rallies on political or social issues. If a community has an academic theme or defined common interest, faculty and staff colleagues can serve as valuable resources in identifying cocurricular learning experiences that reinforce that theme/interest. For example, in a community dedicated to science, community members could visit with a panel of faculty and alumni to discuss alternative careers beyond those traditionally considered. Similarly, students can participate in a community service project at an agency closely aligned with the field of study or common interest, or take a field trip to a related business or agency. Residence life operations should also examine operational processes to find learning opportunities for its students. When the University of Missouri-Columbia needed to upgrade the plans they gave to students on loft designs, they partnered with a Civil Engineering professor and a group of engineering students to develop new plans. These students researched, designed, and even constructed full-scale models, resulting in the set of plans that are now provided to students and parents. Similarly, a group of landscape design students were given the responsibility to design, develop, and maintain a variety of flowerbeds and other plantings. Comparable examples exist on other campuses and represent outstanding "hands on" learning experiences and shared activities for a community.

Customs, Traditions, and Celebrations

Whether it be an Amish barn raising, tossing rice at a sumo wrestling match, bathing in the Ganges, or the changing of the Buckingham Palace guard, a community gives life to its culture and its values through its customs, traditions, rituals, and celebrations. While perhaps not as longstanding, grandiose, or devotional as these events, a vital residence hall community can and should have similar events and practices. It can become a defining element that distinguishes it from others, and that incorporates and bonds its members to one another and the community itself.

Transition rituals. Transition rituals can become very meaningful when a community goes through regular cycles in which old members exit and new enter, like those in our residence halls. Orientation and initiation rituals can become a vehicle to not only celebrate and welcome new members, but to also transmit the values, expectations, and history of the community. Fraternal organizations, including fraternities and sororities, and other leadership and honorary organizations have practiced these traditions for centuries. By participating in these practices, new members demonstrate their allegiance to the community and the values for which it stands. In some circumstances, these rituals and practices have been taken to an extreme and have become detrimental. Appropriately used, however, these events become powerful elements within a community. Most institutions already use them as part of the freshman orientation process, some benignly and passively and some others, such as Texas A&M's Fish Camp, quite powerfully.

While not perhaps as ritualistic, residence hall communities can adopt many of these principles in welcoming new members. The returning members can act as tribal elders in welcoming new members, and actually aid their move into the new community by showing them around campus and taking them to their classrooms before schools begin. Residence life programs, if they have not already done so, are encouraged to identify cadres of returning students for each floor who are willing to arrive a few days early to plan activities, prepare the floor, and welcome new members. These "elders" can also plan customs, whether it is a formal ceremony or a trip to a local pizza shop. The distribution of T-shirts, description of the floor nickname, discussing traditional event participation, or a recollection of past accomplishments of the community help new members understand that they are part of something that has a history and one to which they can contribute. Simply moving into a building with one's parents, finding your name on the door, and bumping into other new members who are equally inexperienced is not enough. Similar rituals for members who are leaving a community can also be established, at which the exploits and foibles are good-naturedly recalled and mementos from the community given.

The benefit of working within a highly transitional community like a residence hall is that customs and traditions can evolve in as few as two to three years. The more constant members, including the staff, can reinforce these traditions to new members quite easily, and current members, who do not stay usually beyond three years, can easily recall them. These customs and traditions can revolve around participation in campus programs or competitions (walk-a-thons, college bowl teams); seasonal or academic calendar events (snowball fights on the first snowfall, a night out dining on the last day of classes); sporting events (block seating at football games, face-painting for spirit rallies); or events that have meaning only to the community (customary birthday rituals for members, noting the birthday of the community namesake).

Academically-related traditions. While many of the customs and traditions are social in nature, communities should be encouraged to create and/or sustain those that reinforce learning and academic success. If a community has a tradition of academic excellence, it should be conveyed to new members as part of the orientation rituals. Likewise, if a community has adopted practices such as studying after dinner, establishing quiet hours, or maintaining legitimate test files, this information must be communicated early. Communities should be encouraged to set grade point average or other academic success goals (e.g., no member receives less than a "C" in a class). Challenges can be issued with staff members or with other communities. Some residence hall communities involve faculty in regular dinners or lunches, or even recognize those who have demonstrated excellence in teaching, advising, or working with students. The Residence Hall Association at the University of Missouri-Columbia borrowed an idea from an engineering community and invites faculty members to deliver a "last lecture" on any topic each month in the residence halls. As noted earlier, communities should establish ways in which to recognize and celebrate the academic accomplishments of its members. At the State University of New York-Binghamton campus, the residence areas are divided into four residential colleges, each with its own faculty master. Although students frequently move into apartments after a few years, they maintain a connection with their college. The residential college hosts a yearly event to celebrate its members' graduation, in which both new and departing members participate.

Celebrations. Boyer (1990) noted that celebration is an essential element of a vibrant community. Jackson and Serrott (1988) recognized the impact of history and celebration in a residence hall community and encouraged each community to appoint a floor historian to chronicle the year's events. They provided these historians with free film for their cameras and free developing to provide a photographic record of the life of the community, which were placed in a community scrapbook. While many residence life professionals have witnessed similar spontaneous occurrences in their communities, this initiative should be actively encouraged. Using technology, which includes scanners, e-mail attachments, and web pages, allows an even wider distribution. One faculty member working with a Freshman Interest Group at the University of Missouri-Columbia scanned photographs of the group's activity and posted them on a web site for the students; they were even sent as attachments to parents with e-mail accounts.

Identity and Commitment

A hallmark for a vital community is the establishment of a recognizable identity. Community identity can be considered from both an internal and external viewpoint. An internal view is when members view their individual identity in the context of their membership to the community or group, and demonstrate a high degree of commitment to supporting the community. When nonmembers of the community can recognize members due to their affiliation with the group, or can easily describe the difference between communities, the view is external. In either situation, the community and its members have a clear sense of identity that describes the community, what it stands for, and what membership in that community means. Not all communities reach, or even aspire to, this stage of development.

Establishing identity. Communities establish their identity through their actions and how they define the previously mentioned elements, either by design or sometimes by default. Ideally, a community explores its common values, relationships between members, its customs and traditions, and the standards and expectations they have of each other. Occasionally, these issues are not explored and the actions of a few individuals can establish an identity that is thrust upon the community whether it seeks it or not. If members do not actively seek to embrace or reject this identity, they may passively resign themselves to it. It is the responsibility of the staff to recognize this, and at least raise questions with the community whether they accept or desire to change this identity. However, it is very hard, if not impossible, for staff to mandate or create a change without the involvement and support of the community.

A group can communicate its identity in different ways. Communities often decorate their territory in ways that reflect their identity. Words, symbols, colors, letters, or significant role models that represent the value or purpose of the community can adorn walls, posters, and clothing. T-shirts often become the uniform of a community, especially when they "do battle" with other communities on the intramural fields, at campus events, or campus competitions. What is significant is that the symbols of the community identity are publicly displayed not only to signify who is a member of the community to others, but also to reinforce the bond among members. As mentioned, language, such as particular idioms and catch phrases, and rituals become powerful ways in which groups reinforce their identity. The assignment or evolution of nicknames for members is a significant step as it represents a new identity for the individuals within the group that is different than when they were not part of the community. Similarly, the roles that members take on or are assigned to support the community become another way of defining who they are in relation to the community.

Staff roles. Staff can play a critical role in the evolution of identity by promoting activities and opportunities for the members to explore so that it happens by design and not by default. In particular, delegation or creation of tasks and roles within the community allows individuals the opportunity to establish their identity in the community. This should be followed up by public recognition to not only support the individual, but the importance of the role itself. Promoting the group to display the accoutrements of identity whether through T-shirts, painting their floor, or encouraging nicknames will reinforce the creation and sustenance of the community identity. The community should also be encouraged to actively participate in the recruitment of new members by promoting their purpose, expectations, and identity to prospective and current students.

Promoting academic success. As identification with a community addresses primarily social needs and takes on mostly interpersonal dimensions, it is also important to promote elements that support student learning and academic success. If they do not do it themselves, staff should ask community members how they want to be perceived academically by others. What is the academic identity as part of their larger identity? Do they want to be perceived as good students or the best students? Is their identity one in which members actively support one another through study groups, informal advisement, maintenance of a learning-supported environment, and celebration of members' academic success? If they share a common academic major or interest, do they want to promote a certain identity with the affiliated academic department, group of faculty, or campus office? Does their identity include service to the campus or local community?

Conclusion

Student affairs and residence life programs may be undergoing a renaissance as we return to our roots and closer affiliation and integration with academic affairs. Many professionals may view this as an abandonment of current student development goals and traditional staffing and programming efforts. While that is not necessary, it is absolutely essential that we examine our current efforts with the recognition "that student learning and development are inextricably intertwined" (American College Personnel Association, 1996, p. 118) and that our primary mission is to support the educational mission of the institutions that employ us. If we have strayed from that central tenet, believing that our expertise and primary focus is on the psychosocial development of the student outside of the classroom, then we must expand our focus. We must also expand our traditional definitions of a community beyond the walls of our residence halls to prepare our students for the leadership roles they will seek or acquire. We must ensure that our residents are integrated within the campus community and the surrounding city and state.

The goals for student learning set by the academic divisions and the institution should be used as a framework for our planning and programming efforts. There is no doubt that we will continue to provide the support, education, and experiences for a wide range of students' developmental needs. However, we must also partner with our faculty colleagues to ensure that our efforts are integrated and not separate, distinct experiences for our students. Residence life and community development is not the end, but a means to an end—student learning and development. Community can be seen as the seat of a three-legged stool, supported by the expectations, experiences, and involvement that students share. However, the purpose of this stool is to support student learning and success. Our residence hall communities remain one of the most potentially powerful educational experiences for students. We not only have the opportunity but also the obligation to ensure that we are providing the richest, learning-conducive environment for students as a foundation for their overall educational experience.

References

American College Personnel Association. (1994-1996). The student learning imperative: Implications for student affairs. *Journal of College Student Development, 37,* 118-122.

Astin, A. W. (1973). The impact of dormitory living on students. *Educational Record, 54,* 204-210.

Astin, A. W. (1977). *Four critical years: Effects of college on beliefs, attitudes, and knowledge.* San Francisco: Jossey-Bass.

Boyer, E. (1990). *In search of community.* Washington, DC: American Council on Education.

Chickering, A. W. (1974). *Commuting versus resident students: Overcoming educational inequities of living off-campus.* San Francisco: Jossey-Bass.

Crookston, B. B. (1974). A design for an intentional democratic community. In D. A. DeCoster and P. Mable (Eds.), *Student development and education in college residence halls* (pp. 55-67). Washington, DC.: American College Personnel Association.

Crookston, B. B. (1980). A design for an intentional democratic community. In D. A. DeCoster and P. Marble (Eds.), *Student development and education in college residence halls.* Cincinnati, OH: American College Personnel Administration.

DeCoster, D. A., & Mable, P. (1980). Residence education: Purpose and process. In D. A. DeCoster and P. Mable (Eds.), *Personal education and community development in College residence halls* (pp. 31-55). Cincinnati, OH: American College Personnel Association.

Ignelzi, M. (1990). Ethical education in a college environment: The just community approach. *NASPA Journal, 27,* 192-198.

Jackson, G. S., & Serrott, S. (1988, March). *The stories students tell: Strategies for assessing residential communities.* Paper presented at the meeting of the American College Personnel Association, St. Louis, MO.

Johnson, W. J., Jr. (1998). Comparisons between FIG and non-FIG freshmen on ratings of the residence hall house environment, Fall, 1997. *Residential Academic Programs Report.* Columbia, MO: University of Missouri-Columbia, Office of Residential Academic Programs.

Kahmi, C., & Thompson, G. (1996). *BASIC: A journal for building a strong involving community.* Columbus, OH: ACUHO-I.

Kalsbeek, D., Rodgers, R., Marshall, D., Denny, D., & Nichols, G. (1982) . Balancing challenge and support: A study of degrees of similarity in suitemate personality type and perceived differences in challenge and support in a residence hall environment. *Journal of College Student Personnel, 23,* 434-442.

Kuh, G. D., Schuh, J. H., Whitt, E. J., & Associates. (1991). *Involving colleges: Successful approaches to fostering student learning and development outside the classroom.* San Francisco: Jossey-Bass.

Pascarella, E. T., & Terenzini, P. T. (1991). *How college affects students: Findings and insights from twenty years of research.* San Francisco: Jossey-Bass.

Pascarella, E. T., Terenzini, P. T., & Blimling, G. S. (1996). Students' out of class experiences and their influence on learning and cognitive development: A literature review. *Journal of College Student Development, 37,* 149-174.

Peck, M. S. (1987). *The different drum: Community making and peace.* New York: Simon & Schuster.

Pike, G. (1996). *A student success story: Freshman interest groups at the University of Missouri-Columbia.* Student Life Studies Abstracts No. 1. Columbia, MO: University of Missouri.

Pike, G. (1997). *Longer-term effects of freshman interest groups (FIGS) on students' college experiences and educational outcomes.* Student Life Abstracts No. 5. Columbia, MO: University of Missouri.

Piper, T. (1997). Empowering students to create community standards. *About Campus, 2*(3), 22-24. San Francisco: Jossey-Bass.

Schlossberg, N. K. (1989). Marginality and mattering: Key issues in building community. In D. C. Roberts (Ed.), *Designing campus activities to foster a sense of community* (pp. 5-15). New Directions for Student Services, No. 48. San Francisco: Jossey-Bass.

Schroeder, C. C. (1980). Territoriality: An imperative for personal development and residence education. In D. DeCoster and P. Mable (Eds.), *Personal education and community development in college residence halls* (pp. 114-132). San Francisco: Jossey-Bass.

Schroeder, C. C. (1981). Student development through environmental management. In G. S. Blimling and J. H. Schuh (Eds.), *Maximizing educational opportunities in residence halls* (pp. 35-49). New Directions for Student Services Sourcebook No. 13. San Francisco: Jossey-Bass.

Schroeder, C. C. (1993). Creating programs with student development goals. In R. B. Winston, Jr., S. Anchors, and Associates (Eds.), *Student housing and residential life* (pp. 517-534). San Francisco: Jossey-Bass.

Schroeder, C. C., & Grant, W. H. (1978). Auburn's engineering alumni house system. *Journal of College Student Personnel, 19,* 567.

Schroeder, C. C., & Jackson, S. (1987). Designing residential environments. In J. A. Provost and S. Anchors (Eds.), *Applications of the Dyers-Briggs Type Indicator in Higher Education* (pp. 65-88). Palo Alto, CA: Consulting Psychologists Press.

Schroeder, C. C. & Mable, P. (1994). Realizing the educational potential of residence halls. San Francisco: Jossey-Bass.

Tuckman, B. (1965). Developmental sequence in small groups. *Psychological Bulletin, 6,* 384-399.

Upcraft, M. L., Gardener, J. N., & Associates. (1989). *The freshman year experience: Helping students survive and succeed in college.* San Francisco: Jossey-Bass.

Whitely, J. A. M., & Associates. (1982). *Character development in college students.* Schenectady, NY: Character Research.

Winston, R. B., Jr., & Anchors, S. (1993). Student development in the residential environment. In Authors (Eds.), *Student housing and residential life* (pp. 25-64). San Francisco: Jossey-Bass.

Appendix 1
Stimulating Community Development

The previously mentioned elements for a viable community contain examples or suggestions on how to promote the development of these dimensions. Following is an outline that will incorporate these elements, but that will primarily focus on creating a learning-supported community. While this outline uses the Six I's framework outlined earlier in this chapter, other frameworks also can be utilized. However, as most have been used to promote traditional definitions of community development, each should be considered in the context of how it can be utilized to develop and support a community with student learning as its focus.

Introduction

- Current members develop an outline of community that summarizes its focus and identity and describes its members, including their academic focus or majors.
- Promotional materials are mailed to prospective members, which outline their values, activities, and expectations, and invites them to request or apply for this community.
- Current members contact prospective members in the spring, and write letters or call new members during the summer for personal touch, to develop relationships and to build anticipatory socialization. List of student majors in the community, floor grade point average, and preliminary academic goals are discussed.
- Current members work with staff and return early to develop orientation activities for new members and welcome back activities for returning members. New members are teamed with other new "study buddies" and a returning student mentor.
- Returning members and staff coordinate first community meetings to discuss community goals, review standards, and discuss roles that do or may exist. Academic goals, quiet hours, and sharing class schedules are discussed and set. Faculty and staff associated with community are invited and encouraged to attend.
- Academic and involvement traditions are discussed with an expectation that new members will participate as that is "what it means" to be a member of the community.
- New members participate in ritualistic incorporation and initiation activities conducted by continuing members.

Interaction

- Community members participate in social and recreational events designed to promote interaction before classes begin. Events are planned for at least one weeknight and one weekend day for the first three weeks.

- Old members lead new members on a tour of campus, including the library, location of their classes, campus "hang outs," recreation center, and others.
- Within the first two weeks, the community participates in outdoor adventure, experiential education, or teams challenge type activities. Faculty and academic staff are invited to participate.
- Either at meetings or posted on doors or bulletin boards, members share class schedules, personal history, favorite activities, career aspirations, and semester goals.
- Cookout or barbecue with faculty and academic staff planned by residence life staff and students.
- Students who have not participated are contacted by old members to encourage interaction; both a social and academic support feature.

Involvement/Incorporation

- Community identifies and selects members for specific roles. At least three roles have academic emphasis (academic chair coordinates schedule sharing and study groups; faculty liaison; and test master, who collects test/quiz/paper deadlines to develop a master calendar for floor)
- Academic Chair forms study groups after common courses or majors are identified.
- Members encouraged to make new "door decs," which outline their interests or coincide with community focus/theme. Signs prepared by staff with individual student roles are posted on appropriate students' doors. Collective list of all roles is posted on floor bulletin board.
- Community discusses semester and yearly goals, to include target grade point average.
- Individual members are encouraged to complete a form listing three goals for the semester, with at least one being academic, and then post goals in room or on room door.
- Community standards are discussed and established addressing issues of involvement, quiet hours, use of public space, visitation, community service, and others.
- Community discusses service project that is consistent with community focus/theme.

Investment

- Floor is given paint and supplies to paint hallways and common spaces to reflect community personality, interests, or theme.
- Community member designs T-shirt that expresses identity or community focus. Members purchase shirts with costs possibly subsidized by floor funds or the department.

Community Development ─────────────────────────────

- Community participates in intramural and other competitions, and issues academic challenges to another community for highest G.P.A. or improvement over last semester.
- Community discusses naming or renaming itself after, or chooses to honor, a successful alumnus or national figure consistent with the community focus or values.
- Community standards are posted in public space and members are encouraged to sign them.
- Faculty members are identified by students for effective teaching, advising, or assisting students. Selected faculty are invited to recognition events and dinner with community.
- Staff discusses development of community profile sheet/information for use in recruitment of prospective students and new members.
- Community allocates how funds are spent.

Influence

- Community reevaluates initial community standards for possible modification, particularly in regards to quiet hours, visitation, and public space use as they contribute to an environment conducive to study and sleep.
- Community discusses and determines selection and assignment guidelines for new members, including the development and review of applications where appropriate.
- Members volunteer to participate in new student recruitment strategies in conjunction with residence life and admissions staff.
- Community evaluates current staff, identifies ideal qualities for staff, and actively participates in the selection of new staff.
- Community discusses room assignment process for following year with staff, and establishes criteria for returning and new members, including G.P.A. standards, levels of involvement, and assignment to single or preferred rooms, if applicable.
- In communities where students are coenrolled or share common courses or academic majors, members initiate or participate in course and instructor evaluations.

Identity

- Members describe the core values, focus, traditions, and distinguishing features of the community when describing it to prospective new members.
- Departing members are recognized and their roles, achievements, and contributions to the community are also recognized. Old members' names may be painted or inscribed on walls of floor lounge or similar space.

- Community evaluates traditional structures (hall associations, student governments, staffing patterns, etc.) and questions need or effectiveness for their community.

Chapter Seven

Considerations When Working With Under-Represented Populations

Kathy Humphrey
Associate Vice President for Student Development
St. Louis University

Considerations When Working ─────────────────────────

"We are all the same," was the chant that resounded through the corridors, quads and classrooms of many colleges and universities during the 70's. This liberal, all-inclusive statement was used to remind whites and assure minority individuals that their intellectual abilities were equal. The volumes of studies completed gave proof that we were indeed all the same. Yet this glorious statement, which appeared to momentarily level the playing ground, had in many ways blinded us to our realities; for although our intellectual abilities were equal, we were not all the same. It is of little wonder that we have struggled to meet the needs of under-represented students; for decades we acted as if minority students' differences did not matter. It was not until the early 1980s that we directed our attention to students' differences. It was not until the early 1990s that we challenged students to engage in the celebration of diversity. This chapter focuses on the needs of under-represented populations; examines what we have done with what we know; and describes opportunities that could enhance the growth, development, and academic success of under-represented populations.

Understanding Student Needs

Every parent, older sibling, aunt, or uncle realizes that on many occasions babies cry when they are not hungry or wet. This is a frustrating time for any caregiver as nothing seems to work until you finally find that perfect position. This is when the baby returns to sleep having found temporary comfort. On many occasions, under-represented students are heard screaming about the injustices they experience. Staff are not always sure why, but students continue to scream. Students are encouraged to form minority organizations and this appears to soothe them for a while; but students who are in the majority question the formulation of the under-represented group's organization. Now, both majority and minority students find themselves in turmoil because the conflict and chaos that surrounds them is real. Before developing programs for under-represented students, a keener understanding of their struggle to survive on our campuses must be gained. What the screaming is all about must be understood; attempts to eliminate student concerns rather than soothe them must be made.

An appropriate place for student affairs professionals to begin to understand the concerns and needs of any student, let alone students from under-represented populations, is the literature on student development theory. However, much of this literature does not adequately take into account the unique dimension of race and culture in the development of minority students. McEwen, Roper, Bryant, and Langa (1990) have suggested nine dimensions that address the development of African American students and should be considered when applying psychosocial theories to these students. They include: developing ethnic and racial identity, interacting with the dominant culture, developing cultural aesthetics and awareness, developing identity, developing interdependence, fulfilling affiliation needs, surviving intellectually, developing spirituality, and developing social responsibility. When applied to conventional theories of student development, these additional factors help to improve one's understanding of the developmental tasks particular to minority students.

Anger, confusion, isolation, and fear are the four threads that run through several racial and sexual development models (Atkinson, Morten, & Sue, 1979; Cass, 1979; Helms, 1984). While finding oneself is a common experience for most traditional college age individuals, the under-represented students search for identity takes second place to the struggle to keep their ethnicity—keeping themselves African-American, Black, Hispanic, Latino/a, Chicano/a, Jewish, Asian, or Island Pacific. They strive to keep themselves connected through their families, which includes those who are blood relatives and those who are ethnically familiar. Keeping themselves in tune with who they are and who they want to be is a weight that many under-represented students carry with them as they begin their college careers. Many under-represented students were reminded before they left home by their families and friends that they need to return like they left, with strong loyalties to their communities, and maintaining all of their identity markings. They were warned about people who do not look like them. Once they arrived on campus and the awareness that statistically the probability for their success is low, fear of failing begins to slowly set in. They meet a few people who do not fit the stereotype that they had been taught and they see those individuals as exceptions to the rules. They are concerned that people will treat them as a color instead of as a person, and the anger begins to set in. They finally decide to disassociate from anyone who does not look like them, as it seems that this approach is so much easier.

Anger

Anger seems to be the catalyst that often propels our marginalized students towards the next developmental stage. While the anger can be difficult to deal with when exhibited, all of the models suggest students who are provided opportunities to deal with their anger can move to a point where they can accept others and themselves. Cass (1979) speaks of the anger that many gay students experience during the identity pride stage. During this stage, many gay students have accepted the fact that they are attracted to the same sex, and they are no longer willing to keep it a secret. Their attitude comes across as "You need to deal with me, because this is who I am." Their anger stems from the pain that they have experienced. However, those experiences moved them to a point where they could accept themselves and disregard what others think of them. Their anger comes from all of the people who express strong religious beliefs, but hate them. The anger comes from those who have reduced them to their sexuality by removing all other pieces of their beings. Their anger comes from their inability to live without fear of hurt or harm. Their anger comes from their feelings of isolation because of the many friends and family members they may have lost.

Confusion

Confusion can be found in the conformity and dissonance stages in the Minority Identity Developmental model (Atkinson et al., 1979). The minority student begins to question why they have bought into the dominant society's ideals, and on many occasions this reflection causes these minority students to feel betrayed and typically provokes anger. This anger manifests itself in the resistance and immersion stage. Moreover, during this period minority students withdraw totally from the dominant culture as they blame it for most of their problems. This is also the stage where many minority students become concerned about becoming a true and loyal member of their own ethnic group. They begin to isolate anything and anyone who is not a part of their group.

Considerations When Working

Fear

Frequently, fear of the unknown turns inside out and manifests itself in the form of anger. The question, "Are we getting better?" is often asked during diversity workshops. After reflecting on my experience as a college freshman almost 20 years ago, I phoned and later met with three women who were sophomores at my alma mater to discuss this issue. I compared their experiences with mine to discover if our society had moved forward in meeting the needs and concerns of minority students. The following narrative was read to each woman, and afterwards we discussed further the similarities and differences.

"Almost 20 years ago, I entered a medium-sized state institution as a freshman, scared of the unknown, afraid of what it would be like to live away from home in a school with predominantly white people, and skeptical that I would never be any more than the "black girl" in class. I checked into the dormitory, which later became a "residence hall," onto a floor where the majority of minority women in the hall had been placed. Not thinking much of it at the time, I unpacked my boxes in my triple room where my bed had been placed only two feet away from my roommate's. At that time, there could not have been more than four percent minorities on our campus, yet I had been placed with three black women. My roommates' race was no coincidence, for many other black women on the floor were also assigned like-race roommates, and I had been well-informed about the statistics of minority failures on college campuses. I felt an incredible amount of pressure to succeed because many people had great expectations of me. I thought it was my responsibility to inform white people that they were misinformed about black people. I felt it my responsibility to show my professors how smart black people are, and as a result, I lost plugs and plugs of hair trying to be an excellent student. Setting the curve was always my goal, and while it did not matter whether I got the highest score, it did matter that I never received low grades in a class. I had something to prove, and I was going to do it by my actions. I studied hard and played little. Joining an organization was not even a thought. I was here to study, and that's what I did."

Kenesha (personal communications, 1998) a first-semester sophomore from St. Louis, Missouri told me that while she was not in a triple room, she had a same-race roommate, but by choice. She had been told not to trust white people all of her life, and she was warned about the prejudices she would encounter in the town. This, of course, alarmed her and she decided before coming to school what she would do if she encountered severe oppression. Kenesha did not get involved with any organizations during her first semester, and she felt the need to prove herself to her peers and professors. Kenesha felt an incredible need to graduate since she was a first-generation college student. She, too, was determined to make it and spoke of how difficult it was to be on a college campus where her family could not help her maneuver the campus environment.

To convince myself that our similarities were not region bound, I contacted a student at a private institution and another at a large major institution in the south, and the similarities were even more glaring, for very little had changed.

Isolation

Why are minority students angry? Why do riots break out, hate crimes occur, and volatile conversations erupt? In the video series, *Talking About Race* (Reid, 1995), students from all over the country answered these questions very well. Students were angry for the following reasons:

1. For many years, they felt ashamed of who they were because of what they had been told (i.e., there is no way they could ever reach the societal standards of beauty, because they did not have the blond hair or blue eyes).

2. For having to watch friends and family members live continuously in oppressive situations.

3. For the insensitivity of administrators who did not establish a way for them to maintain cultural ties on campus.

4. For asking questions that make one feel less human, such as "May I touch your hair?"

5. For being watched and criticized for mixing with their own race while the dominant culture mixed with their race on a routine basis without censure.

6. For being labeled until the labels were proven to be incorrect.

7. For being accused of taking hand-outs.

While we know the feelings of anger, fear, confusion, and isolation are real and intense for our under-represented students, we have done very little to deal with these emotions. After listening to many under-represented students describe their college experience, these words come to mind: very little has changed.

As they sat listening to a woman almost twice their age describing her concerns, issues, and experiences during her freshman year in college, they realized that the connection surpassed the color of her skin. She intimately understood many of their issues, because very little had changed in almost twenty years.

She spoke of the pressure to prove her intelligence to white people and herself, to maintain her blackness, and her determination to beat the odds; it was if, she had lived their lives, for very little had changed.

Confusion, fear, and the need to survive were so evident in her story, but her spiritual guide was her only solace because, on many occasions, she had no one else to lean on. For very little had changed.

Frightened by her inability to manipulate the environment—and finding her family lacking in experience to assist her in negotiating the campus—made her feel even more isolated. And they thought, very little has changed.

They were surprised that she was told not to trust white people, but after further reflection they found that they too were more willing to trust those who looked like them than those who did not. She discussed her mechanisms to cope with oppression, and while theirs were not the same as hers, both were prepared to deal with racism. For very little has changed.

As they talked among themselves, they found themselves more confident in their abilities to succeed. They had not heard of the success rates of minority students until they got to campus, and then some of their confidence began to dwindle. And again they could not help but think that very little has changed.

It wasn't until much later, when they reflected on our discussion that they realized that they too had been placed with roommates or suitemates who were African-American. Was this a coincidence or yet another sign that very little has changed.

Valuing Our Under-Represented Populations on Campus Environments

The 1990's popular diversity question, "Can't we all get along?" appears to be a simple request, but the answer is "no," not until we are ready to deal with the anger of our students. Opening day is a celebration that every housing person eagerly awaits, yet on that day we are actually saying, "Come ye from everywhere, every different size and type of city and country, every ethnic background, every social class, every value system and every orientation. Come ye one and all and live on this floor, and do it harmoniously," never once using the knowledge that we have about the diversity of the floor to head off some of the problems that are lurking around every corner waiting to explode, waiting to give cause for the anger that exists, waiting to move us further and further away from joining hands.

Institutionally, we have already agreed that a diverse student population provides a richer and fuller experience (Wu, 1991). In and out of class, we can see numerous benefits of having a multitude of opinions that are based on various cultural and economic backgrounds. Most of our students still live in cities or neighborhoods where the majority of people look like them. However, their college experience is enhanced by the differences that they see around them on a daily basis. Not only are they able to see the difference on occasion, but they are able to experience the difference vicariously through conversations with their peers, as well as taste the difference by involving themselves in a culture unlike their own. The diverse campus becomes a training ground because we know our graduates will eventually move into the workplace in which they will be challenged to understand and work successfully with a diverse population. Many times, a diverse institution gives students ample opportunities to make mistakes that will not be tolerated in the workplace. At times, students will make comments that are inappropriate, but their ignorance is not a crime at an institution of higher learning. Unfortunately, these comments could be very detrimental to them in the workplace. For example, it is inappropriate to label darker Americans as "colored;" yet if that is the language that the community uses, one may feel it is an appropriate and nonoffensive classification. Yet if that label is used on campus, someone typically will explain the inappropriateness of the label.

A similarly inappropriate label used in the workplace immediately lets those around these individuals know that they are not sensitive to African-Americans, and while they may be informed that their terminology is inappropriate, the possibility of that single comment branding those individuals is great. It is difficult to leave a diverse institution without becoming more sensitive to the needs and concerns of others. So, it makes perfect sense that many institutions include diversity commitments in their goals or mission statements. Many institutions set goals to increase minority populations on their campuses (which is a wise developmental and financial decision since our majority populations are becoming our minority populations). While diverse populations enhance the campus, that enhancement comes with a price.

The Ill-Equipped Environment

About five years ago, I was invited to conduct a workshop for an institution that had recently attracted a large minority population. My first thoughts were that it's never too late for one to receive more information; however some of the mistakes administrators and faculty members make with students because of a lack of knowledge are difficult to overcome. Every year we see more and more under-represented students come to colleges and universities all over the country. But what are we doing to prepare for their arrival? We already know they have different needs, but what are we doing to prepare for them? We already know many of their issues, but what are we doing about them prior to their arrival? When responsible parents find out that they are pregnant, they begin to prepare for the arrival of the new member of their family. They prepare the environment and purchase all the equipment they will need to make the new arrival comfortable. They ensure that digestible foods are ready to help their new family member thrive. They complete their research and they have a good idea what this new experience will be like for them. They have already learned what not to do, and now they are ready. You don't just have a baby, you prepare for its arrival.

Many of our institutional problems exist because we did not prepare the environment for the arrival of our minority students. We did not educate, and in many cases are not educating, faculty and staff about the cultural backgrounds of our under-represented populations. We didn't have time to tell staff and faculty members how important it is to acknowledge the presence of minority students whenever they pass them in the hall or on campus. Assuring minority students that they have nothing to prove because of their ethnicity was never a topic of discussion. Consequently, these small gestures and many others can help to prepare the environment for minority students who are about to arrive to our institutions.

A program that seeks to address these issues was developed at Georgia State University. It is called The Bridge and was created "with the express purpose of providing a jump start at the freshman level and enrichment of experience for African- American students" (LaVant, Anderson, & Tiggs, 1997, p. 48). The program addresses the need to find helpful ways of welcoming students from under-represented groups to a campus culture that in many respects is quite different from the culture in which they were raised. Mentoring is a key component of the The Bridge program and "the developers of the program report that the relationships make the students feel accepted, respected, and supported" (LaVant et al., 1997, p. 48). Programs such as this are certainly a step in the right direction. Not only is this a more personalized means of helping students enter and adjust to the campus culture, but it is also an excellent way for the faculty and staff, who serve as mentors, to be educated and sensitized to the perspectives, backgrounds, and particular needs of incoming minority students.

During the Rodney King incident, many minority students began to reflect upon their institutional conditions, and out of frustration, isolation, and anger, they participated in riots and demonstrations. At one institution, minority students gave the administration a list of demands. Four of the major requests were:

1. Increase the number of minority faculty and professional staff.
2. Provide sensitivity training for the faculty and staff.
3. Make the curriculum more multicultural.

4. Observe Martin Luther King Day as an official holiday.

It is crucial that we understand the power that is involved with hiring a staff that is representative of the minority population on campus. These staff members represent more than a source of identification in that their presence sends a subliminal message of encouragement. Their presence assures minority students that they can indeed complete this process called higher education. Conversely, the disproportionate number of minority housekeepers, dining hall workers, maintenance personnel, and grounds-keepers (all historical jobs for minorities) are also a constant reminder of what they would do if they are not successful students.

Going a step further, as faculty and staff of color are hired in more proportionate numbers, it is imperative that creative and engaging means are developed for facilitating their direct interaction and involvement with students outside the classroom. La-Vant et al., (1997) outline several successful mentoring programs that target African-American men specifically. The Meyerhoff Program at the University of Maryland-Baltimore County, the Student African American Brotherhood founded at Georgia Southwestern University, and the Black Man's Think Tank at the University of Cincinnati are examples of innovative programs that seek to address the developmental and adjustment needs of minority students. A significant component of each of these initiatives is mentoring. Mentoring allow students to receive important information, support, guidance, and encouragement on a personal basis. They also provide much needed role models, especially when mentors belong to under-represented groups themselves.

We can no longer allow major cultural holidays to come and go without notice. Multicultural affairs must become the affairs of all who play a role in our institutions. The presence of our minority students must be felt in every aspect of our institutions. How long will academic freedom be allowed to stand in the way of making the curriculum multicultural? Is it music appreciation or majority music appreciation? Is it world history or European world history? We cannot continue to say that we value diversity but do absolutely nothing to prepare an environment for our under-represented students.

Kuh, Schuh, and Whitt (1991) suggest a number of practical means for incorporating students of color into the institutional culture, thereby influencing that culture and ultimately creating a more inviting and accepting environment. Involvement of under-represented students will promote out-of-class learning for the individuals involved, but perhaps more importantly, it will affect the institutional attitude and heighten the institution's sensitivity to the issues and needs of these students. They suggest practices such as the development of orientation workshops by currently-enrolled students and faculty of color; the creation of forums where minority students and university administrators can discuss concerns; encouraging and facilitating students of color to participate on campus committees, boards, and governing bodies; and recognizing students of color for their academic and service achievements.

The Well-Prepared Environment

Intentionally seeking minority students is a huge commitment. Many benefits result from recruiting a diverse population, but they must be applied to our minority students. How does one prepare the environment for our minority students? This is not an easy question to answer as it will vary depending on individual needs. However, staff must take the time to learn about the various ethnic groups that are coming to campus. Staff, students, and faculty must be trained to understand the development of the minority students, and to expect to see anger on occasion. Know how to address insensitivity when it arises, and make sure the consequences for these types of inappropriate behaviors are clearly stated. Make sure that dining halls provide meals that include ethnic foods. Ask students to provide recipes and initial assistance, if needed. Don't be concerned about additional ceremonies that duplicate traditional ceremonies. For example, if they choose to organize ethnic graduation services, as long as they do not compete with the main ceremony, encourage students in their endeavors. Be aware of the stereotypes that minority students are dealing with. For example, remember that many are taught that the white culture cannot be trusted. Remember that no one comes to the table with an empty plate. Not only do many minority students believe that they are stereotyped, but remember that they also stereotype others. Only through a process of becoming human to one another can students begin to come together with others in recognition of common human ties.

Providing Developmental Opportunities for the Under-Represented Student

I conducted my first diversity program as an undergraduate staff assistant. I gathered my staff and took them to my hometown, and placed them in a position similar to the one that I experienced all of the time at our predominantly white institution. I took them to shopping malls where they could experience what it felt like to be the minority. I let them walk up and down the streets to see what it felt like to walk down a street where very few people shared their ethnicity. Later, we went to my sister's home for a traditional African-American meal. I was determined that white people should understand what my experience was like. I have been educating others in the area of diversity ever since.

A few months ago, I was on the East coast at a small private college and I received my first diversity workshop jolt. An African-American women said to me during the presentation, "You did not plan this workshop for me, you planned this workshop for them (meaning white students)." My first response was, of course, defensive, but I was cool. At the time I thought I was being honest in replying, "No I didn't!" A few months later, I was on the West coast and I gave many groups of people an opportunity to tell how it made them feel when they were oppressed. Unintentionally, I asked no one from the disabled group to share an experience. Afterwards, a legally blind women came to me and said," Never forget us. You may not be able to see us, but never forget us." Two years ago, a young man came to me at the conclusion of a workshop in the Midwest and told me that he really appreciated the materials that I shared, but I needed to speak on the issue of biracial students. After reflecting on all of these instances, it was extremely obvious to me that these workshop participants were correct. I started out educating white people about my own diversity and later about the diversity of others. I felt it my calling to assist others in reflecting on how they cared for their human brothers and sisters. I felt I had developed a program that would enhance the knowledge of white heterosexual people, and I expected the minority students to simply stick around for the ride. Yes, on many occasions the minority students were edified because someone else understood and was speaking on their behalf, but what else were they gaining? It can be difficult to admit that I had missed the mark, but I had.

It is time to develop diversity programs that will heal and attend to the needs of minority students. Why had I missed the mark? Perhaps I had bought into the fact that minority people have always had to learn about white people in order to survive. While this is true for many, a simple analysis should have led me and others to the fact that while minority students have learned about white people, they have not always had the best educators. Stereotypes, misconceptions, and negative experiences must all be dealt with, for these experiences and misconceptions have given many minority students justification for their prejudices. In many ways, some of our minority students need diversity awareness programs even more than their white, heterosexual, able-bodied white peers, because they are not just simply uncomfortable—on many occasions they are in a state of emergency. Their anger and their pain can have devastating effects on their careers, families, and our society.

What Will We Do with What We Know?

Addressing Their Needs

What will we do with the information we have learned about our minority students? What will we do with the anger, frustration, confusion, and mistrust? What will we do with the misinformation that our minority students, on occasion, work with as though it is reality? How will we help them keep their identity while becoming a part of the greater community?

We need to use the information that we have. However, we will not be able to impact the lives of our minority students unless we are willing to invest time in them and establish relationships with them. Human observation has taught us that we can have a bigger impact on people if they think we care about them and they matter to us. Since we have a pretty good idea that some students may struggle with developmental issues, we need to forewarn them of the stages found in the Minority Identity Model (Atkinson et al., 1979) and Gay and Lesbian Development Model. We need to help the under-represented students understand that white students have struggles in formulating their identity, and may not understand them because of where they are in their racial development (Helms, 1984). We need to provide under-represented students with skills to cope with the oppression that they will encounter on campus, as well as to provide them with information and resources that will assist them in addressing their concerns. How many under-represented students feel empowered because they are well informed or aware of the institutional or departmental mechanisms that deal with oppressive behavior? Moreover, we must deal with minority student's stereotypes. In doing so, we must help them understand that trust is not a racial, but a human, issue.

Equally important, we must point out that just as they will find individuals in their own groups that they can and cannot trust, they will also find these individuals in the dominant culture. No longer can we allow minority students to sit with their hands folded during these educational moments. Fairfield University in Connecticut involves students in a total multicultural immersion experience. A diverse group of students is taken to a remote location to live where people and customs are different. The experience ensures that each student will look and feel like a minority during their experience. Through this experience minority students were able to see their white peers as people, for in the immersion experience all of the students were viewed by the dominant culture as minorities. These types of experiences cause both under-represented students and white students to understand their responsibilities to one another as human brothers and sisters (Vendley, 1998).

Under-represented students must become a part of the healing process. Their wounds must be uncovered so that they too can heal. Yes, they may have been hurt, but they must learn to recognize and understand their own prejudices. In doing so, this will hopefully give reason for others to lose their prejudices. We must challenge them to be a part of the bridge that must be built if their children and grandchildren are going to see a better tomorrow.

Where Do We Start?

How will we do all of this? We can start by challenging our student staff members to change the dining practices of colleges and universities across the nation. Why is it that only like groups eat together in the dining halls is a question I have been asking at every institution I have been to in the last two years. "People sit where they are comfortable," is the response I hear from many white students. "I want to sit with someone who I can be myself with," a gay student said. "I don't want to have to explain anything," an African- and Asian-American student said. But I said to them: You are only comfortable with that person that you just met yesterday, because you were willing to take a risk, to get to know that person as a human instead of their group affiliation. You have the power to set the rules during your meal conversation. You simply tell your new acquaintances that you do not want to discuss your differences at mealtimes or any other time if you are not ready to be a teacher yet. Just as the same-race acquaintance you met yesterday can accept you at face value, over time so can someone of another ethnic group.

We must remove the excuses that we have come to rely on that keep us apart. We must also help white students better understand themselves as racial beings (Helms, 1984) so that they understand better the struggles that face under-represented students.

Many times our under-represented students are not given the information they need to be successful on the college campus. I spoke to one student who referred to herself as a first-generation college student and spoke of the struggles she was having because no one in her family could help her maneuver through the environment. University officials must provide more information about the environment. Mentor programs are wonderful but, on occasions, they do not provide the information needed to survive within the campus environment.

We must help under-represented students understand the cultural differences that may exist. For example, for many African-Americans and some international students, "time" is not so exacting. Special events such as birthday parties, house warmings, family reunions, or baby showers in the African-American communities generally start after the scheduled time. This delay rarely upsets the people in attendance; however, in the white culture most events start on time. In essence, time has a different meaning between and within cultures.

Another example or distinction to make is the recognition of someone's presence. Within some ethnic groups the recognition of a person's presence is very important and it does not matter whether that person is known to you or not. While it does not have to be a fanfare, the slightest acknowledgment meets the requirement. However, this is not usually the case in the dominant culture. If the rules are a little different, they need to be shared and discussed in a manner that is digestible and transformable for the under-represented student. Living in a community where one does not understand the rules is very difficult, yet our under-represented students do this routinely.

Because the blood that runs through our veins connects us to each other, we are indeed more alike than different. Yet our socialization process has removed the natural affinity we had for one another at birth. Have you ever noticed little children in a grocery store speaking to everyone they encounter? Did you notice that the child would speak to any human being, small or large, short or tall, black, yellow, or white, able or disabled, rich or poor, heterosexual or homosexual, American or Non-American, cosmopolitan or rural, highly intelligent or mentally retarded? The child could only see their humanness and that outweighs external differences. As these children grow up, we (society), unfortunately, will teach them how to focus on the differences instead of the humanness. We will teach them to trust, admire, believe, and fear. We will teach children how to be "politically correct." And because we will have socialized our children so well on what not to say, they will not be able to find glory in their differences until someone spends a little time helping *them* to *see* their differences in a positive way. If we are to meet the needs of the under-represented student, we must provide them with experiences, relationships, and information that will cause dissonance and lead them to question many of the lessons our society has taught them.

A Final Word

While we have made tremendous strides in understanding the diversity of our under-represented students, we cannot be satisfied with merely understanding the assessment of their needs. Anger, trust, confusion, fear, and isolation have been a part of the under-represented student's experience on our campuses for far too long. We must provide programs that will assist our minority students through their developmental struggles. Alert them to possible developmental pitfalls before they find themselves in the midst of a battle to keep themselves ethnically and culturally secure.

The key to ensuring their success is to provide both subliminal signs and recognizable signs that will lead under-represented students to believe that they are desired, valued, and needed at predominately white institutions. Another key element in providing a thriving atmosphere for minority students is to ensure that the environment is prepared for the diverse population that will enter its doors. Students, staff, administrators, and parents must learn how to celebrate the diversity found on each campus, and address their own fears and issues.

Lastly, under-represented students must be challenged to dismiss the myths they have been taught. They must be challenged to understand they hold a powerful position in the diversity circle, and if they are unwilling to pull together, we may never get past our current state. While we may not be able to "get along" today, tomorrow is coming and if we are willing to proceed past our current location, there is hope.

References

Atkinson, D. R., Morten, G., & Sue, D. W. (1979). *Counseling American minorities: A cross-cultural perspective.* Idaho: WC Brown.

Cass, V. C. (1979). Homosexual identity formation: A theoretical model. *Journal of Homosexuality, 4,* 219-225.

Helms, J. E. (1984). Towards a theoretical explanation of the effects of race on counseling: A Black and White model. *The Counseling Psychologist, 12* (4), 153-163.

Kuh, G. D., Schuh, J. H., & Whitt, E. J. (1991). *Involving Colleges.* San Francisco: Jossey-Bass.

LaVant, B. D., Anderson, J. L., & Tiggs, J. W. (1997). Retaining African American men through mentoring initiatives. *New Directions for Student Services, 80,* 43-53.

McEwen, M. K., Roper, L. D., Bryant, D. R., & Langa, M. J. (1990). Incorporating the development of African-American students into psychosocial theories of student development. *Journal of College Student Development, 31,* 429-436.

Reid, F. (Producer). (1995). *Talking about race* [Video]. Berkeley, CA: Insfilms.

Vendley, G. (1998). Effect of a Multi-ethnic, Multicutural Program on Student Participants. *NASPA Journal, 35*(3), 234-244.

Wu, F. (1991, March 13). Universities' interest in diversity based on belief it is a panacea for racial tension. *Chronicle of Higher Education,* p. B2.

Purposeful Faculty-Student Interaction Programs in the Residence Halls

Mary Ann Ryan
Director of Housing & Residence Life
University of Minnesota-Twin Cities

Purposeful Faculty-Student Interaction

Faculty-student interaction in the residence halls is hardly a new concept. Early in the development of American colleges, faculty first lived in or close to college student housing in residential colleges. "Implicit in the (residential college) model was the assumption that students and faculty would live and learn together" (Winston & Fitch, 1993, p. 316).

Over the decades, their roles and experiences in student housing have varied depending upon the college and the time in history. For example, during the "Bread and Butter" rebellion at Yale University in the 1820s, students, distressed by their demanding classes, protested by rolling cannonballs through their living quarters in the middle of the night while live-in faculty slept (Schneider, 1998). Pillinger (1984) writes that at Vassar College in the mid-1800s, Maria Mitchell, America's first woman astronomer, lived in the campus observatory. On a clear evening, she would stand outside nearby campus student housing and "yell for her students to come and view a specific planet or constellation" (p. 7). Further, she would run through the living quarters and light gas lamps so that the students could see their way out of the building for the observation. Writing of the same time period, Rudolph (1962) reports that on some campuses faculty lived in student housing to function "as spies, policeman and judges" and to "sustain a rigid, minute and often trivial code of laws" (p. 104).

After the Civil War, with curriculum expansion and an increased emphasis on research, the faculty became more disengaged from student life. As a result, some university presidents created the first student affairs positions (NASPA, 1987). By the early 1900s, faculty generally left the cocurriculum to student affairs and focused on the curriculum. This dichotomy between personal development and cognitive learning has been denounced by many in higher education who advocate a coherent student experience that connects what they learn in the classroom to their experiences and lives (Magolda, 1996).

Currently, faculty-student interaction in the cocurricular environment receives considerable attention on many campuses. Living-learning centers, scholars-in-residence, new student orientation, first year experience, and other programs are designed or revitalized, in whole or in part, to create opportunities for meaningful faculty-student dialogue.

"A large part of the impact of college is determined by the extent and content of one's interactions with major agents of socialization on campus, namely faculty members and student peers. The influence of interpersonal interaction with these groups is manifest in intellectual outcomes as well as changes in attitudes, values, aspirations, and a number of psychosocial characteristics" (Pascarella & Terenzini, 1991, p. 620).

The foundation of out-of-the-classroom, faculty-student based programs depends upon collaboration between student affairs and academic affairs. This collaboration was called for in the American Council on Higher Education's *Student Personnel Point of View* statement issued in 1937 (Roberts, 1998). Again in the 1950s, student affairs encouraged the creation of cocurricular programs that engage faculty-student interaction in response to increased enrollment and continued emphasis on research and publication (Lorenz, Schuh, & Hanson, 1989). However, in many cases, a long history of separation between student affairs and academic affairs inhibited meaningful collaboration. In the mid to late 1980s, both higher education's emphasis on the educational value of student experiences beyond the classroom and undergraduate education reform movements began to advocate a coherent undergraduate experience that required collaboration between the two cultures (Zeller, 1996). The climate in higher education continues to promote collaboration. Partnerships, synergy, and cross-functional teams are words and phrases heard across campus reflecting an overall attitude of sharing resources, shrinking barriers, and presenting unified and coherent programs to enhance the student learning experience. Housing and residential life professionals support these concepts by creating, enhancing, and/or promoting programs that emphasize faculty-student interaction in the residence halls.

This chapter examines programs designed to foster faculty-student interaction in the residence halls. The first section examines opportunities for faculty-student interaction in the residence halls and how to develop effective programs. Examining programs that work, teaching classes in residence halls, and faculty-fellow programs are focuses of the second section providing examples from two residential life programs. In the third section, the use and impact of technology in the residence hall faculty-student interaction programs are discussed. Marketing and evaluation of the programs are the focus of the fourth section.

Opportunities and Development

Residence halls are likely environments to host meaningful faculty-student programs that enhance the undergraduate experience. So are campus unions, malls, and even recreational fields, which often are more comfortable to enter as they rarely require an invitation or escort. Clearly, housing and residential life professionals do not expect faculty to frequent residence halls without invitation, role, or purpose. In many cases, the presence of faculty in the residence halls is the result of an undergraduate staff member fulfilling an educational programming requirement. These occasional faculty sightings in the residence halls, although positive and popular, sometimes do not represent a comprehensive faculty-student interaction program. "If undergraduate education is to be enhanced, faculty members, joined by academic and student affairs administrators, must devise ways to deliver undergraduate education that are as comprehensive and integrated as the way students actually learn" (Pascarella, Terenzini, & Blimling, 1994, p. 32).

The development of meaningful and intentional residence hall programs that promote faculty-student interaction requires institutional support and leadership. Program foundation and formation should be based on the institutional mission and goals as opposed to the charisma and commitment of a particular faculty member and a willing residence hall staff member. Linkage to the institutional mission and goals increases program credibility and may ultimately impact the stability of the program on a particular campus. Housing and residential life professionals, using the institutional mission as a foundation, can begin to formulate program philosophy and intended outcomes.

Opportunities to initiate such programs vary by college or university. As with any opportunity, wait for it to come or help create it. If it "comes," the opportunity can evolve with a change in leadership. A new dean or several faculty members' prior positive experiences with a faculty-student interaction program can place the creation of a similar program high on the academic agenda.

Purposeful Faculty-Student Interaction

The ability of housing and residential life professionals to identify and articulate shared goals and agendas of academic affairs and student affairs can also result in opportunity. When Astin (1975) began writing about student involvement as it influenced student retention, he set forth a common campus agenda. In 1993, American College Personnel Association (ACPA) President Charles Schroeder called for an examination of how student affairs could enhance student learning and personal development in response to higher education's focus on institutional productivity. As a result, *The Student Learning Imperative* concluded that "student affairs professionals must seize the present moment by affirming student learning and personal development as the primary goals of undergraduate education" (ACPA, 1996, p. 121). Housing and residential life professionals can invite opportunity for meaningful faculty-student interaction in the residence halls by identifying and articulating student learning and personal development as common ground for faculty and staff.

It does not take an exhaustive search of available literature to identify the division between the academic and student affairs cultures. In writing about the origins of student affairs, Caple (1996) asserts that this "dualistic die was cast" when, "from the beginning, 'student affairs' was charged with the growing responsibility for life on campus, up to but not including the classroom, which was the domain of the faculty and 'academic affairs' " (p. 195). This division can be clearly illustrated on many mid-to-large size campuses by asking residence hall staff to name the dean of a particular college or, conversely, asking a faculty member to identify the director of residential life (unless he or she has been in the student newspaper lately). Often it is incumbent on the residence hall leadership to initiate the partnership with the faculty. Patricia Kearney, Assistant Vice Chancellor for Student Affairs at the University of California-Davis, addressed this point when she said, "If we keep waiting to be asked to dance, we will never be able to develop meaningful relationships with the faculty. Are we willing to share our turf with the faculty? If we are willing to ask the faculty to participate meaningfully in planning and developing the student services agenda, meaningful relationships will follow" (Clement & Rickard, 1992, p. 112).

Residence hall leadership in partnership with academic leadership can approach the development of faculty-student interaction programs in the residence halls in a variety of ways. Generally, to develop and sustain the programs, five components must be in place.

1. *Shared Purpose:* A program to enhance faculty-student interaction in the residence halls must be based on a larger college or university goal and collaboratively developed and defined. This necessitates "buy-in" from vice presidents, deans, and department heads. The housing and residential life professional may initially be the one to "sell" the concept to the vice president who in turn enlists higher institutional support. Actual program formation and definition—either initially or during the evaluation phases with students—is done collaboratively between the faculty participants and housing and residential life professionals. Together, they create a purpose for faculty participation in the residence halls. Whether the faculty teach a class in the hall, adopt a residence hall floor, or actually serve as residence hall directors (as is the case at McGill University in Montreal, Canada), they have a purpose for interacting with stu-

dents in the residence halls. And, ultimately, the purpose is to influence a student's personal and intellectual development (Pascarella et al., 1994).

2. *Commitment and Recognition:* Creating and sustaining programs take time. Since few residential life programs have a "Faculty-Student Interaction Program" position, frequently the bulk of the work, from a housing and residential life perspective, falls on the residential life "program" person or live-in staff whose schedule is already full. Likewise, faculty, who teach full-time and often engaged in research, are the nucleus of the program. These staff and faculty are expected to be committed to the program. Recognition or reward planning, to demonstrate a commitment to the people who make the program work, is a major component of the program. Other forms of public and private recognition are important along with faculty meal plans, t-shirts, and possibly some professional development funding (Carpenter, Paterson, Kibler, & Paterson, 1990).

3. *Appropriate Space*: The residence hall provides physical space for the program environment. Whether it is a dining room, study lounge, or classroom, the space designated for the program must be suitable for meaningful interaction. Thus, the physical characteristics of the space (furniture, lighting, appearance) are important for all program participants. By their nature, residence halls are busy places, alive with activity and noise that housing and residential life professionals describe as signs of community. Determining the level of privacy or quiet the program requires is important to ensure that the designated program space is in an appropriate location within the hall. Adequate classroom space on many campuses is also a concern for academic affairs. Identifying or creating appropriate space for faculty-student interaction can impact the appeal and effectiveness of the program.

4. *Funding:* Some programs require funding for such things as faculty meal plans, educational materials, facility renovation, technology, or stipends. Whether the amount is large or small, this issue should be addressed early in the planning stages. If a large amount of funding is required, it reinforces the importance of program "buy in" from all levels of the administration. For example, auxiliary housing departments could explore the possibility of alternative funding for renovation of residence hall space into classrooms or faculty offices. Contributions from academic departments and externally funded grants have successfully financed programs (Zeller, 1994). Some housing and residential life programs charge students living in halls where special programs exist a higher room rate to offset program costs.

5. *Evaluation*: During the program development, planners should determine how the program process and outcomes will be evaluated. The evaluation should provide information housing and residential life professionals and the faculty can use to assess the effectiveness of the proposed faculty-student interaction program. Naturally, the evaluation results should be used to initiate program change and enhancement. The program outcomes, as derived from evaluation, can be used to promote future participation in the program. For more information regarding program evaluation, see chapter 2 on assessment.

Addressing these five components begins the development of the faculty-student interaction program in residence halls. To further illustrate program development, consider two examples, classes taught in residence halls and faculty fellow (also known as faculty mentor, associate, friend, advocate) programs.

Programs That Work: Classes Taught in the Residence Halls

Faculty teaching classes in the residence halls is very appealing to students, particularly when the hall hosts special-purpose living units that cluster students by academic major and related courses. On some campuses, the classes taught are part of a larger program for first-year students. Because this "one stop" concept reflects an integration of student and academic life, it generally receives widespread university and college support. Some of the most challenging pieces of developing this program are logistical. Work with registration, new student programs, and admissions is necessary to promote class options to the residential students and to ensure that students have registered for the course section being taught in their hall. Residence hall access must be considered when faculty are teaching and for students enrolled in the class who do not live in the residence hall. As "far" is a relative term depending upon the size of the campus, consideration should be given to the hall's location on the campus when choosing a residence hall venue (assuming there is a choice). For example, a residence hall built on the periphery of campus might be an inconvenient class location for faculty members who must teach elsewhere on campus.

The interaction these classes promote benefits all involved. Previously cited literature addresses the student learning that occurs and student satisfaction and retention that are positively impacted. Students experience a physical connection between their academic and cocurricular worlds. The faculty member has a purpose for spending time in a residence hall with students. An opportunity is created to extend the interaction beyond the classroom period by giving faculty members a meal plan; theoretically they can eat lunch with their students after an 11:00 a.m. class, for example. Or, an office space can be designated in the residence hall to promote a faculty member's availability to students beyond the classroom setting.

Another advantage to this program and rationale for investing in quality classroom space (and sometimes instructional equipment) in the residence halls is the multiple ways a classroom can be used. It does not take a lot of imagination to envision hall council meetings, training sessions, social and educational programs, and other staples of residence hall programs occurring in a classroom. During the summer months, the classroom can convert to meeting room space for conference groups housed, emulating local hotels. Classroom design should reflect the intent of meaningful faculty-student interaction. Determine the optimal classroom size with the faculty, and plan accordingly. Select furnishings that allow flexibility. As obvious as it seems, these types of decisions will impact the appeal and usefulness of the space. On many campuses, residence hall space and/or funding are inadequate to develop a classroom. Existing floor lounges or study rooms are effectively used for classes, particularly those with a focus on small group interaction.

If a housing and residential life program does not have significant faculty presence in the residence hall, encouraging faculty to teach in the halls is a good starting point. Beyond asking the faculty member to come to a different location to teach, there is not an implied additional time commitment required. And, despite concerns about civility in the classroom on some campuses, it is generally more comfortable for most faculty to teach in a residence hall than to stop over, unannounced, for an informal chat with students.

Faculty Fellow Programs

Any number of faculty fellow programs are available across the nation. Program definition is often as varied as its title. Basically, a faculty member partners with housing and residential life staff to work with residence hall students in a particular hall or on a particular floor. The smaller the ratio of faculty to students, the better. At the maximum, the ratio should be less than one to fifty (Schuh & Kuh, 1984). The extent of interaction between the faculty and students varies by program and individuals involved. Sometimes the faculty member actually lives in the residence hall, but even in these cases, the extent of involvement between the faculty member and students varies.

The role of the faculty member as a faculty fellow is to interact with students in their residence hall environment. Faculty generally have occasion to interact with students through planned educational programs, meals, attending house meetings, intramural games, social events, residence hall office hours, or, in some cases, informal visits. Benefits of this initiative—besides those derived from the faculty-student interaction—include the presence of another positive role model in the residence halls, support for the residence hall staff, the availability of another caring adult resource in the student environment, personalization of the educational process, and a promotion of positive public relations internal and external to the institution (Jackson & Stevens, 1990).

Selecting a faculty member for the program is and can be done in a variety of creative ways. Some housing and residential life professionals suggest writing a letter from the campus president, provost, or chief student affairs officer inviting faculty to participate. Students then select their faculty fellow from a list of faculty volunteers. Others prefer that students and staff nominate faculty who are then asked to participate. Others, with a predominantly first-year student residence hall population, suggest that the residential life staff select and assign a faculty member so the program is in place for the beginning of fall quarter/semester. Whatever the process, special efforts should be made to recruit a diverse group of faculty participants into the program so as to reflect diversity in the residence hall student population. Some faculty participate in these programs as a result of an affiliation with a residential college or other special-purpose housing unit programs. Other chapters in this volume describe their involvement in more detail.

Program expectations must be reasonable in terms of a faculty member's time. While an undergraduate staff member or other student leader typically is responsible for overall communication between the faculty member and the students in a particular community, other connections with the faculty member must be in place. A collaborative faculty fellow program has a smaller oversight committee consisting of faculty coordinator(s), residential life coordinator(s), and student leader(s). The oversight committee ensures that the program structure is both in place and continually effective. The program structure includes:

1. Orientating the faculty and residential life staff to the faculty-student interaction program.

2. Familiarizing the faculty member with the residence hall environment.
3. Providing the faculty member with information about the student and residence hall culture, structure, and policies.
4. Scheduling meetings of all faculty fellows and the oversight committee on an ongoing basis to discuss concerns and experiences.
5. Establishing special communication to alert the faculty member of any crisis or issues that may arise on the floor and impact the faculty member's interaction with the student.

In beginning a faculty fellow program, a campus may want to pilot the program in select communities. This helps in two ways. First, residential life staff and key faculty have time to cultivate their relationship with affected students and refine the program. Second, it takes time to develop these programs and to increase faculty participation. Successful pilot programs establish a solid foundation and positively promote the program, thereby increasing interest and involvement.

Examples of Programs that Work:
Hamline University and Central Missouri State University

Hamline University is a liberal arts college in Minneapolis, Minnesota, with a residence hall population of approximately 750. Over the past three years, Hamline has successfully integrated faculty into the Residence Life program. In 1996, as a result of goals set by Hamline University's First-Year Experience Task Force and subsequent task force projects, students in four first-year seminar classes were assigned to special housing units (a wing in a residence hall) designated as a Living-Learning Center. Resident assistants assigned to Living-Learning Centers are specially trained. Living-Learning Center program components include first-year seminars taught in the residence hall, informal faculty-student interaction through social programs, and extensive consultation between faculty and Residence Life staff regarding student issues and involvement. In essence, the residence hall director and faculty serve as cocurricular advisers for students and collaboratively design and implement informal opportunities for faculty-student interaction. The residence hall director also communicates student academic concerns to the faculty member (Deppe & Davenport, 1996).

By the third year of the program, eight first-year seminars were taught in the residence halls. The focus of all seminars is critical thinking. Each seminar involves the class in two activities a month outside of the classroom so as to give students a different opportunity to participate in learning. These activities vary and usually reflect the diverse interests of the faculty. For example, one class went to the Ordway Theatre in St. Paul, while another class visited a waste treatment center. Activities are funded jointly by academic departments and Residence Life.

At Hamline University, students sign up for the seminar first, then are assigned a room based in part on their course section. But Matt Rader, Director of Residence Life, doesn't advocate any particular order in course selection or room assignment. "It's a toss up on which way is better. At Hamline, when some students found out their hall assignment and were unhappy with it, they then wanted to change seminars" (M. Rader, personal communication, May 1998).

With a class size of 16 students, seminars are taught in floor lounges. The traditional lounge atmosphere is comfortable. Residence Life provides all audio-visual equipment when requested. The faculty choose the readings for the students in their seminar. Sometimes faculty will eat in the dining hall with the students after class. Seminars taught in the halls are also offered elsewhere on campus. In 1998, retention for students enrolled in the seminars in the residence halls was 14% higher compared to students not enrolled in residence hall classes.

In this case, Residential Life staff members ask faculty to participate in the program. Rader believes that residential life professionals need to go out and talk to faculty to learn of their interest in residence hall programs and to encourage participation. To him and many others, it begins with the establishment of effective relationships between faculty and residential life professionals (M. Rader, personal communication, May 1998).

Central Missouri State University is located in Warrensburg, Missouri. With a residence hall population of approximately 2,400, Central has created opportunities for meaningful faculty-student interaction in the residence halls. In 1998, approximately 40 faculty members volunteered to work with students in the residence halls through the "Faculty Friends" program. Faculty are primarily assigned to first-year living environments (floor clusters of approximately 35 students), although some faculty work with larger communities housing upper-class students. The role of the faculty friend is to serve as a role model in the community and to assist students with their academic and personal development.

To solicit participation in the program, University Housing sends out a letter to the faculty inviting them to become a Faculty Friend and asking those interested to indicate a preference for working either with first-year or upper-class students. University Housing staff also meet individually with each new faculty member to introduce the program and to determine the faculty member's level of interest in the program. After compiling a list of faculty volunteers, the University Housing staff then assigns faculty to a community. Early in the fall, University Housing hosts a social for the undergraduate staff and Faculty Friends. Pictures are taken, connections between the faculty and residential life staff are made and/or renewed, e-mail and phone lists are distributed, and expectations for the program are defined. After an orientation to the residence hall, faculty are given an opportunity to participate in the "move-in" process. Along with the traditional "thank you" note and evaluation form sent to each Faculty Friend who volunteers for opening weekend, Elizabeth Schulte, Associate Director of University Housing, personally calls each Faculty Friend to thank them. She also e-mails the University President to tell him who participated, in case, she indicates, "he (the President) would see them on campus and want to thank them himself" (E. M. Schulte, personal communication, July 1998).

After opening, the University Housing staff contact their Faculty Friend once every two weeks, on average. The faculty become members of the community by attending floor programs and intramural events, eating meals with students in the halls (sometimes bringing their families with them), helping students with their study skills, and participating in other informal opportunities for interaction. Some faculty invite students to their homes in the Warrensburg community.

Purposeful Faculty-Student Interaction

A Faculty Friend advisory committee consisting of faculty, University Housing administrators, and students meets once a month to discuss program enhancements and concerns. Faculty Friends are invited to monthly luncheons in the residence halls to discuss their perceptions of the program with residential life administrators. A monthly Faculty Friend newsletter distributed by University Housing completes the on-going components of the program.

The Faculty Friend program is funded by University Housing and the cost (printing and food) is minimal. The true investment is in the time devoted to the program by all participants. At Central, the grade point average of the first-year students living in residence halls is significantly higher than those students living off campus. "The gap between the grade point averages of these two groups widens each year as we involve more faculty in the residence hall environment," notes Schulte (personal communication, July 1998).

At both Hamline University and Central Missouri State University, faculty presence is evident in the residence halls from the beginning of the academic year. For a first-year student, seeing faculty in their living environment becomes commonplace. For the faculty member, there is a reason to be in the environment. These conditions increase the likelihood of meaningful interaction. The housing and residential life staffs are key to creating and maintaining this climate. Their role is generally that of program facilitators. Engaged in creating and maintaining the structure of the program, the staff takes care of program logistics, administration, and facility issues. Attending to program details (how do the faculty access the hall, where do they park, how do they get a free lunch, or where's the chalk), the staff plans in advance and communicates these plans to the faculty. Staff solicit feedback on program effectiveness and negotiate change in program structure when necessary. They insure that the basic needs of students and faculty are met in the residence halls so that learning can occur (Chickering & Reisser, 1993).

As titles of the programs (faculty friends, mentors, fellows, associates, etc.) and the interactive nature of courses taught in the residence hall suggest, these faculty-student interaction opportunities can result in positive and mutually beneficial relationships. "Students benefit from contact with experienced adult role models and may identify faculty members who will serve as resources to aid and support them during their college years. At the same time, faculty members can learn about student interests, problems, and lifestyles and can use that information to improve teaching" (Day, 1985, p. 31). Housing and residential life staff also benefits from the program. Research indicates that students want to live in an academic environment and that, along with their peer group, residence hall staff influence the students' perceptions of the climate of the residence hall (Denzine, 1997). By promoting faculty-student interaction in the residence halls, the staff contributes to the academic climate in the halls that will likely have a positive impact on student behavior. Stamatakos (1984) wrote of the absence of faculty role models in the residence halls. "In the absence of significant or credible adult role models, it is possible that peer pressure, characterized by students' high need for quick gratification, may be a major contributor to the development in students of relative values that permit the justification of almost any kind of behavior" (p. 13).

The staff also has the opportunity to form significant relationships with faculty members. Often, housing and residential life professionals can become fairly secluded in their housing world. Relationships with faculty expose the staff to a bigger picture of campus life and sensitize staff to issues in academic affairs.

Use of Technology to Enhance Faculty-Student Interaction in the Residence Hall

Technology enables students, faculty, and staff to communicate at anytime and from anywhere. As residence hall professionals deliberate about the impact of distance learning on the future of on campus housing, they often invest significant resources in ever-changing technology to keep residence halls in pace with campus technology and competitive in the housing market. Only a few years ago, residence halls were considered state-of-the-art if they were wired for cable television and telephone and had a computer lab. Today, students expect high-speed access to the campus network from their residence hall room. Students can e-mail the college president with questions or complaints; a resident assistant can send a voice mail message to each member of the community reminding them of a house meeting; and prospective students can apply for admission to the college and campus housing simultaneously, on-line.

The full impact of technology as a means of enhancing faculty-student interaction in the residence halls has not been determined. Pinheiro (1997) writes that "student-student and student-faculty communications is enhanced when computers are used" (p. 25). At "The Changing American College Student" teleconference in April 1998, Alexander W. Astin, John Gardner, and Linda J. Sax discussed the impact of technology on campus. Astin indicated that although it appears word processing improves students' writing skills, the effect of other components of technology needs to be seriously studied. Gardner said the "jury is still out" on determining the impact of technology on the student learning experience (National Resource Center, 1998).

Students today want more privacy and control over their environment. The notion of privacy in the residence halls does not suggest isolation or a lack of participation in the floor community. Rather, according to Altman (as cited in Banning, 1996, p. 4), privacy means that students control when they are alone and when they are with others what information is presented about themselves. Expanding upon this concept, Banning (1996) suggests that as residence hall rooms become more fully functioning—a result of student preferences for more privacy (single rooms/apartments), space, and technology—some students may retreat from traditional community building activities common in residence halls today. These "cocooning" students "should be able to move toward community at their own pace . . . and be able to bring with them their diversity" (p. 5). He offers that the computer might be the in-between that allows students to enter the community at their own pace. So, for the student who does not want to participate in the "get-to-know-our-faculty-friend ice breaker," an opportunity is provided to connect with the faculty member through e-mail or chat groups, which, by their nature, disinhibit interaction.

Communications technology also may impact the faculty-student interaction because it is asynchronous. "Asynchronous communication is communication not limited to having all parties participate at the same time" (Barksdale, 1998, p. 95). Check your e-mail Monday morning, when are students writing you? What were you doing at 2 a.m. when they decided to write to you about a problem, concern, or with a question? The faculty mentor becomes more accessible with technology. Students do not have to wait for the faculty member to come to the hall or leave a voice mail message to connect with them. For the resident assistant whose schedule is typically hectic, e-mail becomes a natural and efficient means of inviting the faculty member to floor events, or of copying the faculty member on communication going out to floor residents.

This technology should not replace the actual presence of the faculty member in the residence hall; rather, it should be used to supplement and support the program. As examples, create a chat room for students enrolled in the first-year experience class taught in the residence hall so that classroom discussion and sharing can continue beyond scheduled class time; distribute newsletters for faculty fellows through e-mail so recipients can comment on articles and/or share experiences; or use video or audio clip to lend excitement to traditional programs and other forms of communication.

Housing and residential life professionals historically have adapted well to "new" challenges impacting their environments. What other profession requires knowledge and some competency in topics such as asbestos, ADA, Astin, and alcohol abuse? As campus initiatives increasingly focus on technology, housing and residential life professionals, faculty and students need to creatively explore the use of technology in residence halls, particularly as it relates to faculty-student interaction. Within the "electronic university, . . . student and faculty collaboration can be enhanced by a residential setting designed to maximize these interactions" (Zeller, 1996, p. 12).

The University of Minnesota, Twin Cities Campus, created a virtual residence hall to connect off campus first-year students with the residence hall environment as part of their Commuter Connection program. The virtual residence hall, called "Gopherville" (http://www.umn.edu/housing/go4ville.htm), is an interactive web site where participants appear on the screen as avatars and talk to one another through words imprinted in cartoon-like balloons in a variety of different rooms and offices. The site has a number of bells and whistles (an amphitheater for speakers to use to address student groups, checkers and backgammon game rooms, interfaces with campus offices) and has the potential for much more. In the site design, it was intended that activities and interaction initiated in Gopherville would lead to face-to-face contact. For example, off campus students participating in Gopherville would be invited to special lunches hosted by administrators and faculty in the halls; the championship round of a backgammon tournament initiated in Gopherville would be held on-campus. During site development, the Associate Provost extended an invitation to the 40 faculty who taught the largest freshmen classes. These faculty members were invited to hold office hours in a Gopherville office. At the time of this writing, students, other than those who helped plan the Commuter Connection program, have not experienced Gopherville as the program will actually begin Fall Quarter 1998. However, embedded in its design is opportunity for faculty-student interaction on-line that will hopefully evolve into face-to-face interaction.

The housing and residential life professional can speculate about the future of technology and how it will impact their environments and interaction within those environments. But technology is rapidly growing, expensive, and changing. The impact this change will have for residence halls, for students, and for attempts to create community has yet to be fully evaluated. In developing faculty-student interaction in the residence halls, the use of technology as a means to enhance the program should be purposeful and in keeping with campus-wide technological goals.

Marketing and Evaluation

To sustain, expand, and/or enhance faculty-student interaction programs, housing and residential life professionals should plan for effective marketing and evaluation. Marketing the program, both internally and externally, contributes to program participation and value. Several cohorts on campus are critical to marketing success.

1. *Admissions:* Admissions professionals have expertise in marketing and promoting programs both on and off campus. Admissions' publications reach prospective students and send a message about what is valued on campus. The concept of interacting with faculty in the residence halls can be introduced to the student as a campus-life expectation before the student arrives on campus through publications and information shared by admissions office representatives.

2. *New Student Orientation:* This program generally involves faculty and administrators from across campus. As previously mentioned, on many campuses new students register for classes during orientation and, with proper planning, students will know how to enroll in a course taught in their residence hall. This planning generally is done with the faculty member, the housing office, and the registrar's office, but is promoted through the new-student orientation program. Orientation leaders and advisors should receive information about the residence hall classes and enrollment so they can promote the program and advise students on course selection.

3. *Faculty:* Recently this author received an e-mail from her University's Associate Dean in the College of Liberal Arts (CLA). The Associate Dean asked if Housing and Residential Life would like to collaborate with CLA's Global Studies Program to create a residential living-learning experience for students interested in global studies. In subsequent meetings to plan the program, the Associate Dean indicated that she thought of proposing the concept because she heard such positive comments from faculty working with students in the Biology House and Honors Housing programs in the residence halls. Faculty will share the good news about their residence hall experiences. Faculty currently involved in faculty-student interaction programs can be asked to help promote the expansion of the program to other academic departments. In essence, they become an important program reference.

4. *Campus Community:* A housing and residential life department's marketing materials targeting program benefits and opportunities should be widely distributed on campus. The department's web page, application, newsletters, and brochures are obvious vehicles used to promote the program to a larger community. Educating peer offices in student affairs about the program and its benefits can be done through all levels of the housing organization. Some faculty-fellow programs have expanded to faculty-and-staff-fellow programs wherein a faculty member and student affairs staff member work jointly with a residence hall community.

Faculty-student interaction in the residence halls ideally should be as natural and commonplace for students as having cereal available for dinner in the dining hall. That which was once new and innovative becomes a student expectation of their residential experience. Collectively, as campus partners learn about, read about, talk about, and, in some cases, experience the program, program marketing is perpetuated.

During program development, housing and residential life professionals and the faculty determine how the program's process and outcomes will be evaluated. Chapter 2 explores assessment issues in residential education, but it is important to note here that beyond determining how and when the evaluation will occur, housing and residential life professionals and the faculty should determine how to use evaluation data to promote the program to the campus community and prospective students.

Astin (1984) wrote, "Frequent interaction with faculty is more strongly related to satisfaction with college than any other type of involvement or, indeed, any other student or institutional characteristic. Students who interact frequently with faculty members are more likely than other students to express satisfaction with all aspects of their student experience, including student friendships, variety of courses, intellectual environment, and even the administration of the institution" (p. 304). Pascarella and Terenzini (1991) reported that there is strong evidence indicating that the outcomes of educational aspirations, persistence, and attainment are positive for the student in relation to the student-faculty interaction outside of the classroom.

Given these findings, in studying the retention of students between their first and second years of college, program design might focus on any differences in retention between students participating in the program and those who did not. Assuming that the retention of students participating in the program was higher and that increased retention was one of the purposes of the program, there is a real success story to be shared, to be celebrated, and to be recognized by the campus community. It is incumbent upon housing and residential life professionals to take a leadership role in spreading the good news.

A Final Word

This chapter focused on two purposeful faculty-student interaction programs—classes taught in residence halls and faculty fellows. Other chapters in this volume describe other purposeful programs (living-learning centers, special purpose housing, residential colleges) that also emphasize the out-of-the-classroom connection students can have with faculty in the residence hall environment. Each campus is different in terms of the culture, climate for collaboration, and politics. Consequently, no textbook formula exists for developing an ideal program that would be universally successful on each campus. As a general guide presented in this chapter, the program developed should be based on the institution's mission, goals, and direction. Working with faculty and students will help housing and residential life professionals develop the program and tailor it to best respond to the needs of individual campuses.

As this chapter suggests, establish long range program goals with faculty and students that address the potential impact of technology, the attrition of involved faculty and housing and residential life professional staff, and the future financial demands on the program. Patience is necessary in developing programs. Pilot programs with students in one hall or on one floor with faculty from one academic department or college.

A trial-and-error period will, in the long term, help establish a coherent and collaborative foundation for the program.

But, most importantly, the program needs to continually emphasize the integration of academic and student affairs to create a "seamless learning environment" (Kuh, 1996) for students in the residence halls. All levels of the housing and residential life organization must recognize this integration as a primary goal of the department; it should understood that housing resources (time, financial, facility, staff) will focus on program success. This understanding makes it somewhat easier for staff to accept relocating their breakroom so that space can be made available for a faculty office or advising center.

In closing, opportunities for faculty involvement in residence halls require institutional support. The development of these programs must include a shared purpose between academic affairs and student affairs, recognition of those involved, appropriate space to house the programs, varying levels of funding, and systematic evaluation. A good starting point for a faculty-involvement program would be classes taught in the residence halls.

Successful faculty-involvement programs include an orientation of the faculty to the residence hall environment, an oversight committee that monitors the program, and comprehensive and on-going communication. Using technology in these programs may enhance community and communication. Collaboration with a variety of campus constituents helps market these programs. Programs that support faculty-student interaction can help positively determine the impact of college on the student.

It is the responsibility of housing and residential life professionals to initiate, create, promote, and sustain these programs for our students. Beyond providing and managing student housing, supporting student learning in the residence halls is the very core of housing and residential life work.

References

American College Personnel Association. (1996). The student learning imperative: Implications for student affairs. *Journal of College Student Development, 37*, 118-122.

Astin, A. W. (1975). *Preventing students from dropping out.* San Francisco: Jossey-Bass.

Astin, A. W. (1984). Student involvement: A developmental theory for higher education. *Journal of College Student Personnel, 25*(4), 297-308.

Banning, J. H. (1996). Designing for community: Thinking "out of the box" with porches. *The Journal of College and University Student Housing, 26*(2), 3-6.

Barksdale, J. L. (1998). Communications technology in dynamic organizational communities. In F. Hesselbein, M. Goldsmith, R. Beckhard, & R. F. Schubert (Eds.), *The community of the future* (pp. 93-100). San Francisco: Jossey-Bass.

Purposeful Faculty-Student Interaction —————————————

Caple, R. B. (1996). The learning debate: A historical perspective. *Journal of College Student Development, 37*(2), 193-202.

Carpenter, D. S., Paterson, B. G., Kibler, W. L., & Paterson, J. W. (1990). What price faculty involvement? The case of the research university. *NASPA Journal, 27* (3), 206-212.

Chickering, A. W., & Reisser, L. (1993). *Education and identity revisited* (rev. ed.). San Francisco: Jossey-Bass.

Clement, L. M. M., & Rickard, S. T. (1992). *Effective leadership in student services.* San Francisco: Jossey-Bass.

Day, J. F. (1985). Faculty involvement in residence halls: A student managed program. *The Journal of College and University Student Housing, 15*(2), 31-34.

Denzine, G. M. (1997). Assessing the academic climate in University residence halls. *The Journal of College and University Student Housing, 27*(1), 19-24.

Deppe, M. J., & Davenport, F. G. (1996). In practice: Expanding the first year experience: A report from Hamline University. *About Campus, 1*(4), 27-30.

Jackson, G. S., & Stevens, S. (1990). Incorporating faculty and staff into residence halls. *The Journal of College and University Student Housing, 20*(1), 7-10.

Kuh, G. D. (1996). Guiding principles for creating seamless learning environments for undergraduates. *Journal of College Student Development, 37*(2), 135-148.

Lorenz, N., Schuh, J. H., & Hanson, A. (1989). Student-faculty interaction in the residential setting. In J. H. Schuh, (Ed.), *Educational programming in college and university residence halls* (pp. 74-96). Columbus, OH: ACUHO-I.

Magolda, M. B. B. (1996). Cognitive learning and personal development: A false dichotomy. *About Campus, 1*(3), 16-21.

National Association of Student Personnel Administrators. (1987). *A perspective on student affairs.* Washington, DC: Author.

National Resource Center for the First Year Experience and Students in Transition (Producer). (1998, April 21). *The changing american college student.* University of South Carolina: Teleconference.

Pascarella, E. T., & Terenzini, P. T. (1991). *How college affects students.* San Francisco: Jossey-Bass.

Pascarella, E. T., Terenzini, P. T., & Blimling, G. S. (1994). The impact of residential life on students. In C. C. Schroeder, P. Mable, and Associates, *Realizing the educational potential of residence halls* (pp.23-32). San Francisco: Jossey-Bass.

Pillinger, B. B. (1984). Early residential life: Vassar college in the nineteenth century. *The Journal of College and University Student Housing, 14*(1), 7-9.

Pinheiro, E. (1997). The electronic campus—Universal access through mobile computing. *On Campus, 2*(2), 25-27.

Roberts, D. C. (1998). Student learning was always supposed to be the core of our work: What happened? *On Campus, 3*(3), 18-22.

Rudolph, F. (1962). *The American College and University.* New York: Random House.

Schneider, A. (1998, March 27). Insubordination and intimidation signal the end of decorum in many classrooms. *The Chronicle of Higher Education,* pp. A12-A14.

Schuh, J. H., & Kuh, G. D. (1984). Faculty interaction with students in residence halls. *The Journal of College Student Personnel, 25*(6), 519-527.

Stamatakos, L. C. (1984). College residence halls: In search of educational leadership. *The Journal of College and University Student Housing, 14*(1), 10-17.

Winston, R. B., Jr., & Fitch, R. T. (1993). Paraprofessional staffing. In R. B. Winston, Jr., S. Anchors, and Associates, *Student housing and residential life* (pp. 315-343). San Francisco: Jossey Bass.

Zeller, W. J. (1994). Residential learning communities: Creating connections between students, faculty and student affairs departments. *The Journal of College and University Student Housing, 24*(2), 37-43.

Zeller, W. J. (1996). Two cultures united: Residential programs of the 21st century. *The Journal of College and University Student Housing, 26*(2), 7-13.

Chapter Nine

Leadership Development and Governance

Kenneth L. Stoner
Director of Student Housing
University of Kansas

Leadership Development

Working collaboratively and productively with leadership development and student governance staff is one of the most important duties that challenge student affairs administrators daily. It must be noted that the author has made two assumptions as a basis for this chapter. One, leadership can be learned from others in a variety of formal and informal settings. Two, leadership can be learned from environmental circumstances and challenges. It is true that the social and political context impacts the development of leadership. It is also true that individuals can be taught how to develop individual leadership skills.

Depending on which "great leader" might be under consideration, the discussion could be lively as to whether the individual's personal leadership skills or the circumstances of the times played the greater role. Separated from World War II, Dwight E. Eisenhower might never have been catapulted into a position of world leadership. In the absence of the Great Depression, Franklin Delano Roosevelt might have been just another president. From the other viewpoint, without Martin Luther, the Protestant Reformation might have stalled. Without Florence Nightingale, nursing might never have become a profession; without Joan of Arc, France might never have emerged from the Hundred Year War as a country. Both positions have merit; leadership results from a blending of personal attributes as may only be applicable within the social and political context of the times.

These two assumptions are critical; comments within this chapter address a range of issues broader than just housing and residence life programs. Some suggestions are institutional in nature, but if implemented, have positive ramifications for leadership development and governance within residence life facilities. The social and political context, or the environmental milieu, of the entire campus and the importance attached to student involvement, leadership, and governance can be arranged purposefully to enrich the educational experience of all students. In this fashion, we are all being challenged to think outside our "housing box," knowing the positive impact of university initiatives culminates in a "multiplier effect" for those students residing on campus.

Kuh (1998) in his article, "Lessons from the Mountain," shared incidents in which highly trained professional forest firefighters lost their lives because they refused to follow orders which were to abandon their heavy equipment packs and escape to a nearby area of refuge. The question is germane to our profession, why do we have difficulty abandoning our burdensome equipment, with which we are comfortable, when we know these tools will not work in present circumstances or in the future? In the foreseeable future, even more collaboration on initiatives with our academic and administrative colleagues in the development of leadership and governance will be expected from housing professionals. Thus, this chapter takes a broader view of leadership development and governance. University-wide techniques or tools that significantly contribute to a campus environment conducive to the development of individual leadership and involvement in governance have been included for consideration. Most institutional initiatives have positive ramifications for residence life operations and must be embraced accordingly.

Over the years, professional staff members have been successful in developing leadership within residential units. Emerging interest among administrators at the institutional level signals that the time is right for collaboration with our faculty and staff colleagues to invest energy in campus-wide initiatives that will exponentially enhance existing programming efforts within residential life operations. This chapter introduces foundation documents that provide the basis for this emerging interest. In addition, this chapter states the case for residence life professionals to embrace and support the implementation of broader initiatives that will validate leadership within the curriculum; institutionalize some form of community meeting; and, facilitate attempts to connect with "generation next." Additionally, it offers suggestions for enhancing our traditional leadership programming efforts with brief discussions on the importance of meaningful affiliations among representative student organizations and the inclusion of historically under-represented populations, empowerment, entropic flow, and the educational use of themes and tokens.

Foundation Documents

It is difficult to restrict the literature review to a few key works that can be considered foundation documents utilized in the development of this chapter. However, in preparation, several publications and manuscripts provided useful insights and were considered critical in support of leadership development and governance in the collegiate residential living environment. Coupled with the compilation of articles in this monograph, a "starter kit" for anyone desiring to investigate this topic could be assembled by collecting: *What Matters in College* by Astin (1993); *Involving Colleges* by Kuh, Schuh, Whitt, and Associates (1991); *How College Affects Students* by Pascarella and Terenzini (1991); the Volume 37, Number 2 issue of the *Journal of College Student Development* (1996); *Educational Programming in College and University Residence Halls* edited by Schuh (1989); *Exploring Leadership for College Students Who Want to Make a Difference* by Komives, Lucas, and McMahon (1998); *Advice for Advisers: The Development of a Residence Hall Association* by Dunkel and Spencer (1998); and Advising Student Groups and Organizations by Dunkel and Schuh (1998). These works, among others, were reviewed as a basis for this chapter.

Validating Leadership Within The Curriculum

In 1972, Brown wrote, "It is time now for student development functions to become curricular—with no prefix added. This means legitimizing current out-of-class experiences by making them available more systematically to all students and by giving them some type of academic recognition." (p. 42). This challenge has been vigorously debated over the last quarter of a century, yet it still remains time to embrace the validity of the experiential components of leadership and educationally based community service activities within the curriculum and on the transcript. Schroeder and Hurst (1996) powerfully documented the educational value of integrating the curricular and cocurricular experiences in learning communities. Further, results from a national study of 3,450 students attending 42 institutions indicated that involvement in community service initiatives during the undergraduate years substantially enhanced the academic and life skill development of participating students, and increased their sense of civic responsibility (Astin & Sax, 1998). This section provides a sampling of academic options that reinforce involvement and develop leadership among students attending institutions of higher education.

A renewed emphasis on "Leadership Transcripts" is again surfacing on campuses across the country. Beginning with the fall semester of 1996, Central Michigan University implemented a "Student Development Record" (SDR) that charts developmental growth through university experiences; validates cocurricular activities; complements the academic transcript; documents career path experiences; and internally supports scholarship and award applications. The SDR documents memberships, leadership, and paraprofessional positions; and awards and honors community and university service activities, participation in varsity athletics, and other enrichment commitments evidenced by conference and workshop attendance. Although generated under the Office of Student Life umbrella, the SDR is distributed through the Registrar's Office along with the transcript.

The University of Tennessee at Martin has packaged an interdisciplinary "leadership minor" through the School of Arts and Sciences with applications processed by the Office of Student Affairs; the leadership minor requires 21 hours of specified course work and receipt of the Certificate of Leadership Achievement. To receive certification, the student must complete an individualized self-examination of skills and personal attributes; participate in a variety of applied leadership challenges; work with a selected campus mentor for a minimum of 40 hours to include an experiential component; and receive a "leadership accomplishment rating" at term-completion of a significant leadership role within the campus community. In addition, Freshman Leaders in Residence Scholarships of $1,000 each are credited toward on-campus room and board expenses of entering students receiving this designation, which is determined and subsequently awarded on the basis of their leadership involvement and academic record in high school. The Freshman Leaders in Residence are required to live on-campus to receive the scholarship and are required to enroll in a two credit-hour leadership seminar taught by the Dean of the School of Arts and Sciences during their freshman year.

A "leadership minor" is also in the process of being established at the University of Kansas as well as on numerous other campuses across the country. In fact, there are now about 700 college programs offering some form of leadership development, double the number from just four years ago (Reisberg, 1998). At Kansas, it has been agreed that the minor will be in tandem with a recommended experiential leadership component culminating with one or more capstone courses; the experiential components will be identified according to a graduated scale or level of involvement (exploratory, participatory, contributory, and leadership) of the individual.

Credit for Alternative Spring Break (ASB) projects and other work/internship assignments affiliated with the academic major of participating students also is a movement worth supporting. Although academically based, many work groups consist of a collection of individuals that know one another and work together through residential living units. Some individuals obtain necessary credit in their major courses of study, others receive elective credit, and others participate for no academic credit, but as a personal commitment to service-learning opportunities. A specific program with a residential base is "Natural Ties" at the University of Kansas coordinated as part of the service-learning Center for Community Outreach (CCO). Physically or mentally-challenged individuals are matched with living units or clubs to promote participation in a variety of activities in a natural setting. On behalf of their living unit or club, coordinating individuals can enroll in a two credit-hour class that prepares sponsors to facilitate a positive and interactive community inclusion experience.

The University of Maryland at College Park implemented the first approved academic program in the country that encourages participants to seek elective office. The Academy of Leadership arranges opportunities for students to build an academic foundation and to participate in experiential public service. The proximity of the state and nation's capitals coupled with the large diplomatic community serves as a unique laboratory for students desiring to become the citizen-leaders of the future. Field trips have included visits to the U.S. Capitol, Maryland General Assembly, Holocaust Museum, Annapolis, Habitat for Humanity, plus an excursion to South Africa. Academic credit is provided for service-learning or experiential initiatives that require prior placement approval of the instructor. A minimum of 3 hours a week for 12 weeks or 36 hours of community service complements a weekly 1½ hour seminar where issues related to their experiences are shared and discussed. Assignments vary but typically relate to hunger and homelessness, adult literacy, community health care problems, and related issues of poverty.

In 1972, the University of Colorado at Boulder established the Student Leadership Institute as a separate nonprofit corporation. Over the years, this initiative has progressively evolved into one of the most innovative residential leadership programs in the country. The Leadership Residential Academic Program (LRAP) component reflects institutional, state, and national agendas, and includes the collaborative efforts and funding commitments from the University's Foundation as well as grants from the Ford Foundation and IBM. The LRAP mission is synthesized as "nurture and enable the capacity, ability, and commitment of leaders, while reinforcing within each an authentic sense of service to communities." This program has been attractively packaged for sharing with other campuses in a manual titled *Community Trusteeship: A Guide for a Leadership Residential Academic Program* that includes an interactive CD-ROM (Student Leadership Institute, 1997) about the Student Leadership Institute; an electronic address (*sli@colorado.edu*); and a web site (*www.colorado.edu/SLI/LPAP/*) to consult for further information (Goodman & Ravine, 1997). Currently, LRAP participants live in on-campus residence halls; beginning with fall semester of 1999, participants will be clustered within the same facility to further enhance the instructional impact. Plans are in process to build a new "academic-residential" complex, which will accommodate 250 participants following completion of phase one construction. It is anticipated that this multimillion dollar, state-of-the-art facility will be ready by 2001 at the latest, and will have the design flexibility to include 400 residents as part of a phase two expansion. The proposed financing of the project incorporates investors through the "triple-net lease" arrangement and also reflects futuristic "partnerships" that are continuing to emerge on campuses across the nation. The LRAP has professionally blended academic and residential components into a world-class leadership program. A review of this program challenges us all to plan long-range in program development, to work collaboratively, and to think outside "our box."

Leadership Development

The University of South Florida has established a "Leadership House" in a small residence hall on their campus. The concept for the house is based on the book, *Teacher as Servant: A Parable*, by Robert Greenleaf (1987). This program provides another excellent example of partnerships that are emerging in higher educational communities. In this case, the arrangement was forged between the University of South Florida and The Greenleaf Center for Servant-Leadership in collaboration with AT & T.

Similar to programs at Maryland, Colorado, and South Florida, other institutions, including the University of Missouri, are also pursuing specific learning communities focused on leadership and learning. Missouri is developing a Civic Leadership Residential College patterned after the Maryland model; this initiative also will include a leadership minor with integrated coursework, team teaching, capstone experiences, service-learning components, as well as involvement of community and government officials.

Residence life and housing administrators should support the cocurricular movement actively. Residence halls and other university student housing operations provide a unique laboratory environment for developing leadership skills. For examle, residents who cannot successfully negotiate the volume of the stereo down the hall will never be able to broker world peace. Residents who cannot reach harmony with their neighbors in achieving a balance between individual rights and the "common good" will never be able to develop progressive social policy. Residents who cannot allocate monies among competing funding priorities and requests will never be able to address the issues of homelessness and poverty. Residents who cannot learn to celebrate diversity within the living unit will never be able to conquer hatred and bigotry or the tragedies of racial or ethnic prejudices that plague our world community. Indeed, the future success and viability of university student housing operations is inextricably linked to the academic mission of the institution and the residential "leadership laboratory."

Community Hour

The importance of the academic calendar and subliminal messages that can be effectively communicated through scheduling priorities of the institution must not be underestimated. Even nonverbal messages, consistently communicated over time, can have a powerful influence on student attitudes, public and constituency relations, goal achievement, and even alumni giving. It is not difficult to deduct the priority of an expectation intuitively when time is reserved for that activity through the "Official Timetable" of the university.

Since it was founded in 1971, Evergreen State College in Washington has preempted Wednesday afternoons as "governance time." Philosophically, everyone (students, faculty, and administrative staff) within the campus community at Evergreen is expected to participate in governance activities. This arrangement supplements the mission by institutionalizing the availability of all stakeholders to one another for discussions, open forums, meetings, walk-in contacts, and other essential collaborative efforts. All standing committees as well as "Disappearing Task Forces" at Evergreen are required to have significant student representation.

Similarly, at Slippery Rock University in Pennsylvania, every Tuesday and Thursday from 11:00 a.m. to 1:00 p.m. is "blocked" as "common hour." No classes or appointments are formally scheduled during these two periods of the week; all members of the faculty and staff are expected to make themselves available for "walk in" student traffic. One day a month during this time, a public forum (prescheduled and included in the official university timetable and on the official university calendar of events) is held in which the entire campus community participates. Student representatives often give reports about organizational agendas and activities, express concerns, and question members of the university administration. In the twelve years since implementation, "common hour" has been positively evaluated as one change that has strengthened the institutional community.

It appears that administrators of these two institutions spend less time fighting the mythical assertions that often distract other campuses. For example, many campus officials frequently hear that faculty and administrators are not conveniently available to students and that no one listens to student concerns. Through purposeful scheduling and attention to mission, such perceptions are minimized on the campuses of Evergreen State College and Slippery Rock University.

The power of the peer group and other community experiences suggest that professional student affairs administrators should take a much more active role in academic planning and policy making (Astin, 1996). The literature review provided by Terenzini, Pascarella, and Blimling (1996) forcefully documents the importance of out-of-class experiences on the learning and cognitive development of students.

Connecting With Generation Next

Working with the current generation of college students has always presented challenges to residence life and university administrators over the years. The pendulum has swung from the intense activism of the Vietnam and civil rights era of the late 60s and early 70s when students sought to become involved, but were kept from the table, to the "disconnected" students now in attendance. However, unlike thirty years ago, current administrators are actively attempting to bring students, who are now acknowledged as legitimate stakeholders, to the table. This challenge has increased the attention being given to learning styles and suggested additional opportunities for reaching students, particularly those functioning in leadership roles. Momentous adjustments will be required to realize our respective educational missions.

The June 1, 1998 issue of the *National On-Campus Report* ran the front page headline of "UCLA Study Finds College Freshmen Not Connected" in summarizing the 32nd annual report, titled *The American Freshman: National Norms for Fall 1997* by Sax, Astin, Korn, and Mahoney (1997). Among the more notable findings was the conclusion that current college freshmen are less connected with academics and less involved in political action than any previous class entering as freshmen in the 32-year history of administering the annual survey. Interestingly, the rate of volunteerism has reached an all-time high among these same students. Considering the disengagement in other areas, these trends may reflect the increase in efforts to promote volunteerism and even requiring it as a condition for graduation. Further, the driving motivation behind the pursuit of a degree has migrated, over the years, from love of learning to receipt of an academic credential (Sax et al., 1997).

Two texts offer insights for understanding and proactively addressing these phenomena. The edited work by Oxedine (1997) titled *So You Want To Be President . . . How To Get Elected On Your Campus* is a valuable reference, documenting the extremely creative techniques and innovative campaign strategies used by students seeking election to the highest student office on campus. Individuals tell the reader in their own words why they ran for office, what they considered the issues to be, how their campaign strategy evolved, and what gave them the edge in being elected.

Engaging students in discussions of issues presented in this text can have positive consequences. Issues worthy of careful consideration and discussion—such as ethics, values, voting-blocks, campaign finance and fundraising, volunteers, public relations and media strategies, coalitions, platforms, use of polls and feedback mechanisms, debating, and understanding campus concerns—all emerge from the first-hand account of individuals who were successful in their campaign bids. The book would be extremely useful as a resource for initiating discussions at student leadership retreats.

The value of the text compiled by Komives et al. (1998) is in provoking thought and presenting an array of issues for discussion and further consideration by those active in student government. This work is organized around four themes: leadership in a changing world; relationships as the foundation of leadership; leadership applicable within groups, organizations, and communities; and, leadership and renewal. The approach of the authors is appreciated; the content is applicable to any individual desiring to "make a difference" and is based on the premise that leadership skills "can be learned." In combination with the Oxendine publication, these two books provide substantive content for undergraduates interested in leadership; they frequently constitute the readings for introductory leadership classes or are selectively utilized as the foundation for discussion groups among students pursuing leadership opportunities as an enhancement to their academic program.

Minimally, leadership forums on topics of interest can be very productive. The annual election of officers provides an opportunity to schedule meetings that focus on the "preparation of candidates," "campus issues," "filing one's candidacy," and "involvement through leadership." Learning from readings and discussions in the classroom or from the shared experiences of others is always helpful, but personal leadership is an experience unique to the environmental milieu and dynamics of institutional setting, individual personalities, and understanding the context of campus issues at a given point in time. There is no substitute for involvement.

And, there is absolutely no doubt that advances in technology have changed traditional "connect points" significantly with students attending institutions of higher education. Almost escaping notice is the fact that many entering students no longer have the ability to read cursive. Elementary students are taught the English alphabet and know how to read and write in an uppercase and lowercase printed format, and from that point are immediately taught "keyboarding." Depending on the public school, a "handwritten" paper may never be required from a pupil, or, in some cases, not accepted in preference to printed format generated by computers. Members of the faculty are discovering that feedback or comments penned, in cursive, directly on students' papers either cannot be read or are often misunderstood. In addition, many students prefer to communicate electronically and some class papers are being submitted with web sites listed for all references. Although new learning technologies could be used to enhance interactions between students and faculty, from some perspectives, it could be argued that computer technology actually has reduced meaningful contact (Astin, 1996). "Connecting with the disconnected" will continue to challenge all of us in higher education; although current students may seem "disconnected" from traditional academia, many correctly note that students are "connected technologically."

Enhancing Leadership Programming

Within residence life organizations, traditional programming efforts toward developing leadership can be tremendously enhanced by structuring meaningful affiliations with similar state, regional, or national student organizations; making a commitment to empower the students in leadership positions; understanding the reality of entropic flow; and, incorporating themes and tokens as learning tools.

Meaningful Affiliations

The value of exchanging ideas and programs with peers is a tremendous supplement to campus and residence life staff efforts. Institutional membership with NACURH provides abundant opportunities for involvement and leadership development. The various regional affiliates of NACURH, such as the Intermountain (IACURH) and South Atlantic (SAACURH), offer additional possibilities. Further, there are numerous subregional groupings within each regional affiliate, such as Kan-Neb (Kansas and Nebraska); MACURH in the Midwest region; and a host of state associations such as IRHA in Illinois, OKRHA in Oklahoma, NCARH in North Carolina, and TRHA in Texas. Every campus should be involved at whatever level is appropriate and this involvement can be sustained as a continuing supplement to campus leadership development.

Involvement in other leadership-based organizations also has merit. For example, the LeaderShape" Institute with a historic affiliation with of the University of Illinois at Champaign-Urbana is a one-week experience of a lifetime for college-aged students. Both the curriculum and social activities are focused not only on developing leaders in the 17 to 25 age group, but also on inspiring, supporting, and committing students to "lead with integrity." LeaderShape" touches the lives of 60 students from all over the country each week in Allerton, Illinois; many institutions across the nation have now established LeaderShape" as an annual retreat in conjunction with other campus leadership development and governance programs. "LeaderShape" activities include learning leadership theories, interacting with guest panelists, developing a personal vision, helping to support others in their developmental stages, and real-life "games" such as "StarPower" and "Earthquake" with very understandable manifestations of power and oppression. By participating in this nationally recognized program, students are exposed to a variety of motivated, committed, visionary, and high integrity individuals.

Leadership Development

Hosting conferences always increases the number of students on-campus involved during that period of time. The additional students involved in the hosting function of the RHA tends to generate continued and increased involvement for several years. And, the more students that are involved, the greater the individual and organizational impact.

Historically Under-Represented Populations

Affiliations that foster leadership development within and among historically under-represented populations are also noteworthy in the residential environment. In 1984, the University of Georgia created a Minority Assistant position to enhance and support the role of the live-in Resident Assistants. This position has since evolved into CLASS (Continuing the Legacy of African-American Student Success) Advocates or CAs. This extremely successful initiative offers tremendous leadership opportunities for participants. The program also aids in retention and academic success by focusing on the specific needs of the African-American students within established communities. CAs are trained to address concerns of under-represented populations as an inhibitor to community development (Department of University Housing, 1998).

The Housing and Residential Life Office (HRLO) at San Diego State University encourages and supports a variety of special interest committees such as the "Ujima," "Asian and Pacific Unity," and the "La Familia." These committees organizationally interface and interact with both the Residence Hall Association (RHA) and the HRLO organizational structure and administrative personnel. In addition to supplementing programming initiatives within the halls, one of the specific goals of these committees is to develop and nurture a potential pool of student leaders for the benefit of the university community (Housing and Residential Life Office, 1998).

Many campuses now sponsor a variety of summer institutes and leadership academies designed to acclimate and motivate students from under-represented populations. The African-American Partnering Talent (APT) program at the University of Central Arkansas provides one excellent blueprint for success (APT Summer Academy, 1998). Without doubt, these institutes and academies have a "multiplier effect" and positive leadership outcomes for the institutions chosen by graduates of these programs, as well as the living communities in which participants will reside while pursuing their respective degrees.

Empowerment

Rasche and Stoner (1989) identified four basic rules essential to working effectively with student governments. These rules to be successful advisors were listed as: (1) genuinely care; (2) understand the governing documents; (3) utilize resources; and (4) be available. The rules as developed and presented in that chapter are worth re-reading and are no less important today. However, in the last decade, another precept has increased in importance to the point that a fifth rule emphasizing "empowerment" must be added to the list. Advisors should "empower" the students to accomplish mutually established goals. Empowerment promotes development of participants by reducing obstacles to involvement (Komives et al., 1998).

As we know, regulatory requirements and bureaucratic procedures often complicate the abilities of even seasoned professionals to complete assigned tasks and organizational objectives. Procedures that may be seen as minor nuisances to professionals with years of operating experience may be seen as insurmountable to students. Making arrangements to bring a speaker to campus, to host a conference, or to travel to a student government meeting can become an experiential nightmare for students attempting to negotiate the institutional maze—particularly the first time. As part of their supportive role assignment, advisors must facilitate outcomes and "empower" students to realize legitimate goals. It is easy for students to become frustrated; advisors must keep pace with students and help focus their efforts in outcome-specific channels.

Entropic Flow

The concept of "negentropy" (negative entropy) provides one useful theory for understanding the challenges of working with students and their governing associations. Entropy, in theory, describes the proclivity of any system to gravitate towards a more disorderly arrangement. The term "organizational creep," occasionally used within the student affairs profession, would seem to also reflect this phenomenon. We accept the fact that a tremendous investment of energy, including staff time and resources, is required to implement organizational change. However, negentropy implies that substantial investments are required just to maintain the stability of the status quo and offset the natural entropic flow of the organization. Even greater investments will be required to implement and sustain meaningful organizational changes.

This notion of energy investment (negative entropy) within organizations was suggested by C. F. Frederiksen (1980). He wrote:

> A beautiful lawn may be used as an appropriate analogy. Granted, energy has been expended to make the lawn beautiful; however, over time, even greater amounts of energy will be required in the form of watering, mowing, trimming, and fertilizing just to maintain the lawn in its original condition (negentropy). Even the most beautiful lawn, if unattended, will quickly become an eyesore (entropy) (p.5).

As administrators working with students and student governments, we invest tremendous amounts of energy packaged in staff time and financial resources to implement changes. However, as housing professionals we must acknowledge and accept the reality that significant allocations of energy continue to be required towards the maintenance of working relationships with student governing bodies. Well-planned, meaningful, and continuous investment of staff time and supporting resources will foster a stable as well as a productive student government.

Typically, advising the hall governments as well as the RHA is delegated to hall directors or younger professionals on the administrative staff interested and enthusiastic about such an assignment. Staff serving in advisory capacities must routinely keep all professional and support staff not only informed, but also periodically involved in supportive roles. Like the unattended lawn, representative student governing associations can quickly become problematic if left unattended and if allowed to gravitate into the role of an adversary.

Leadership Development

Themes and Tokens

In our sound-bite, bullet comment, snippet society, using short messages or themes as learning tools to stimulate additional and continued thought is important. As one example, LeaderShape" graduates receive a small glass drop as a symbol of unity and belonging. Given to each participant that completes The LeaderShape" Institute, these drops serve as a tangible reminder of the friendships, learning experiences, and challenges met. Each student leaves the conference with the small token as a reminder not only of all the experiences, but also the role each played in the lives of others and that the synergy created with people is greater than any one individual's energy. After a week of close interactions and development of leadership skills, the small token almost seems trivial, but it is always accepted with a smile and often tears. The students return to campus with priceless memories, new friends, and a small clear stone to remind them of the experience.

Possibilities are limited only by one's imagination. Successful leadership programs have boasted themes such as: The Gold Banana, One Thousand Sandals, Passing the Baton, The Deep Water, The Walls of Sparta, The Winds of Change, The Prism Holder, New Directions/Past Reflections, Make a Difference, Marking Your Place, At the Window, The Wind and the Lion, Rock of Sisyphus/Cistern of Danaides, The Dream Catcher, "A" is for Teaching, The Puzzle Mosaic, Your Moccasins are Too Hard, The Sword of Damocles, and The Monarch and the Viceroy, to list but a few. All of the programs with these themes have "keepsake tokens" given to the participants.

A Final Word

Participation of students in leadership and governance activities is always an educationally enriching experience to the individual. Although membership and activity attendance will certainly be remembered, any lasting individual impact will be minimal unless the students go on to actively participate, assume positions of leadership, and accept planning roles on their respective campuses. Further, the involvement of officers in establishing goals and objectives, planning activities, participating in leadership training, and attending conferences are excellent training opportunities for developing skills essential for, and applicable to, holding positions of community leadership in the future.

Whatever is good for the students and the RHA is good for the housing organization, the university, and this democratic society. University administrators appreciate the positive publicity generally associated with campus events. Further, the goodwill among students and potential return from our future alumni are immeasurable.

Use of the foundation documents referenced in this chapter introduces the basis of the emerging interest mandating that residence life professionals embrace and support the implementation of broader campus leadership initiatives. Efforts must be vigorously supported to validate leadership within the curriculum, to institutionalize some form of community meeting, and to facilitate attempts to connect with "generation next." Additionally, a number of unique programs have been highlighted that enhance traditional leadership programming efforts within the residential setting. In closing, this chapter reaffirmed the importance of meaningful affiliations among representative student organizations, historically under-represented populations, empowerment, entropic flow, and the educational use of themes and tokens.

Yes, leadership can be learned from others. University administrators are obligated to intentionally develop a comprehensive program that provides maximum opportunities for learning. Leadership can also be learned from environmental circumstances and challenges; university administrators are further challenged to provide the organizational framework, an enriching environment, and meaningful involvement that facilitates learning by students attending the institution. One of the best places for achieving leadership-learning and educational goals is the residential learning laboratories readily available through the student housing facilities and program operated by the institution.

References

APT Summer Academy. (1998). Office of Minority Recruitment and Retention: University of Central Arkansas.

Astin, A. W. (1993). *What matters in college? Four critical years revisited.* San Francisco: Jossey-Bass.

Astin, A. W. (1996). Involvement in learning revisited: Lessons we have learned. *Journal of College Student Development, 37*, 123-134.

Astin, A. W., & Sax, L. J. (1998). How undergraduates are affected by service participation. *Journal of College Student Development, 39*, 251-263.

Brown, R. D. (1972). *Student development in tomorrow's higher education: A return to the academy.* Washington, D.C.: American Personnel and Guidance Association.

Department of University Housing. (1998). History of the CLASS Program. Division of Student Affairs: University of Georgia.

Dunkel, N. W., & Schuh, J. H. (1998). Advising student groups and organizations. San Francisco: Jossey-Bass.

Dunkel, N. W., & Spencer, C. L. (Eds.). (1998). *Advice for advisors: The development of an effective residence hall association (2nd Ed.).* Columbus, OH: ACUHO-I.

Frederiksen, C. F. (1980). The future is now. *The Journal of College and University Student Housing, 10*(2), 3-6.

Goodman, A. J., & Ravine, H. (1997). *Community trusteeship: A guide for a leadership residential program.* Boulder, CO: Student Leadership Institute.

Greenleaf, R. K. (1987). *Teacher as servant: A parable.* Indianapolis: The Greenleaf Center for Servant-Leadership.

Housing and Residential Life Office. (1998). HRLO special interest committees. Division of Student Affairs: San Diego State University.

Journal of College Student Development. (1996). *37*(2).

Komives, S. R., Lucas, N., & McMahon, T. R. (1998). *Exploring leadership for college students who want to make a difference.* San Francisco: Jossey-Bass.

Kuh, G. D. (1998). Lessons from the mountain. *About Campus, 3*(2), 16-21.

Kuh, G. D., Schuh, J. H., Whitt, E. J., & Associates (1991). *Involving colleges: Successful approaches to fostering student learning and personal development outside the classroom.* San Francisco: Jossey-Bass.

Oxendine, B. (Ed.). (1997). *So you want to be president . . . How to get elected on your campus.* Gainesville, FL: Oxendine Publishing, Inc.

Pascarella, E., & Terenzini, P. (1991). *How college affects students: Findings and insights from twenty years of research.* San Francisco: Jossey-Bass.

Rasche, C. M., & Stoner, K. L. (1989). Working with students and student government. In J. H. Schuh (Ed.), *Educational programming in college and university residence halls* (pp. 63-73). Columbus, OH: ACUHO-I.

Reisberg, L. (1998). Students gain sense of direction in new field of leadership studies. *The Chronicle of Higher Education. 45*(10), A49-A50.

Sax, L. J., Astin, A. W., Korn, W. S., & Mahoney, K. M. (1997). *The American freshman: National norms for Fall 1997.* Los Angeles, CA: Higher Education Research Institute, UCLA.

Schroeder, C. C., & Hurst, J. C. (1996). Designing learning environments that integrate curricular and cocurricular experiences. *Journal of College Student Development, 37,* 174-181.

Schuh, J. H. (1989). A framework for student involvement. In J. H. Schuh (Ed.), *Educational programming in college and university residence halls* (pp. 12-25). Columbus, OH: ACUHO-I.

Student Leadership Institute. (CD-ROM). (1997). Boulder, CO: ProMotif Media.

Terenzini, P. T., Pascarella, E. T., & Blimling, G. S. (1996). Students' out-of-class experiences and their influence on learning and cognitive development: A literature review. *Journal of College Student Development, 37,* 149-162.

UCLA study finds college freshmen not connected. (1998). *National On-Campus Report, 26*(11), 1, 6.

Chapter Ten

Conclusions and Recommendations

Thomas W. Dukes
Former Director of Counseling and Dean of Freshmen
St. Joseph's College

John H. Schuh
Professor and Chair, Educational Leadership and Policy Studies
Iowa State University

Conclusions and Recommendations

This chapter summarizes the conclusions from previous chapters and presents a series of recommendations for housing officers who are interested in developing the learning environment in their housing facilities. Clearly, it is important to remember that what works at one institution may not work at others. So, in reviewing the conclusions and recommendations, we urge readers to remember the contexts of their institutions and to tailor the principles identified in this chapter to the specific needs of their campuses.

Conclusions

The first part of this chapter summarizes the conclusions drawn from the various discussions presented by the chapter contributors. Taken together, these conclusions provide a foundation of recommendations for housing officers and others interested in developing rich, residential learning environments.

The Body of Research on Student Learning in Campus Housing

The literature on the effects of residential life experience on student learning and development is rich and nearly unequivocal. Residents who interact with faculty over serious matters grow and develop as a result of that experience. They are also more likely to persist and graduate than students who live in other circumstances. It is clear that simply living on campus will not necessarily expedite student learning. The studies reported in this book indicate that there may be little difference in student growth between living at home or living in a residence hall. But when a rich environment is crafted—one which places students in contact with faculty—and when the resulting interaction has an academic focus, good things will happen.

Housing assignments also seem to make a difference in student learning. Students with similar academic or extracurricular interests seem to thrive when they are assigned in the same proximity. This seems to be a strong argument for assignments targeted by academic major, interest in service learning, or other interactions an institution wishes to promote.

Assessment in Residence Halls

Assessment has moved from being perceived as a frill to a necessity in the housing officer's portfolio of activities. In the residential context, assessment helps housing department staff deliver services and programs that are more effective, more responsive to student needs, and more consistent with institutional expectations.

Assessment plays a particularly crucial role in measuring the extent to which interventions such as those described in this volume are successful. If a housing officer claims that certain forms of growth or development result from specific residential programs, then that claim needs to be supported by local data. Assessment is essential in sustaining local programs because, quite frankly, people are not interested in what works elsewhere, they want to know what works on the local campus. As a consequence, assessment needs to be incorporated into the annual routines of housing officers.

Transition Experiences

All students undergo transition experiences, but housing offices can develop interventions which will help minimize the negative aspects of the transition experience. Students can experience difficulty as they try to make sense of their new environment and how to behave in it. Excellent foundation studies are presented in this book, which help describe the transitions of students.

It is important to remember that students from under-represented populations have two transitions to make; to the college environment from their high school environment and to the new culture, where people may be very different than in their home towns. Consider, for example, the challenges faced by a student transitioning from an inner city to a small college town. Outside the campus community, the number of people of color may be very small. Finding restaurants which serve familiar food, places where their hair can be cut, entertainment outlets, and so on may be difficult or impossible. As a consequence, their adjustment may be considerably more difficult than other students from majority cultures.

Residential Colleges

The history of residential colleges can be traced from Oxford and Cambridge, going back a number of centuries. Examples of contemporary applications of the residential college model vary considerably and are linked to the mission and culture of individual campuses. These applications, however, tend to result from partnerships formed between the department of residence life and academic affairs. In addition to the need for a strong partnership. a commitment of human and financial resources is necessary to develop a rich learning environment.

Living in a learning environment of this kind helps students in large, impersonal institutions feel like they are in a small, personalized one. It provides a focal point for student experiences and facilitates serious student-faculty interaction.

Academically Sponsored Residential Learning Programs

Student housing and academic affairs staffs can form a variety of partnerships to improve the residence environment and foster improved student learning and growth. The primary motivating factors for the development of these partnerships include improving pedagogical practices, and enhancing and measuring the attainment of curricular objectives.

The models that exist for these kinds of program are numerous. Among them are service learning, freshman interest groups, peer teaching, supplemental instruction, and learning communities. These models and others contribute to enriched student learning in the residential setting.

Community Development

Community development is seen by some housing officers as an end in itself. In the context of developing a rich learning environment, community development should be seen as a factor that facilitates student learning as well. A byproduct of this ap-

Conclusions and Recommendations

proach is that as an individual contributes to the enrichment of the community, the community contributes to the individual's growth.

Often community development is left to whatever occurs, meaning that specific steps are not taken to shape the community environment. In the case of developing a learning environment, specific interventions can be developed to help shape the residential unit.

Programming for Under-Represented Populations

Traditional student development theory needs to be supplemented with an understanding of how members of under-represented populations grow and develop. While progress has been made in developing a more inclusive environment, the work is far from over. Additional steps need to be taken to provide a better environment for student populations who are comparatively new to the campus.

Majority students, faculty, and staff need to understand the challenges faced by members of under-represented populations who move into campus housing. After developing this understanding, they can take specific steps to make sure that the environment is welcoming and more inclusive.

Purposeful Faculty-Student Interaction

In the residential setting, faculty-student interaction that is focused on serious topics tends to result in student growth and development. Institutional support and leadership are important ingredients in developing environments that support faculty-student interaction. Equally important are shared goals by housing officers and faculty.

Programs that promote student-faculty interaction tend to result in promoting student learning, student satisfaction, and student retention. These outcomes are consistent with the overall objectives for residential programs, and as a consequence, are highly desirable. Many examples demonstrate that these programs can be developed regardless of institutional type, without a substantial infusion of campus resources or highly complex support systems. Most importantly, treating these programs as central to the residential experience, rather than seeing them as peripheral or marginal, will result in student learning and growth.

Leadership Development and Governance

The field of leadership development provides a rich opportunity for linkages between residence hall programming and the academic mission of the institution. Students who are empowered by residence life staff to take an active role in hall governance, organization of community service projects, and other planning and decision-making roles are afforded an opportunity to develop skills that come only from direct experience.

Housing officers can provide an organizational framework, an enriching environment, and meaningful involvement opportunities for students that will facilitate this kind of learning and development. Clearly, the residential environment offers an extraordinarily rich setting for students to apply the principles they have learned from their classes.

Recommendations for Practice

The next section contains a summary of the various recommendations from each of the chapters. These recommendations form the heart of developing residential programs that contribute to student learning.

Program Development

Make sure that academic programs are consistent with the institutional mission and philosophy. Programs that promote student learning must be consistent with the institution's mission and philosophy. Consider a commuter campus which is designed primarily to serve adult students. Since a campus of this type has a very modest housing capacity, programs are likely to be less extensive than at a residential institution. Programs which facilitate learning in the residence halls can be very effective without necessarily being complex. At a commuter institution it is unlikely that the programs found at a residential college will be implemented. However, smaller scale faculty-student interaction opportunities still exist. For instance, a meal program whereby students have lunch with a faculty member once a week to talk over class material could be developed.

Develop a shared vision for residential programs with faculty and other academic leaders. Before programs designed to systematically involve faculty are developed in the residence halls, it is important to engage in thorough discussions with faculty and academic leaders. Programs are improved by such input and are more likely to be viewed as consistent and with the concerns of all involved. Faculty may have a slightly narrower view of the college experience than housing officers and, even if they moderate their views, their perspective is likely to focus on academic learning. Most housing officers concur that the academic nature of their institutions is preeminent. Many positive byproducts are likely to occur when programs are carefully conceived, even in institutions that place a heavy emphasis on the academic learning.

Form partnerships with faculty and academic leaders that meet the needs of students and faculty. One should not assume that simply because programs are developed with the best of intentions that faculty and other academic leaders will automatically want to participate in them. Faculty may have a slightly different view of student learning and the academic experience, and they will want to make sure their perspectives are integrated into the learning opportunities that are developed in the residence halls.

Spend time understanding faculty culture and the faculty reward system. Student affairs staff may not understand the faculty reward system and what is useful in terms of their faculty evaluation. At research institutions, such activities as publishing in refereed journals and securing grant funding are highly prized. Interaction with students outside the classroom is a fairly low priority and is unlikely to be considered in the promotion and tenure process. So, while interaction with students can be fun and rewarding for faculty, this is not helpful in terms of their career advancement. As a consequence, it is important for student affairs staff not to rely too heavily on a small group of cooperative faculty members and instead try to spread the commitments over a wide variety of faculty.

Conclusions and Recommendations

Develop programs that facilitate purposeful interaction between students and faculty. The research literature is very clear on this point. Simply expecting learning to occur when programs place students and faculty in close proximity is to miss the point. What seems to foster student learning is purposeful programming designed to accomplish certain objectives. So, for example, programmers could plan a meal during which students discuss course materials with faculty.

Connect out-of-class learning with academic objectives. A number of activities can be organized in the residence halls to support the application of classroom learning. The development of service learning projects, for example, is a natural for the residence halls. Tutoring programs for underserved children, taking children to campus events, or working with voter registration programs are all examples of linking classroom learning with out-of-class activities.

Use residential facilities and technology to support programs designed to enhance student learning. As residence halls become more academically oriented with the development of classrooms, computer labs, and the like, they can become quite attractive to faculty as teaching facilities. Clearly, the residence hall budget is not an inexhaustible resource, but as funding is committed to the development of classrooms and support facilities, residence halls can be quite attractive to faculty members as a place to teach.

Develop an awareness of innovative instructional techniques and integrate them into residential education programs. Along with the application of technology, other opportunities for innovation can make teaching students in the residence halls attractive to faculty. They can try new ways of teaching, perhaps using a more student-centered approach to instruction. Faculty can learn which instructional techniques provide benefits for everyone involved, including themselves, housing staff, and most importantly, students.

Recognize faculty and staff for their contributions to the development of residential education programs. The contributions of those who develop learning programs in residence halls should never be taken for granted. On a regular basis the contributions of these individuals should be acknowledged through formal activities such as receptions or dinners, and through less formal but equally important gestures such as thank-you notes and certificates.

Working with Students

Know the developmental theories that apply to students. A variety of theories can be used to aid in understanding how students learn and grow. When planners apply these theories to program design, they enhance student learning. Students tend to be more receptive to programs which address their most pressing concerns. Theory helps planners identify which issues are the most salient for various groups of students. For example, entering freshmen are probably less ready to begin serious career planning activities and more ready to deal with issues related to establishing their autonomy and independence.

Recognize that students from under-represented populations will grow and develop differently than students from the majority culture. The experiences of students from under-represented populations often are very different than those of students from the majority culture. The challenges they face in attending a primarily white college are substantial. They will need support from role models and other individuals who understand their developmental issues.

Educate all levels of staff about the challenges that students face in making the transition from high school to college. Emphasize that many students from under-represented populations will be making the transition from their home and community environment to a very different cultural environment, in addition to the high school to college transition. All students entering college, be they freshmen or transfers, face transitions. Staff needs to be prepared to help students make these transitions.

In working with students of color, hire role models, involve current students of color and faculty in planning various activities and programs, such as orientation, homecoming or other significant events in the lives of students, and in the decision-making process of the organization. While progress has been made in diversifying institutions of higher education, the work is far from done. Simply recruiting more students of color does not begin to address many of the systemic problems in institutions. Besides understanding developmental theory for assisting in transitions, resident hall staff must devise direct interventions to make sure that students persist. Programmers can use the ideas suggested in this book to facilitate this process.

Leadership and Community Development

Link programs to academic departments. It is not difficult for housing officers to identify and establish links between programs and academic departments. Many programs already have a natural link to academic programs such as a foreign language house, programs for under-represented populations in certain majors (such as women in engineering), or programs that bring together US and foreign nationals interested in international exchange programs. Community development in these cases can be built around the academic theme. Leadership in these units can be structured to advance the collective experiences of the group. For example, students from language houses can participate in Model UN or similar activities on campus.

Make use of assignment procedures to help develop community. Rather than making assignments on a random basis, assign students with similar academic or out-of-class interests as a first step in developing community. Often these students should have classes together or, at a minimum, take similar courses. They can form study groups, tutor each other, prepare for exams together, and engage in other academically related activities which will help develop a sense of community.

Plan specific interventions to develop communities with an academic focus. It is a mistake to assume that communities will develop automatically when students live in close proximity. One of the best ways to develop communities is to plan them with an academic focus. We mentioned using the assignment process to facilitate community development. The use of the Freshmen Interest Group (FIG) concept, as an illustration, has tremendous potential for the development of community. Students live together, take classes together, have similar academic goals, know the same faculty, and can support each other in their academic endeavors. This approach seems to work very well in establishing community. It will also help to ensure that community develops along educationally purposeful lines.

Conclusions and Recommendations

Try to find ways to integrate community and leadership development in the curriculum. Building on the concept of service learning, opportunities exist to integrate community and leadership development in the curriculum. Courses which advance these concepts can be developed and team-taught by housing staff and members of the teaching faculty. If courses cannot be developed on these topics, then there may be ways that class projects, practical experiences, or other activities can enhance community and leadership development.

Recognize that leadership can be taught and skills can be improved with practice. If one simply assumes that leaders are born and not developed, then there would be no point in worrying about leadership development. The body of research seems clear on this point: leadership skills can be learned. As a consequence, the intentionally designed residential unit can be an excellent way of organizing leadership development activities. Many leadership positions exist and, just as importantly, the residence hall provides a good training ground for students to try out their leadership skills, often in a very low-risk setting.

Assessment Activities

Consider assessment as a long-term commitment. Assessment should not be considered as a one-shot activity or conducted on an occasional basis. Assessments work best when they are conducted regularly, whether there is a crisis or not. Clearly all the forms of assessment cannot be conducted each year, but a planned rotation of assessments including needs assessment, satisfaction assessment, and most importantly, outcomes assessment will serve the department well. Assessment provides critical feedback concerning the student condition and a means of knowing the extent to which programs work. This approach also leads to a process of continuous improvement for the department, a critical element in contemporary higher education.

Carefully determine the approaches you will use to assess important matters. Determine who will be involved in the assessment process, what kinds of assessments to conduct, and who should receive reports of assessment projects. These issues are quite important because a planned, deliberate approach to assessment is far more effective than simply diving in the assessment pool and swimming to the nearest ladder. Good models of assessment are available for the serious investigator. Sound methodology is the critical criterion for selecting a model. Choose one which provides a systematic approach and then implement it.

In the middle of a crisis is the wrong time to begin taking assessment seriously. A far more useful approach is to create a multiyear assessment strategy which includes a number of assessments to be completed each year. Data generated and reported on a routine basis will assure program planners, participants, and other housing department staff that programs are valuable. Waiting for external audiences to challenge effectiveness is a serious mistake. Integrating assessment into the annual work plan is by far the best approach.

A Final Word

We conclude this book by observing that the timing seems to be ideal for the implementation of learning opportunities in campus residence halls. The research literature is robust and consistent: purposeful learning experiences facilitate student growth and persistence. We know students grow from these experiences. We know what kinds of experiences are most effective. The technology has matured to a point where no reasonably informed housing officer should wonder how to implement learning experiences in residence halls. And, measures have been developed to the point whereby determining success or failure of interventions can be accomplished unequivocally. In short, no impediments block the development of purposeful learning programs in campus residence halls. Our students deserve nothing less than the best learning environment we in higher education can provide. Why not start now?